WHITE

HURRICANE

WHITE HURRICANE

A GREAT LAKES NOVEMBER GALE

and

AMERICA'S DEADLIEST MARITIME DISASTER

David G. Brown

INTERNATIONAL MARINE / MCGRAW-HILL
Camden, Maine ~ New York ~ Chicago ~ San Francisco ~ Lisbon
London ~ Madrid ~ Mexico City ~ Milan ~ New Delhi ~ San Juan
Seoul ~ Singapore ~ Sydney ~ Toronto

The McGraw·Hill Companies

1 2 3 4 5 6 7 8 9 10 DOC DOC 9 8 7 6 5 4

The Library of Congress has cataloged the hardcover edition as follows:

Brown, David G. (David Geren), 1944–
  White hurricane : a Great Lakes November gale and
America's deadliest maritime disaster / David G. Brown.
    p.   cm.
  Includes bibliographical references and index.
  ISBN 0-07-138037-X
  1. Shipwrecks—Great Lakes—History—20th century.
  2. Severe storms—Great Lakes Region—History—
  20th century.   I. Title.
  G525.B8575 2002
  977—dc21   2002008265

Paperback ISBN 0-07-143541-7

Maps by Equator Graphics

THIS BOOK IS DEDICATED

TO THE SAILORS

WHO NEVER RETURNED

FROM THE 1913 WHITE HURRICANE,

AND TO THE FAMILIES WHO

NEVER GAVE UP LOVING THEM.

CONTENTS

MINNESOTA

Thunder Bay

Scottish Hero
(loc. unknown)

Leafield

Lake Superior

Duluth

William Nottingham

Turret Chief

L.C. Waldo

Keweenaw Bay

Henry B. Smith

Huronic

Major

Whitefish Bay

F.G. Hartwe

Sault S

Superior

Marquette

J.T. Hutchinson

St. Marys River

Meaford

Plymouth

Halsted

Louisiana

M I C H I G A N

WISCONSIN

Green Bay

Lake Michigan

Waukesha

Milwaukee

IOWA

Chicago

ILLINOIS

INDIANA

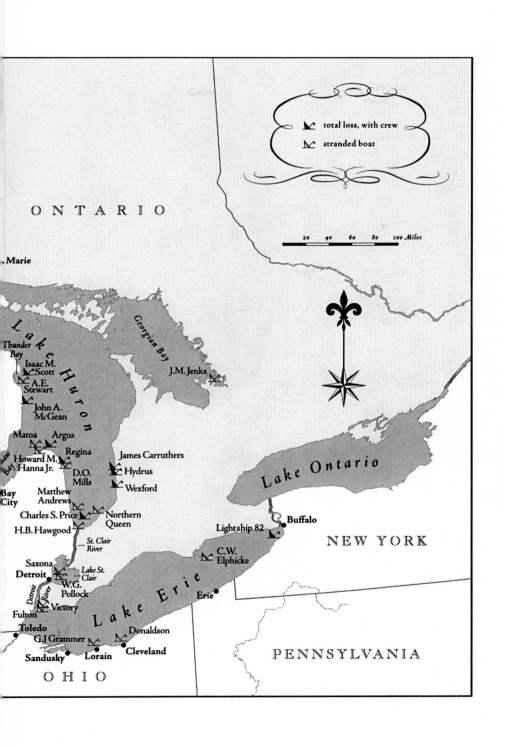

ONTARIO

total loss, with crew

stranded boat

20   40   60   80   100 *Miles*

. Marie

Lake Huron

Thunder
Bay

Isaac M.
Scott

A.E.
Stewart

John A.
McGean

Georgian Bay

J.M. Jenks

Matoa   Argus

Regina

Howard M.
Hanna Jr.

D.O.
Mills

James Carruthers

Hydrus

Wexford

Bay
City

Matthew
Andrews

Charles S. Price

Northern
Queen

H.B. Hawgood

St. Clair
River

Saxona

Detroit

Lake St.
Clair

W.G.
Pollock

Detroit
River

Victory

Fulton

Toledo

G.J Grammer

Sandusky   Lorain   Cleveland

OHIO

Lake Ontario

Buffalo

NEW YORK

Lightship 82

C.W.
Elphicke

Lake Erie

Erie

Donaldson

PENNSYLVANIA

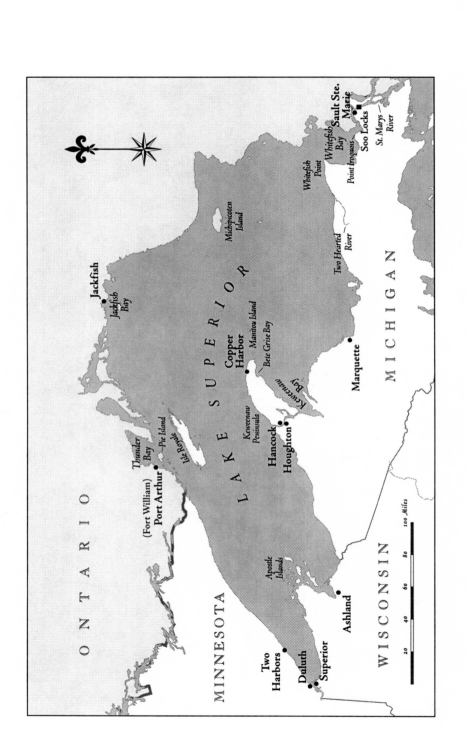

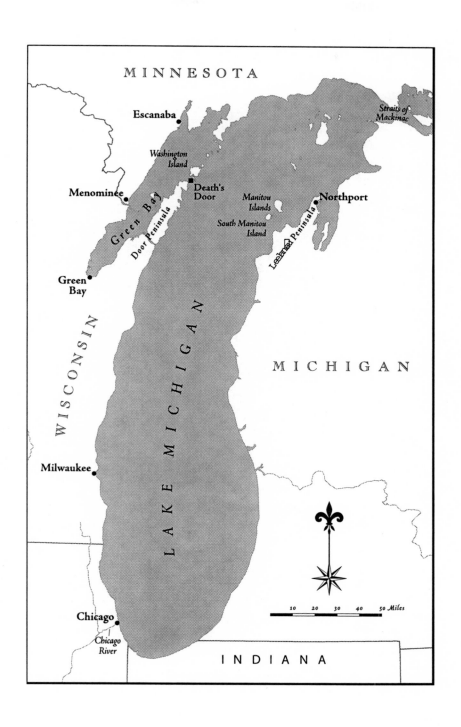

MINNESOTA

Escanaba

Washington Island

Menominee

Green Bay

Death's
Door

Manitou Islands

Northport

South Manitou Island

Door Peninsula

Leelanau Peninsula

Straits of Mackinac

Green
Bay

WISCONSIN

LAKE MICHIGAN

MICHIGAN

Milwaukee

Chicago

Chicago River

INDIANA

10   20   30   40   50 *Miles*

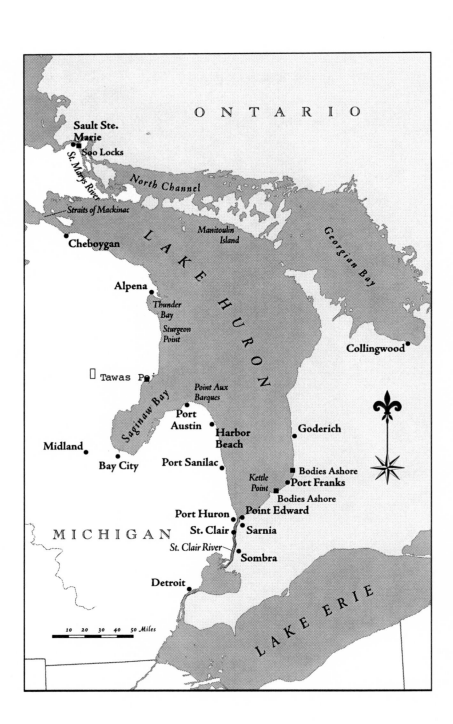

ONTARIO

Sault Ste.
Marie
Soo Locks

St. Marys River

North Channel

Straits of Mackinac

*Manitoulin
Island*

Georgian Bay

Cheboygan

L A K E   H U R O N

Alpena

*Thunder
Bay*

*Sturgeon
Point*

Collingwood

☐ Tawas Pt

Saginaw Bay

*Point Aux
Barques*

Port
Austin

Harbor
Beach

Goderich

Midland

Bay City

Port Sanilac

Bodies Ashore
*Kettle
Point*
Port Franks

Bodies Ashore

Port Huron

Point Edward

St. Clair

Sarnia

MICHIGAN

St. Clair River

Sombra

Detroit

10   20   30   40   50 *Miles*

L A K E   E R I E

PREFACE

SURVIVORS OF THE November 1913 storm on the Great Lakes dubbed it a "White Hurricane," and they had good reason. The first gale of November that year was more than just another disturbance in the atmosphere. It was the defining event in the lives of the sailors and captains, stewards, engineers, and life savers who fought to save their ships and the lives of victims in Great Lakes history.

One youngster who watched snow swirl around his house was Charles Franklyn Brown. My father was only eight that year, but never forgot looking down from his second-story bedroom window at a snowdrift climbing the side of his family's home on Cleveland's east side. For a boy, that drift represented the opportunity of a lifetime. His mother, Bessie, reluctantly opened the window and he paused only a moment before launching himself in a face-first belly slam down the snowdrift. Fifty years later he still laughed when he recalled that cold, two-story plunge to the ground.

The first time I can recall hearing this tale was in November 1950, when a less destructive winter gale once again buried Cleveland in snow. My most exciting memory of that storm is of National Guard tanks pulling city buses through the snow-clogged streets. Tanks were exciting, but nothing to compare with jumping from an upstairs bedroom window.

My father's reminiscences helped stir my interest in the men and ships of the lakes. As an eighth-grade student I purchased a copy of Dana Thomas Bowen's *Shipwrecks of the Lakes*. It was the first book in what would become a library of Great Lakes material. But reading was not enough. By the late 1950s I was charting courses for our family boat as we explored lake ports and islands where the stories in those books took place.

The ghost of the White Hurricane still haunts my adventures. On a beautiful summer day on Lake Superior I imagine the hulk of the *L.C. Waldo* being battered by thundering waves off the Keweenaw Peninsula, its crew trapped inside by a sheath of ice. On the Port Huron to Mackinac Island race, while sailors watch jib tell-tales, I think about the overturned hulk of Lake Huron's famous "mystery ship."

Initially, this book was to be a simple sea story—a sailor's yarn of wind and waves. In the quiet halls of Cleveland's Public Library a microfiche reader took me back in time to 1913. Pages of newspapers clicked before my eyes. Within those often fuzzy images the surf still pounded and snow swirled. Words of sailors, hypothermic and half-drowned from their ordeals, came out of the screen with undiminished intensity despite the passage of nine decades.

The White Hurricane roared across seven states and a good portion of Ontario, Canada. It covered an area of North America equal in size to western Europe. Had the storm struck the British Isles and then gone on to attack Denmark, France, Germany, and Northern Italy, it would have been world news.

No single library can contain all the newspapers and other records of a storm that size. The material is spread through collections hundreds of miles apart. Fortunately, there are angels called "librarians." A few phone calls started searches in Duluth, Marquette, Chicago, Buffalo, and Washington, D.C. Suddenly, it became necessary to find a way to organize a blizzard of photocopied newspaper articles.

Newspapers of that day were filled with lurid details from survivors of the huge waves, hurricane-force winds, and blizzard conditions. Despite these chilling eyewitness accounts, the one aspect of the story that was consistently missing was the storm itself. Even the weather forecasters of that day did not really know what happened. Their lack of knowledge was eventually laid bare in political bickering in Washington, D.C.

As my research progressed, it became clear that the storm was not just central to the story, it constituted the narrative backbone. Understanding the course and chronology of the storm's birth and development became not just a matter of interest, but an absolute necessity. But, what really did happen? Forecasters did not obtain the knowledge and tools to understand the weather events of that November until many years later. The story of the storm itself was missing from those contemporary newspaper accounts simply because nobody had the ability to understand the cascading nature of events in the atmosphere that surrounded them.

With the help of two meteorologists—Robert Shiels and Ken McKinley—I set out to provide a likely explanation for a natural cataclysm of almost 90 years ago.

Tracking down the necessary weather data from 1913 proved daunting. Daily records from the Cleveland weather station had been headed to the scrap heap until somebody thought to donate them to the Historical Collections of the Great Lakes at Bowling Green State University in Ohio. We found them there in a bound volume that may not have been opened in 80 years.

Additional daily records from weather observers in Detroit, Duluth, Marquette, Sault Ste. Marie, Toledo, Chicago, and Buffalo were generously provided by NOAA's National Climatic Data Center in Raleigh, North Carolina. Rolls of microfilmed newspapers yielded contemporary weather maps, crude though they were.

Using all these sources, we have reconstructed the Great Lakes storm of 1913. The storm scenario laid out in these pages isn't the only possible explanation for the apocryphal weather experienced on the Great Lakes between November 7 and November 10, 1913—lacking upper-atmosphere data, we can never know for sure—but it is perhaps the most feasible. It also agrees in broad outline with the scenario posited by William R. Deedler in his article "Hell Hath No Fury Like a Great Lakes Fall Storm," posted on the Internet at http://www.crh.noaa.gov/dtx/stm_1913.htm.

Forming a clearer picture of what happened in the atmosphere did not make writing about the storm any easier. Newspaper reports of events during and after the White Hurricane were often at odds both with one another and with an informed retrospective analysis. Some 1913 news reports were logically impossible—either confused or downright incorrect. (The same is often true today of accounts of breaking news.) One ship was reported downbound on Lake Superior when it was really making an upbound passage to Duluth. Wind shifts were sometimes described in print as occurring at the wrong time of day. Each of these discrepancies had to be studied and reconciled.

Detail by detail, we reexamined large portions of the record, seeking to untangle the narrative skein. This process transformed what began as a simple sea story into what I hope is a rich tapestry of human drama set against a backdrop of winter chaos.

This retelling of the quintessential Great Lakes storm almost came too late. Many 1913 records were not as fortunate as those of the Cleveland weather station. For instance, no history of the White Hurricane would be complete without Captain S. A. Lyons' letter describing the steamer *J.H. Sheadle's* battle to survive on Lake Huron. That letter is reproduced in its entirety in appendix 1 because of its historical significance.

Captain Lyons' personal carbon copy was donated to the Great Lakes Historical Society museum in Vermilion, Ohio, some five decades ago. Since then, it has disappeared. Fortunately, a barely legible electrostatic copy still exists in the Bowling Green archives. That sole copy keeps Captain Lyons' words with his original typographical errors alive.

There is no way to know how many other documents have disappeared. Of course, the most valuable records erased by time are human memories of the storm. Like my father, the people who battled the storm are gone. They took with them their first-hand remembrances. All that remains are a few family stories and the fading newspapers that recorded the events of those four days.

And what a four days they were. A dozen modern steamships were sunk like bathtub toys. Another score of ships were battered into submission or cast ashore. Perhaps 250 or more sailors died in those hurricane-force winds; we don't really know how many. The names and faces, the surfboats and the sunken or stranded ships, the stalled locomotives and swirling snow merge into a confusion of details as the story unfolds. This confusion was the reality when 90-mile-an-hour winds, whiteout snow squalls, and 35-foot waves combined to produce a the storm for which survivors could find no better name than "White Hurricane."

David G. Brown
May 2002

PROLOGUE

NOVEMBER 5, 1913

Erie, and Ontario, and Huron, and Superior, and Michigan—possess an ocean-like expansiveness, with many of the ocean's noblest traits . . . they are swept by Borean and dismasting blasts as direful as any that lash the salted wave; they know what shipwrecks are, for out of sight of land, however inland, they have drowned full many a midnight ship with all its shrieking crew.

—HERMAN MELVILLE, *Moby-Dick*

As MILTON SMITH PREPARED to leave the steamer *Charles S. Price* on Wednesday, November 5, he did not think of himself as a superstitious man. He simply could no longer ignore feelings of uneasiness growing inside him. Throughout the summer and early autumn of 1913 he had served as the *Price's* first assistant engineer. He liked the work, and his wife and children depended upon his pay of $84 per month, quite adequate by 1913 standards. Most of all, however, Smith's family needed him alive. The universal foreboding among Great Lakes sailors for the gales of November made him choose this particular moment to get off the ship and go home to Port Huron, Michigan.

A pleasant 50-degree southeasterly breeze rustled the ship's flag when Smith gave his resignation to Captain William M. Black. Sunlight through the porthole made a spotlight circle on the deck of the small cabin. Captain Black and Chief Engineer John Groundwater tried to convince their reluctant engineer to make one final trip. From outside came the sounds of the huge steam-powered coal dumper as it lifted loaded railroad hopper cars, tipped them over, and dumped whole carloads of coal down a steel chute into the hold. Their ship was docked in Ashtabula, Ohio, on Lake Erie, where it was taking on its last upbound cargo of the season. The *Price* was scheduled to go into winter layup in two weeks—after it returned from Lake Superior with one last downbound load of iron ore.

"Why not finish out the season?" Captain Black must have asked, but Smith was adamant about getting off that day. He apologized for leaving the *Price*'s engineering department shorthanded, but he just had to leave. The best arguments of the ship's top officers could not change his mind. Former engineer Smith left the captain's wood-paneled cabin and walked aft to the more spartan accommodations he had shared with another engineer all summer. He lifted his duffle off the bunk and looked around one last time to make sure he had left nothing behind.

Smith was not the first sailor to feel uneasy about working the lakes in late autumn. From the earliest Native Americans in their fragile canoes, Great Lakes sailors have always worried about late-season gales. Each autumn, even while golden sun still sparkles off gentle waves, deckhands and captains instinctively glance at the western horizon. They search involuntarily for signs of an impending storm—and with good reason. Violent weather sweeps across North America's five inland seas with little warning. Storms develop at any time of year, but the most deadly are those that occur in late autumn, just about the time the commercial sailing season ends. Sailors expect gales to haunt the lakes during those late fall days when golden October darkens into dreary November.

A 1959 report published by the U.S. Office of Climatology as part of the opening of the St. Lawrence Seaway said, "The location of the Great Lakes in the interior of the North American continent . . . gives the region more complex and rapidly changing weather patterns than those of more maritime locations." Storms come up quicker on the lakes than they do on the world's saltwater oceans. "The development of a storm of major proportions sometimes occurs within less than 24 hours. Such rapid developments have resulted in extreme alertness on the part of the forecaster to provide adequate warning for shipping in the Great Lakes."

Native Americans did not need government reports to warn them of the dangers of the Great Lakes. They were well versed in the changing moods of these giant bodies of fresh water across which they paddled their long trading canoes. That may be why more travel was done by walking around the shores of the lakes than by making open-water passages in those impressive but frail vessels. It remained for French explorer Rene-Robert Sieur de LaSalle to initiate more than three centuries of commercial navigation on the lakes. LaSalle believed that a European-style sailing ship could stand up to freshwater gales. In the winter and spring of 1679 he ordered construction of a two-masted vessel similar in design—though smaller in size—to the French ship that a short time before had carried him across the stormy Atlantic to New France. His tiny ship was built near what is now Black Rock, New York, not far from present-day Buffalo and Niagara Falls.

In those days, the land surrounding the Great Lakes was a vast forest. Even with so much standing wood available, the task of building a timber-framed ship in the wilderness proved daunting. LaSalle ordered the keel laid in January, when heavy timber could be skidded on snow and ice, but working outdoors was nearly impossible. European shipyards often aged their timber for a decade or longer before using it in a ship. In the New World wilderness, shipwrights found that the green wood with its frozen sap refused to yield to their tools. And local Iroquois openly objected to the project, trying everything short of a full-scale attack on the French camp to stop construction. Despite these problems the hull was launched in early May and fitted out by June.

LaSalle's ship was named *Le Griffon*, after a mythical beast that is half lion, half eagle. A carved lion figurehead looked forward from the stem, and a carved eagle guarded the stern. Gathering his adventurers, LaSalle sailed west the length of Lake Erie. They hauled their way up the Detroit and St. Clair Rivers before continuing northward the length of Lake Huron and passing through the Straits of Mackinac. On Lake Huron the French were caught unprepared by a summer squall that threatened to capsize the small vessel. After calm returned, the band of explorers crossed Lake Michigan to what is now Wisconsin, where they spent the summer hunting and trapping.

On September 19, 1679, LaSalle watched from shore as *Le Griffon* sailed out of Green Bay, downbound to Lake Erie. Prophetically, the tiny vessel went through what is known today as Les Portes des Morts—

Death's Door Passage—between the Door County peninsula and Washington Island. *Le Griffon* carried the Great Lakes' first commercial cargo: fur pelts intended for sale in Europe. Profits from those furs were supposed to fund additional expeditions into the North American wilderness.

LaSalle knew enough about the Great Lakes' autumn gales to want *Le Griffon* to beat them back to Lake Erie. Even so, the ship apparently sailed too late in the season. Friar Louis Hennipen, a Jesuit priest who documented the LaSalle exploration, described the end of the Great Lakes' first commercial vessel: "The ship was hardly a league from the coast when it was tossed up by a violent storm in such a manner that our men were never heard from since. And it is supposed that the vessel struck on the sand and was there buried."

Historians now believe that *Le Griffon* sailed well beyond Hennipen's sight before coming to grief. It is thought the tiny vessel successfully passed out of Lake Michigan through the Straits of Mackinac before it was wrecked in upper Lake Huron. Pieces of a small wooden ship that may belong to the French vessel have been found near Tobermory, Ontario, at the entrance to Georgian Bay, but so little of this obviously ancient wreck exists that a positive identification has not been possible. *Le Griffon* was the first of an estimated six to ten thousand vessels that would litter the lake bottoms over the following three hundred years.

Almost 160 years after LaSalle, the first steamboat to operate above Niagara Falls, met a similar fate in yet another autumn gale. Built in 1819 by shipwright Noah Brown, the *Walk-In-The-Water* was launched on Scajaguada Creek near Black Rock, New York, not far from where *Le Griffon* was built. This new steamboat supposedly got its name from a Native American's description of the ship's two side paddle wheels, which seemed to "walk" the ship across the water. The full name of the ship was too cumbersome for waterfront conversation or publication in newspapers, so everyone referred to the *Walk-In-The-Water* as simply "the steamboat." Nobody asked, "which steamboat?" in 1820–21. This modified two-masted, topsail schooner was the only one above Lake Ontario. (The steamboat *Ontario* had operated on that lake since 1817.)

Although *Walk-In-The-Water* made at least one trip partway up Lake Huron, its primary route was plying Lake Erie between Buffalo and Toledo. The steamboat was 135 feet long with a beam of 32 feet and a burden of 338 gross tons. The side paddle wheels were exactly amidships, following plans drawn by steamboat pioneer Robert Fulton. Despite the cumbersome machinery, the steamship relied heavily upon its masts and sails when the winds were favorable.

"The steamboat" chugged out of Buffalo for the last time on the evening of October 31, 1821. Not far into its final voyage, the schooner with paddle wheels encountered a typical fall storm. The sky darkened under the weight of clouds that seemed to press down on the lake. With these clouds came a northwest gale that churned up Lake Erie's infamously choppy waters. Captain Jedediah Rogers pushed westward into the storm until pounding waves started the seams of his wooden craft. With water rising in the hold and threatening to put out the fires in the boiler, he turned back toward Buffalo.

Water was pouring into *Walk-In-The-Water* faster than the men at the pump brakes could send it overboard. It became clear to Rogers that he would not reach the haven of Buffalo's harbor in time. He tried to anchor, but the ropes were apparently rotten and could not stand the strain. First one, then the other anchor cable snapped. Rogers was as helpless as any passenger while his vessel drifted toward shore, driven by the unrelenting gale. At 4:30 A.M. on the first day of November, the tiny ship fetched up on the beach at the foot of what is now Buffalo's Main Street. Passengers and crew were landed safely, but the first steamboat of the upper lakes was a wreck.

The loss of *Walk-In-The-Water* was not quite total. Great Lakes historian Dana Thomas Bowen claimed the vertical engine, with its 36-inch-diameter cylinder and 4-foot stroke, was carefully removed from the twisted hull. After refurbishing, the steam engine and boiler were installed in a brand-new vessel. This iron machinery outlived that wooden hull as well. It was placed in yet a third ship before being retired from lake duty around 1840. After that, the cylinder head was reportedly used daily as part of a factory engine until the early twentieth century.

Settlers who pushed their way west into the heart of the North American continent discovered that weather here moved faster and was more violent than what they had experienced in Europe. Understanding the mechanisms behind tornadoes, blizzards, and summer hailstorms became an important quest of American scientists. Throughout the nineteenth century the Holy Grail of that quest was a "law of storms" that would allow forecasters to predict the North American weather. In 1859, New

York professor Elias Loomis noted in a paper presented to the American Scientific Association that "when violent storms are raging, they generally advance from West to East." He also wrote that winter storms take several days to reach what he termed their "greatest violence."

Although the work of American weather scientists paved the way, what today is known as "The Law of Storms," is credited to a Dutch meteorologist, Christoph H. Diederick Buys Ballot, who published his law of wind direction in 1857. Buys Ballot's Law states that an observer in the Northern Hemisphere facing into the wind has the center of low pressure to his right and somewhat behind him. Buys Ballot demonstrated his theory by simply adding up a series of observations in which it proved true and comparing that with the relatively small number of times it proved false.

Earlier, James H. Coffin and William Ferry had come to the same conclusion, but based upon scientific principles such as the Coriolis effect and centripetal force. Several other foundations of modern meteorology were laid during the sixty years prior to 1913. William Redfield and Robert Fitzroy showed how barometric pressure and wind direction could be used to predict storms. Fitzroy founded the British Meteorological Service in 1859, an accomplishment that proved his undoing. Scientific methods were not sufficiently developed to predict weather with the certainty desired by the military. Fitzroy's suicide in 1865 followed stinging criticism of his work by the British Navy.

The search for "The Law of Storms" was spurred in the United States by the high price of sunken ships, damaged buildings, and lives lost each year. *Walk-In-The-Water* was not the last ship—steam or sail—to be lost in a gale on the lakes. An 1835 storm was said to have "swept the lakes clear of sail." Lake Erie was blasted by 60-mile-per-hour winds on November 22 and 23, 1874, with the resulting loss of four ships. A blow that struck all five lakes on November 25, 1905, sank or stranded at least sixteen ships with winds of more than 70 miles per hour. More recently, the "Armistice Day Storm" on November 11, 1940, wrecked a dozen vessels, including two modern steel freighters that disappeared without a trace.

Meteorologists describe the Great Lakes as a "climatological battlefield" where cold polar air and warm, moist tropical air wrestle for control of the North American atmosphere. In spring and fall, the "no-man's-land" separating these atmospheric combatants lies across the five Great Lakes. Sharp contrasts in temperature trigger intense, fast-moving, low-pressure cyclones along the dividing line between the two air masses. These are the fabled "gales of November" that make Great Lakes sailors like Milton Smith so wary.

Smith was a steam engineer, not a trained meteorologist. He apparently relied more on his instincts about the weather than scientific instruments. During his service in ship engine rooms he had seen his share of foul weather. Perhaps he was uneasy about staying aboard the steamer *Charles S. Price* for its final voyage simply because the fall of 1913 had been so pleasant. In any case, it was apparently with a feeling of relief that he packed his kit and said his good-byes. He was not alone among the *Price's* crew in having concerns about November gales. Wheelsman Arze McIntosh stopped Smith before he walked off the freighter.

"Milt, is it true that you are going to leave the ship?" Smith later recalled his friend asking. The men talked for a moment before Smith started down the ladder to the pier. McIntosh helped the former engineer get his sea bag safely to the quay. Although Smith was leaving the ship, he would make much the same journey as his former shipmates—at least as far as his hometown. Both were headed for Port Huron, a small city at the southern end of Lake Huron where it empties into the St. Clair River. Smith's family was waiting there for him. The former engineer would make the trip by land, the wheelsman by water. Both wondered if they might see each other again soon.

Indeed, Smith did see his friend again within days, although not in Port Huron. The unemployed engineer probably didn't even catch a glimpse of his former ship as it passed within a few thousand feet of his house in the darkness early on the next Sunday morning. Smith's unpleasant final meeting with Arze McIntosh and his other shipmates came a few days later in a small Canadian storeroom under far different circumstances than any of them could have imagined.

On this Wednesday, though, the two men still had parting words to say. According to Smith's account of events to reporters, the shipmates talked about going home to their families. "Dammit! I wish I was going with you," Smith recalled McIntosh saying with conviction. And then he said again, "I wish I was going with you."

WEDNESDAY, NOVEMBER 5

MILTON SMITH stepped ashore from the *Charles S. Price* onto the acres of iron ore, coal, stone, and railroad tracks that made up the docks of Ashtabula, Ohio. He had to hike the length of the coal dock, perhaps pausing to let an empty railroad hopper car roll down the "hump" at one end of the unloading machine. Coal from that car was still thundering into the *Price's* hold when the unmanned hopper clattered past Smith and slammed into a string of other empties on the siding. The hump and gravity allowed the empty cars to recouple themselves into a train so they could be hauled back for reloading at some open pit mine in southern Ohio or West Virginia. It was a noisy business. The now-former ship's assistant engineer tramped perhaps a half-mile to the highway. Everything around him—buildings, streets, lampposts, and even the scrub grass was stained the same peculiar black with an underlying hint of red. This color, distinctive of lower Great Lakes ports, was a combination of black dust from nearby coal loaders and red grit from the open piles of iron ore. The same blackish-red color stained buildings and streets in virtually every port on the lower lakes. Gary, Indiana, shared this dark red grunge with "the Flats" along the Cuyahoga River in Cleveland, Ohio. It can still be seen on the steel mills of Zug Island and the Ford River Rouge complex near Detroit, Michigan.

The "sailor town" adjoining the docks on the west bank of the Ashtabula River was known as a place where a man could satisfy all his appetites during the few hours his ship was in port. In sharp contrast, Ashtabula's "downtown" district, where the locals shopped and dined, was up the hill and as far from the disreputable waterfront as possible. Ashtabula was a "large" small town, its modest size belying its importance in the iron ore and coal trades.

Ashtabula's port had grown behind an arrowhead breakwall built in stages by the federal government at the mouth of the river. The east wall was under construction in 1913. One of the largest man-made harbors on the Great Lakes, it was even more heavily used then than it would be ninety years later. This deepwater port was favored by railroads because it was directly north of the Appalachian coalfields and equally well situated to handle the flow of iron ore south to the steel mills in Youngstown and Steubenville, Ohio, and Pittsburgh, Pennsylvania. Steel was the driving force behind the fleet of cargo ships on the Great Lakes. By 1913, the United States had an insatiable demand for goods manufactured from steel. The blast furnaces, rolling mills, and factories satisfying that demand were clustered along the south shore of Lake Erie and on lower Lake Michigan, where they were convenient to the nation's heartland. Raw iron ore lay in huge deposits on the remote shores of northern Lake Michigan and western Lake Superior. Ships carried the ore down the natural water highway of the Great Lakes to the waiting blast furnaces.

The presence of this heartland waterway, so critical to the exploration, development, and commerce of North America, was the result of a geological accident. When the glaciers that scooped the Great Lakes basins last receded some ten thousand years ago, they left behind the largest freshwater reservoir in the world. Today, 20 percent of the world's supply of fresh water is contained in the five lakes: 5,473 cubic miles, or 6 quadrillion gallons in all. It is enough water to cover the lower forty-eight states to a uniform depth of 9.5 feet. The combined surface area of the lakes is 94,000 square miles—larger than the states of New York, New Jersey, Connecticut, Rhode Island, Massachusetts, Vermont, and New Hampshire combined. Stretched end to end, their shorelines would reach nearly halfway around the equator. Michigan, which borders four of the five lakes, has 3,288 miles of coastline, more than any other state except Alaska.

Lake Superior is the largest and deepest of the five lakes—489 feet on average—and contains more water than the other four together. From Duluth it stretches 350 miles east to Sault Ste. Marie, Michigan (known as the "Soo" to lake sailors). Water from Lake Superior flows down the swift St. Marys River to Lakes Huron and Michigan. On a map, these lakes hang like diverging pendulums on north–south axes, Lake Michigan to the west and Huron to the east. From the southern end of Huron the St. Clair River, Lake St. Clair, and the Detroit River roll south to the western end of Lake Erie. From there it is a 200-mile steam northeast to the Welland Canal around the thundering waters of Niagara Falls. Lake Ontario, which receives water from the falls, is the lowest of the Great Lakes. At its eastern end it flows into the St. Lawrence River, the great waterway giving access to the North Atlantic.

As if the lakes themselves were not enough good fortune, other geological accidents conspired to put massive deposits of coal in southern Ohio, Pennsylvania, and West Virginia. The happy orientation of the Appalachian Mountain valleys north to south made it easy to lay track from the coalfields to the lakes. Railroads could earn sizable profits hauling coal to Great Lakes ports for shipment to the iron ore mining communities on the upper lakes. Coal gave lake freighters a two-way business: coal upbound and ore downbound. By the first decade of the twentieth century, the Great Lakes fleet represented considerably more than one-third of the cargo capacity of the U.S. merchant fleet. Annually, ships on the lakes carried more than 50 million tons of ore. The 860-mile waterway from Duluth to Ashtabula and surrounding ports was one of the most heavily traveled in the world in 1913.

Milton Smith strode uphill (everything was uphill from Ashtabula's waterfront) with his sea bag to catch a ride to Ashtabula's gingerbread-trimmed "railroad gothic" train depot. There he purchased the ticket that carried him over the land route around the western end of Lake Erie via Cleveland, Toledo, and Detroit. The trip took more than 12 hours with train changes, but the next time he went to sleep it was in his own bed. Smith's former shipmates would cast off on almost the same journey—only by water—three days later, on Saturday morning, after their cargo of coal was loaded.

The train carrying former Assistant Engineer Smith rolled along the southern shoreline of Lake Erie, passing through Cleveland's east side on an elevated roadbed. Cleveland in the early twentieth century was a city of wooden homes. In those pre-automobile days, working-class homes were built almost on top of one another. Most were large, two-story duplexes, and it was common for the owner to live in one of the apartments and rent the other. Garages were almost unheard of, because autos were still toys of the rich. Working men and women walked to the corner where they waited to catch one of the city's famous trolley cars for the ride to work. Housewives in babushkas also walked, but not to the trolley. They carried the day's groceries home from neighborhood stores in cloth totes known across northern Ohio as "shopping bags."

Cleveland bragged of being "The Forest City" in those days, and for good reason. Residential streets in both working-class and wealthy neighborhoods were lined with lacy American elms. Stout sycamores with their bark peeling in sheets grew on nearly every street. The narrow strip of land between the sidewalk and the street was known by Clevelanders as the "tree lawn," because every home had at least one full-grown tree in that narrow space. Homes often had one or more mature maples or elms in their front yards as well. By the first week of November, the leaves were mostly off these trees. They had been raked into neat piles that, as they burned, provided the heady aroma that marked the fall season.

WILLIAM H. ALEXANDER may have caught a whiff or two of the last smoldering piles of leaves as he rode the streetcar to work from his east-side home that morning. New to northern Ohio, Alexander had recently been named Cleveland's chief weather observer after serving in Baltimore, Maryland. As usual, one of his main tasks that day was to read the tele-graph copy to decipher the morning weather map sent from headquarters in Washington, D.C. To the untrained observer, the coded data were just gibberish. In fact, the words were part of a complex system left over from the days when the Weather Bureau was part of the U.S. Army Signal Corps. The code allowed the maximum amount of data to be transmit-ted in a minimum amount of time. The code saved money by reducing the number of words needed to convey complex information. One word of code represented an entire phrase in ordinary English.

Creation of weather maps in 1913 was a complicated undertaking. Each local weather station transmitted observations twice daily to Wash-ington—nominally at 8 A.M. and 8 P.M., Washington time. It seems strange today, but coordinating weather observations was a serious problem fac-ing the U.S. Army Signal Corps when it established a national network of weather observers in 1870. In that year the United States had seventy-five different time zones. Rural communities still used old-fashioned local time based on "high noon," when the sun was directly overhead on the town square. The railroads started untangling the mess in 1885 by divid-ing the country into four time zones. But few rural communities fol-lowed suit. Standard time made it easier to schedule train service, but farmers maintained that cows and chickens ran on God's time, not the railroads'.

Alexander and his fellow Weather Bureau workers used the railroad system of standard time to synchronize their twice-daily reports to Washington. This meant that the observer in Duluth, Minnesota, took his 8 A.M. readings (Washington time) at 6:52 A.M. local time. The clock in Buffalo, New York, read 7:44 when the 8 A.M. observations were recorded there. Railroad standard time would not become the official time for everyone— farmers and meteorologists—until 1918, in the aftermath of World War I.

Cartographers in Washington plotted the twice-daily data, creating detailed national maps of what the weather had been at the time of the observations. Fax machines and wire photo transmitters had not been invented, so significant data from each map were then extracted and sent back to the local offices using the complex telegraphic code. Men like Alexander had to carefully replot the data to build their own simplified copies of the national map. Naturally, the "latest" weather map in any office was hours behind the actual weather outside the window. The Washington office also mailed printed copies of the 8 A.M. weather map to each station, but these did not arrive for a day or two.

Scientific weather forecasting was still in its infancy during the fall of 1913 in part because of the American Civil War. In 1849 the secretary of the Smithsonian Institution, Joseph Henry, spent $1,000 to start a network of 150 volunteer weather observers. By 1860 he was spending $4,400 per year on the project and posting a daily weather map, which became a favorite attraction for museum visitors. But the Smithsonian's network of volunteer observers was torn apart by the War Between the States and never reassembled.

Although meteorology would not come of age until weather forecasts took on military significance during World War I, in 1870 the U.S. Army initiated a national weather service under the command of General William B. Hazenin. This military service provided the framework for the U.S. Weather Bureau. The Army Signal Corps had its own school of meteorology by 1881. The first weather stations on the Great Lakes opened at Oswego, Buffalo, Cleveland, Toledo, Detroit, Grand Haven, and Milwaukee. It was a low-priority project, and about half the weather stations on the Great Lakes were closed in 1883 in a round of federal budget cutting.

Farmers were the prime consumers of weather forecasts during the nineteenth century, so the government transferred the weather services to the Department of Agriculture in 1891, and the Weather Bureau was born. (It would later become part of the National Oceanographic and

Atmospheric Administration's National Weather Service.) Despite set-backs, there were steady improvements in forecasting during the late nineteenth and early twentieth centuries. The Canadian government also established a weather service, and a uniform system of storm warnings for the U.S. and Canadian Great Lakes was adopted. As the nineteenth century closed, Canadian forecasters were claiming that nearly 90 percent of their forecasts were verified by the actual weather.

Two hurdles still facing observers in 1913 were a severe lack of data and a rudimentary knowledge of how the atmosphere swirled around them. Only a small number of surface reporting stations, spread thinly across the continent, provided reports of surface weather conditions. For practical purposes, there were no stations in the sparsely populated regions to the north and west of the lakes. Significant weather often developed in that wilderness without attracting notice.

No useful data were collected from the air because airplane pilots in those days ventured only a few hundred feet aloft in machines that were little more than motorized box kites. Nothing was known about the jet streams that steer surface weather systems from more than 5 miles over-head. These high-altitude rivers of air were not discovered until the 1920s by the Japanese and by U.S. Air Force B-29 pilots in the early 1940s. Today, forecasters use the jet streams to predict both fair and foul weather, but that was not the case ninety years ago, in an era when forecasters did not yet understand the basic mechanisms of cold and warm fronts. Lacking com-puters, meteorologists in Washington manually plotted each day's data on their maps. Given the lack of reporting stations, isobars were drawn in as much by eye as by certainty. This painstaking process delayed the creation of forecasts and weather warnings, but it was the best they could do.

Although the local mapmaking for Cleveland was done by weather observer William Alexander, every symbol, line, and word of his forecast had been first approved by headquarters in Washington. Even so, that cumbersome process of drawing, encoding, and then redrawing weather maps represented a marked improvement on the attempt at a national map made by Professor Cleveland Abbe in 1869. That map resulted from Abbe's collaboration with Frank A. Armstrong, the manager of the Cincin-nati office of Western Union. The telegrapher collected weather reports from outlying offices, and Abbe attempted to make sense out of that data by plotting it on a map. In the 1880s Abbe convinced the Ohio legislature to create a statewide weather service. Abbe's pioneering work influenced the early development of the national Weather Bureau.

On November 5, 1913, weather observer Alexander plotted the data from Washington using a French curve drawing template to create sweeping lines of equal temperature—isotherms. He used the same technique to ink lines of equal pressure, or isobars. As he finished the last line his eye examined the curves to see if anything unexpected was developing. The morning's map was almost clean of foul weather. Freezing rain in northern Maine was moving offshore into the Atlantic. Blustery conditions in Texas and Kansas were too far south and west to be of immediate concern. Except along the northern border of the Dakotas and a few points in the Rocky Mountains, temperatures across the country were above freezing. For northern Ohio, as for most of the country's midsection, the extremely mild autumn of 1913 was going to continue another day.

After Alexander completed his map, he added a local forecast for Cleveland and a regional one for Lake Erie before sending it to a printer who made copies for distribution to the city's newspapers. Additional printed copies went to post offices and other places where the public could view them.

Alexander was glad of the pleasant November conditions. A native of Hunt County, Texas, he remembered boyhood summers that had been blistering hot, and he had recently returned from postings at Weather Bureau stations in Basseterre, St. Kitts, West Indies, and San Juan, Puerto Rico. The maps told Alexander that he did not have to fear Cleveland's cold and blustery November weather at least for another 36 hours. The temperature would rise into the 50s that day.

NOT EVERYONE was so pleased with the unusually warm November temperatures. The autumn of 1913 created a problem for onion growers and distributors. Their crop was sprouting in storage. The same thing had happened the previous fall, with the resultant loss of thousands of dollars of income. According to a November 7, 1913, article in the *Cleveland Plain Dealer*, the onion producers decided to drop their prices during early November in an effort to sell off as much of the crop as possible before it spoiled in storage.

Sixty miles west of Cleveland at Marblehead, Ohio, warm temperatures were being blamed for outbreaks of diphtheria and scarlet fever.

Doctors claimed the unusual October weather was prolonging a local epidemic of diphtheria that had swept through the small village at the entrance to Sandusky Bay. As a precaution, the town had been under quarantine for almost a month. Some of the dead were buried beneath slabs of poured concrete to prevent the feared disease from "rising from the ground."

About a week earlier, on October 29, a case of scarlet fever had been diagnosed in Marblehead, causing health officials to tighten the existing diphtheria quarantine. Work continued in the nearby limestone quarry in spite of the illnesses. Crushed stone from Marblehead was needed for road construction and to feed blast furnaces in Cleveland, where the production of steel continued 24 hours a day during the summerlike conditions of early November. There was no hint in Cleveland, Detroit, Chicago, or Milwaukee that the weather over northern Lake Superior was deteriorating. The national map for Wednesday, November 5, was dominated by a large fair-weather high-pressure area centered roughly over Ohio's capital city, Columbus.

AT ASHTABULA, on Lake Erie, the 504-foot *Charles S. Price* continued loading coal without Milton Smith. The ship's captain was unaware of the gathering gale over Lake Superior, but even if he had known about this first "blow" of November, Cleveland-born shipmaster W. H. Black probably would not have been concerned. The *Price* was one of the newest freighters on the Great Lakes. Shipbuilding was more advanced than weather forecasting in 1913. Built of steel, Black's vessel offered the latest in conveniences, including electric lights, hot water showers, and flush toilets, in an era when American farms still burned "coal oil" for light and had a privy out back.

Steel ships like the *Price* were replacing wooden vessels in the Great Lakes fleet at a rapid pace. In fact, demand for new steel ships had created a shipbuilding boom around the lakes. Roughly half the vessels built by U.S. shipyards during the first decade of the twentieth century were launched on the lakes. These larger steel ships took work from the aging fleet of smaller wooden hulls that had been built at the close of the nineteenth century. Constant launching of new vessels meant that by 1913 the Great Lakes fleet was growing younger in average vessel age with each passing year.

The largest vessel on the lakes in 1900 was the *James J. Hill*, at 498 feet. The *J. Pierpont Morgan* reached 600 feet in 1906. The launching of the *Col. J.M. Schoonmaker* in 1911 set a new benchmark for the longest lake freighter, at 617 feet. The *Schoonmaker* had a single 2,600-horsepower, triple-expansion steam engine. Just to prove this new giant was no fluke, a sister ship was launched a year later.

Wednesday's national map painstakingly plotted by Weather Bureau headquarters in Washington showed a low-pressure area over the far northwest in Washington State and British Columbia. This weather system was expected to move east and dip down into the Dakotas. If it followed a typical path, it would bring stormy conditions to Cleveland in three or four days. Forecaster Alexander probably expected it would arrive Friday or Saturday at the latest. But unknown to Alexander (or any other U.S. weather forecaster) a complicated chain of atmospheric events would soon be churning the waters of western Superior. In retrospect it seems likely that another low, farther east but north of the map coverage, was approaching the Hudson Bay region, and trailing south from it was a long cold front advancing toward Superior, though still more than 24 hours to the west.

At Fort William, Ontario, on Lake Superior's northern shore, Captain Neil Campbell of the steamship *Sarnian* needed only his November forebodings to warn him that the unusually fine autumn weather was coming to an end Wednesday evening. It was a chilly 35 degrees at Fort William's grain docks when, as midnight approached, Campbell gave orders to single up the mooring lines in preparation for the last downbound trip of the season. There was little wind, but a change was in the air.

THURSDAY, NOVEMBER 6

WEATHER FORECASTING during the second decade of the twentieth century remained more divination than science. Only a few key forecasters at headquarters in Washington were authorized to do this arcane work. The process involved studying the daily map for similarities with the historical records of weather for the date in question. Sometimes the system worked. Often it failed spectacularly, as on March 12, 1888, when forecasters divined cold and brisk but fair weather for New York City. Nearly two feet of snow fell that day in what has been known on the East Coast ever since as the "Blizzard of '88."

Forecasting had improved in the twenty-five years since that disaster, but in 1913 it still relied greatly on educated guesses based on the historical record. Careful collection of weather data from around the country was aimed at finding natural patterns to the weather that meteorologists hoped would allow more accurate forecasts. This method of weather forecasting was called "weather typing" by Edward Garriott, the chief Washington forecaster in 1901, who promoted it. Garriott believed that the more meteorologists knew of the past, the better they could predict the future. Toward that end an elaborate system of cross-indexed weather maps was developed. It was a flawed process if only because the amount of data that a forecaster had to sort through to make each day's predictions was beyond human capacity. One person simply could not remember all of the maps, and the volume of printed catalogs proved cumbersome.

Over the next half-century, meteorologists would come to understand frontal structures and wave cyclones. They would begin to understand the three-dimensionality of the atmosphere, and how upper-level conditions affect surface weather. The first mathematical models of atmospheric processes would be developed, and still later the invention of high-speed computers would permit the use of these models for predictive purposes. But in 1913 none of these concepts and tools was available.

Ship captains in 1913 trusted their own weather instincts over government forecasts issued by deskbound bureaucrats who had never sailed the lakes. Captain Neil Campbell did not rely on either U.S. or Canadian forecasters to alert him that foul weather was on the way. By late Wednesday evening, as the *Sarnian's* mooring lines were being singled up in preparation for departure from the Canadian harbor of Fort William (now Thunder Bay) on northern Lake Superior, the approaching cold front was probably heralded by early clouds as warm, moist air over the lake was pushed aloft.

Great Lakes sailors handled their ships' lines both on deck and on the piers in 1913. Few ports provided stevedores to assist. When docking or undocking, a deckhand or two would be swung over the side using a rude bosun's chair that was little more than a short wooden plank. These members of the ship's crew would secure the lines to bollards for docking and would retrieve them for departure. The *Sarnian's* crew now did the latter, knowing they would have to go ashore in "the chair" again to handle lines in the locks at Sault Ste. Marie, at the lake's lower end.

When his ship departed early Thursday morning, Campbell noted another change. "My barometer was falling," he later recalled for reporters, "but the wind had not sprung up yet."

Campbell planned to hug the Canadian shore on the north side of the big lake. "When I got around Thunder Bay cape it began to blow from the southwest," he later recalled. In fact, the wind on Lake Superior had been blowing south to southwest for a day or two, the result of circulation around the large area of high pressure that covered much of the eastern United States. But now those winds were picking up strength as the northern low moved toward Hudson Bay, creating a sharper local pressure gradient. The *Sarnian* could also have encountered squall lines ahead of the approaching cold front. This blow from the southwest transformed the rocky Canadian shoreline to Campbell's north into a dreaded lee shore. The triple-expansion steam engine of the 320-foot *Sarnian* developed just 1,000 horsepower—not a lot for a ship of its size—and the freighter was unable to avoid being blown toward the craggy Canadian mainland. "I saw my boat could not make it with wind from that direction, so I went back behind the cape," Campbell said. "Five times I made the effort to get out."

■ ■

BY 1912 there were more than 2,050 employees and volunteer observers working for the Weather Bureau. Most were simply field observers, not trained meteorologists. The bureau gave these observers only six weeks of training, none in weather science. They were taught how to maintain and read the various instruments. Most important, they learned how to properly fill out government forms. Observers were to observe, and little else. All of the collating of the data and the forecasting were to be done by the small cadre of professionals in the Washington office.

Experienced weather observers such as Alexander in the Cleveland Bureau office gained much of their knowledge from on-the-job experience. Alexander was undoubtedly well aware of the relationship between high or low pressure and the weather. Highs were recognized as bringing fair conditions, while lows brought stormy weather. But no one, either observers or meteorologists, understood cold and warm fronts.

It would take another six years for Norwegian scientist Jacob ("Jack") Bjerknes to develop the concept of weather fronts. In 1919 he began a revolution in weather forecasting with the publication of a short paper titled "On the Structure of Moving Cyclones." The twenty-one-year-old Bjerknes suggested that low-pressure systems were preceded by "warm fronts" and followed by what he called "cold fronts." Prior to Bjerknes, forecasters were aware of what they called "steering lines" and "squall lines" but did not know how they fit into the overall picture of the weather. The concept of "fronts" has been refined over time, but Bjerknes' work remains a keystone in modern weather forecasting.

None of this was available to Alexander and his fellow observers in November 1913. Their lack of understanding of weather dynamics is illustrated by the bureau's record keeping. Barometric pressures, so vital to modern predictions, were monitored hourly, but many stations recorded a single daily reading in their official logs. Wind direction was often overlooked as a critical factor in weather forecasting. Records available for many stations show only the predominant direction of the wind for an entire month and the direction of the maximum gust of wind during that month. Wind directions were not reported to newspapers on national summary maps.

The incomplete collection of data on wind direction is an indication that its importance in changing weather patterns was not fully appreciated. Ship logs and captain reports from 1913 show the same lack of understanding about wind direction and storms. Captains always recorded the strength of gusts, but only occasionally was the wind direction written down. In many cases, it is necessary to deduce the direction of wind described in a ship captain's log by studying a map to see what geographic feature he chose for protection from the gale. A ship that anchored in the lee of land to its north was most likely escaping a northerly wind. That much is obvious. But, was it a northwesterly or a northeasterly wind? The records are often mute on such details.

Thirty-two years earlier, in 1881, Canadian scientist Dr. Joseph Workman had pointed out the mortal danger to Great Lakes sailors of ignoring the weather. As an example, he used the wooden steamer *Zeeland*, which foundered on Lake Huron during a November gale in 1880. "Had the master of the *Zeeland* consulted his barometer and noted the prevailing under and upper cloud carriages, he would not have left port," he wrote in a letter circulated to Canadian newspapers. "No very small proportion of those in command of our inland shipping are not only imperfectly acquainted with meteorological science, but actually regard the whole subject with self-satisfied contempt." As events played out in 1913, the intervening three decades had done little to change the attitudes of Great Lakes captains.

On Monday's map a low-pressure system had been shown over northern Lake Superior, but the meteorologists in Washington had placed it east of Montreal on Tuesday. Wednesday's map indicated that only a solitary high-pressure system centered over Ohio was affecting weather on all five Great Lakes. The movement of this anticyclone from Oklahoma on Tuesday appeared to have pushed low pressure and stormy weather to the east, out of the area. The biggest weather system shown on Thursday morning's map was still this fair-weather high-pressure center, which forecasters positioned over eastern Virginia, where it was affecting the middle Atlantic coast. It was expected to continue sliding to the east and disappear over the Atlantic Ocean. The high was centered on Washington, D.C., but the curve of its isobars showed that it was still the dominant influence all the way west to Detroit and north to Toronto. While the *Sarnian* was waiting for relief from building southwest winds on Lake Superior, Cleveland observer William H. Alexander studied maps that showed no evidence of any gales near that lake.

Alexander knew that winds rotate clockwise around a high-pressure

center in the Northern Hemisphere. This was one of the facts collected
into "The Law of Storms" by nineteenth-century scientists. The Great
Lakes were now on the "back side" of the high, so its "anticyclonic"
(clockwise) rotation helped pump warm, moist air northward from the
Gulf of Mexico. That was the logical explanation for the unusually pleasant temperatures recorded by Alexander's official thermometer.

A coded telegraph message from Washington grabbed Alexander's attention shortly after 9 A.M. Although they were warm, the rising winds on the
lower lakes required the lowest-level storm warning—a small-craft warning, which, according to a 1913 bureau publication, predicted moderately
strong winds and sea conditions that might be dangerous to small craft.

The term *small craft* had no specific definition but loosely applied to
vessels under 65 feet, such as fish tugs and small coastal schooners. (Curiously, an exact ruling on the size of a "small craft" still does not exist. This
lack of a specific definition is currently before the U.S. courts because of
the proliferation of lawsuits involving weather-related accidents.)

Captains of large steel freighters have always excluded their vessels
from small-craft warnings, and usually pay little attention to them. That
Thursday, however, the increasing wind that prompted this advisory did
cause problems for some ships. Several freighters became trapped by a
fluctuation in water levels on Lake Erie and Lake St. Clair. Water level
changes of this type are called *seiches*. Northwest winds on Wednesday
that backed to the southwest and south on Thursday literally pushed
water out of the shallow west end of the lake toward the deeper eastern
basin. The water depth near Toledo, Ohio, decreased because of the
seiche, resulting in a corresponding increase in water depths at Buffalo,
New York. The difference between water levels at the east and west ends
of Lake Erie has occasionally exceeded 15 feet. On Lake Michigan, the
water has risen as much as 7 feet at Chicago.

The seiche caused several groundings of ships at the mouth of the
Detroit River and in Lake St. Clair Thursday, though these minor inci-
dents escaped attention except for brief mentions in the shipping news
of local newspapers. The steamer *Price McKinney* became stuck in the
Grosse Pointe Cut near Detroit, Michigan. It was not seriously damaged
and was quickly floated free. At nearby Russell's Island, the *S.J. Albright*
also became stuck in the mud until it could be lightered.

Otherwise, ships on the lower lakes took advantage of pleasant

November temperatures to finish their last voyages of the season. Except on western Lake Superior, pleasant south and southerly winds were blowing throughout the Great Lakes region. A total of twenty-eight vessels locked upbound through Sault Ste. Marie during the day, while twenty-four others locked through downbound. Thursday was a perfectly ordinary workday for the majority of captains, mates, and sailors of the Great Lakes fleet. Captain Campbell of the *Sarnian* might have been hunkered down against a November southwesterly "blow," but just 50 miles to his south sailors were still enjoying unusually fine weather.

Along with offhand comments about the unusual weather for November, talk around Lake Erie that Thursday focused on the sandsucker dredge *Doville*. This hapless workboat was in the shipyard at Toledo, Ohio, after crossing beneath a closed railroad bridge in that city's harbor. The ship's superstructure had been swept off in the accident along with some of its pumping equipment. As indicated by an article in the November 6, 1913, *Toledo Blade*, it was generally agreed that the *Doville*'s captain must have been an embarrassed man.

Sailors visiting the locks at Sault Ste. Marie talked about the collision of two freighters on Monday in the upper approach canal to the American locks. The steamers *Queen City* and *Siemens*, both owned by the Pittsburgh Steamship Company, sustained considerable damage to their bows. Damage to the downbound *Queen City* was on the starboard side, while the upbound *Siemens* was crumpled on the port. After temporary repairs both vessels completed their last runs of the season.

No matter which accident was the topic of conversation, somebody would mention how safe a year 1913 had been on the lakes. There had been fewer sailors injured or killed in sinkings or other accidents than in any other year of recent memory.

St. Clair River — Sombra, Ontario
REGINA

One captain with little concern over building foul weather on Lake Superior was thirty-four-year-old Edward McConkey. His 249-foot Canadian package freighter, *Regina*, spent Thursday docked at Sombra, Ontario, about halfway up the St. Clair River near the foot of Lake Huron. Conditions on the river remained exceptionally mild for early November—sunny and 58 degrees at midday, with a light southerly wind. Winter seemed far in the future.

In 1913, Sombra was hardly more than a crossroads with a riverfront wharf. The Chesapeake & Ohio Railroad main line ran a few blocks east of the town's business district without even a siding to serve the docks. Sombra, however, is centrally located in a large agricultural area, and it was a crop from those farms that drew *Regina*. The ship stopped to load bales of hay (some reports say straw). A dry spot had to be found in the hold where they would not grow moldy. The small freighter's two jib cranes lowered the bales into a protected corner of the hold. Not only did the hay have to be protected from moisture, but it had to be stowed where the bales would be handy for unloading at their destination.

McConkey's Canadian vessel looked like a half-size Great Lakes straight decker even though it was never intended to carry bulk cargoes like coal or iron ore. *Regina* had been built six years earlier in Dumbarton, Scotland, as a sort of floating delivery van for the Canadian wilderness. Known on the lakes as "package freighters," ships like *Regina* carried all manner of goods to isolated ports along the Ontario shoreline of Lake Huron, mostly inside Georgian Bay. Prior to modern highways, package freighters served as the delivery trucks of the Canadian north woods, linking communities virtually inaccessible except by water. Naturally, the final ship visit of the season was particularly important for residents of those isolated communities. It represented their last contact with the outside world for four or perhaps five months.

The relatively short length of Canadian package freighters was mandated by the size of locks in the canals connecting Lake Ontario to the lower St. Lawrence River. The modern St. Lawrence Seaway was only a dream in 1913; it did not become a reality until the 1950s. The available locks limited ships to about 250 feet in overall length. A whole class of Canadian Great Lakes vessels known as "canalers" was built to fit those locks.

Regina was owned by the Merchants Mutual Line of Toronto, Ontario. Its crew of twenty-two men consisted mostly of Canadian sailors, although there were also men from England and Scotland aboard. Canada was a dominion of the British Empire in 1913, explaining the nationalities of the crew aboard the Scots-built ship. Sailors and ship were subjects of the same king.

Regina was taking on its cargo of hay at Sombra at about the same time as weather observer Alexander was noting a near-record high temperature of 66 degrees in Cleveland. Northern Ohio newspapers commented that Thursday and Friday were "the warmest November days in years." Readers were cautioned that the unseasonable conditions were about to end. Alexander was already forecasting freezing weather for Saturday and Sunday as the result of cold sweeping down from the Dakotas. But the official forecast made no mention of a major storm anywhere on the Great Lakes. In the November 7, 1913, *Cleveland Press*, the worst weather predicted was a cold November rain.

Lake Superior — Duluth, Minnesota
SAMUEL F. B. MORSE

The upbound steamer *Samuel F.B. Morse* finally pushed its way into Duluth about 11 A.M. Thursday after an unexpectedly rough trip from Sault Ste. Marie. At the 10 mile-per-hour speeds typical of 1913 freighters in open water, the 394-mile trip usually took 40 hours. But rough conditions were beginning to slow upbound ships, and the *Morse* was one of several that arrived up to 11 hours late that day. A significant factor in the delayed arrivals was the size of engines in Great Lakes steamers. Typically, they were smaller than those of oceangoing ships because the many canals and rivers on the lakes did not require high speed. In foul weather, however, the smaller engines left lake freighters at a disadvantage. Many lacked the power to maintain their schedules when pounding through storm waves. The actual speed made good into a head sea often dropped to as little as 8 or 9 miles per hour.

Lake Superior — Jackfish, Ontario
SARNIAN

By Thursday afternoon, ships on northwestern Lake Superior were pressed between leaden clouds overhead and tumultuous gray-green waves. The overcast had begun building at dawn, and by midafternoon daylight had lost the golden color of autumn and taken on the gray light of early winter. Bright hues disappeared about noon, painting the world in somber shades of gray. Despite this gloom, the weather hardly qualified as a full-fledged November gale—not yet.

Captain Campbell of the *Sarnian* may have been telling a bit of a sea story when he related to a *Port Huron Times-Herald* reporter days later that conditions on Superior were the worst he had ever seen. "Thursday brought me as far as Jackfish," he said. "Laid under the bluffs there until Friday night," the captain added. His local knowledge allowed him to find shelter behind a headland at the small port of Jackfish, Ontario, some 90 miles east of Thunder Bay on the Canadian side of the lake. As luck had it, Campbell chose a harbor more protected from the northwest gale that was about to sweep across Lake Superior than from the current southwest wind.

Lake Superior — Fort William, Ontario
JAMES CARRUTHERS *and* J.H. SHEADLE

Late Thursday afternoon two captains rested against the counter in the office of the grain shipping dock at Fort William, Ontario, at the northwestern corner of Lake Superior. This was the same port that *Sarnian* had departed nearly 18 hours earlier. Posted nearby was the latest weather information from Canadian forecasters. It was the practice of the Canadian weather service to telegraph storm bulletins to harbormasters and major shipping dock operators. These warnings were displayed in special frames provided for the purpose by the Dominion government.

Captain W. H. Wright commanded the largest and strongest ship in the Canadian Great Lakes fleet, the *James Carruthers*. It was also one of the newest ships on the lakes, having been launched at Collingwood, Ontario, only the previous May. Extra steel framing had been built into this 529-foot "straight decker" to make it one of the stoutest hulls on the lakes. This strength came at a penalty, however. The *Carruthers* had slightly less cargo capacity than other ships its size.

Next to the Canadian shipmaster stood Captain S. A. Lyons of the American ship *J.H. Sheadle*. His 530-foot bulk freighter was in its seventh season. The two captains chatted as they waited for the clerk to finish their paperwork. In view of the rising winds outside the snug office, they agreed to go down Lake Superior together. Contrary to their plans, however, the loading of grain into the *Carruthers* was unexpectedly delayed, and the *Sheadle* would set out on its own shortly after 8 P.M.

Although of different nationalities, the Canadian and American ships were of such similar design they might have been mistaken as sisters. Both were straight deckers, a type of bulk freighter unique to the Great Lakes. Their design derived its name from the long expanse of straight deck between the forward pilothouse and the boilerhouse at the stern. Straight deckers originated as wooden lake freighters in the years following the U.S. Civil War. The pattern on the lakes was to locate a single steam engine in the stern of freighters. This configuration provided the maximum length of uninterrupted cargo hold amidships.

The first straight decker is believed to have been the *R.J. Hackett*, launched at Cleveland, Ohio, in 1869. In 1882 the *Onaka* also came down the ways in Cleveland. More than 300 feet in length, this ship's pilothouse in the bow and engines aft fixed the style of the Great Lakes bulk freighter for all time. The straight-deck freighter proved ideal for handling bulk cargoes, such as iron ore, coal, limestone, and grain. Straight deckers dominated the 1913 fleet because those bulk raw materials were the dominant cargoes on the Great Lakes. Of the three, iron ore was the most profitable. At the time, mines at the western end of Lake Superior were producing ore so pure it could go directly into a blast furnace without refining. The supply of ore seemed as endless as the demand for steel. About 40 million tons of iron ore were moved down the lakes every shipping season during the years immediately prior to World War I.

Straight deckers would remain the quintessential Great Lakes freighter long after 1913, although by 1980 most were equipped with self-unloading booms. Nobody has ever considered the straight decker a graceful design. A naval architect for the American Shipbuilding Company once admitted, "We build shoe boxes with a point at one end and a propeller at the other."

When the last of its cargo of grain had tumbled down the chutes and into the *J.H. Sheadle*, it was time for the crew to begin the laborious process of closing the yawning hatches with telescoping steel covers. Every movement left footprints in the grain dust on the deck in the lee of the hatch coamings, where it was protected from the rising wind. The majority of those gaping hatches were still uncovered as the ship crew singled up its lines in preparation to depart Fort William. The same blustery southwesterly winds that dogged the *Sarnian* on its way to Jackfish whistled around the grain loading docks. "When I left, the barometer was below normal, but stationary," Captain Lyons would later write.

Just offshore from Fort William in Lake Superior lies Isle Royale, a long island with its axis oriented northeast to southwest. The channel between this island and the mainland acted like a wind tunnel Thursday evening. Southwest winds were funneled between the island and the mainland, causing sizable waves to build in the channel. "The wind had been blowing for some time," Captain Lyons observed. "After getting outside of Thunder Cape, there was a heavy sea running from the southwest and a strong breeze. I went back under Pie Island, letting go the anchor at 10 o'clock and laying there." Captain Lyons chose his shelter wisely. Pie Island is a midsize chunk of land nestled in the entrance to Thunder Bay. This island and Thunder Cape to the northeast provide natural protection to the bay from lake waves. For the moment, the *Sheadle* was well guarded against swells rolling up the Isle Royale channel.

For whatever reason, the *Carruthers* did not start on its downbound trip immediately. The Canadian freighter may have remained in Fort William to escape the strong southwest winds and seas. Certainly, Captain Wright took advantage of this time to secure the hatch covers of his ship. Meanwhile, throughout Thursday, the U.S. weather station at Saulte Ste. Marie recorded mild south and southeasterly winds. The winds went east after midnight, but speeds remained light, in the 5- to 7-mile-per-hour range. No precipitation was recorded. Similar conditions were reported at Marquette, Michigan, where south to southeast winds at 11 to 12 miles per hour were recorded. According to the *Toledo Blade* on November 6, gale conditions were still confined to the upper lake.

The moon was ringed by a well-defined halo during the evening twilight at Detroit that Thursday. Observer George W. Pitman carefully noted it in the station's permanent log. As he wrote, he may have been thinking about a weather rhyme handed down over the generations:

When halos ring the moon or sun . . .
Rain is coming on the run.

FRIDAY, NOVEMBER 7

FRIDAY MORNING the foul weather around the Great Lakes was still confined to a November gale on western Lake Superior. Mild conditions continued on Lake Erie, where Cleveland still enjoyed kinder-than-normal autumn weather. Bureau Chief Alexander noted that the sky was partly cloudy and the temperature was 50 degrees at 6 A.M. The weather map telegraphed from Washington to outlying offices that morning showed an area of low pressure that had appeared seemingly from nowhere overnight to center some 100 to 150 miles south of Duluth, but this low would drop off the map again by Sunday and probably never really existed as a closed-surface system. Rather, low pressures in that region were the result of an upper-level trough. Early Friday, the bureau was not yet alert to the Superior gale.

Noting the warm, 16- to 18-mile-per-hour wind blowing from the southeast in Cleveland, Alexander warned that the moderate temperatures could not last. His published weather forecast called for pleasant conditions to end overnight in rain as the presumed low over southern Minnesota moved through. Freezing temperatures would arrive for Saturday and Sunday as a result of cold air sweeping down from the Dakotas on the back side of the low. The steadily falling barometer, the increasing overcast, and the southeast winds at Cleveland were sure signs of an approaching weather change.

Lake Superior —— Pie Island, Ontario
J.H. SHEADLE

The grain-laden *J.H. Sheadle* spent most of Thursday night behind Pie Island in northern Lake Superior. No Great Lakes captain would have anchored simply to avoid discomfort. Captain Lyons' ship probably had real need for shelter. It was (and occasionally still is) common practice on the Great Lakes for vessels to begin departing harbor while the tedious task of closing hatch covers was incomplete. The *Sheadle* likely sailed from Fort William in this condition. Captain Lyons quickly realized his mistake and sought a calm patch of water where his crew could safely secure their vessel without fear of the building waves. Whatever Lyons' reasons for anchoring, by 4 A.M. Friday the experienced captain got his vessel underway again, steaming for Whitefish Bay, 220 miles to the southeast. Captain Lyons avoided any mention of hatch covers in his letter about the storm sent to the owners of the *Sheadle*. He chose a simple, equally believable reason for getting underway again—a wind shift to the north.

Well before dawn on Friday morning, long before weather observer Alexander awakened in Cleveland, Captain Lyons realized his tiny shelter at Pie Island had disappeared with the approach of a squall line. Although he did not know it, the *Sheadle* had just experienced the passage of what is today called a cold front. According to his official report, Lyons remained anchored, "until 3:30 the morning of the 7th (Friday), when the wind went north and we proceeded on our voyage."

Captain Lyons was still raising anchor when the same veering wind was noted at the weather station in Duluth. The wind went west there during the 3 o'clock hour before veering northwest at 6 A.M. This wind shift was accompanied by a gradual decrease in wind speed to almost calm during the 7 o'clock hour. After that, the wind built steadily to 28 miles per hour at noon. By 5 P.M., men and women on their way home from work would be holding onto their hats in the 42-mile-per-hour gusts. As wind speeds went up, the temperature in Duluth dropped steadily from 48 to 29 degrees.

Lake Superior — Two Harbors, Minnesota
L.C. WALDO

Just after dawn Friday, the modern 472-foot steel bulk freighter *L.C. Waldo* started downbound from Two Harbors, Minnesota, an ore-loading port about 25 miles northeast of Duluth. In the straight decker's hold was the final cargo of rust red ore for the season. Captain Duddleson had no way of judging just how rough conditions would become when he reached open water. Strong southwest winds had been blowing while he prepared to depart the ore docks. The wind went north after the ship cleared the entrance, promising a "lumpy" trip down to the Soo locks.

The *Waldo's* pilothouse was typical of Great Lakes ships. It was a tiny, D-shaped room with windows around the curved front to give unobstructed vision forward and to each side. Smaller windows gave a view aft. There was just enough space for a compass binnacle and steering wheel in the middle of the room and a chart table along the back wall. An empty patch of deck forward of the wheel was reserved for the captain's stool. Next to it stood the engine order telegraph (universally called a "chadburn" on the lakes, after the Chadburn Company, which produced a large number of these telegraphs during the early years of the twentieth century). Jutting up from the deck near the chadburn was a large bronze whistle pull. Steam radiators lined the forward walls to provide heat needed in spring and fall. On ships equipped with an electric searchlight, the hand control poked downward through the roof above the captain.

It has never been the custom to call the pilothouse of a lakes freighter "the bridge," even though it serves that function. However, walkways to either side of the structure have always been called "bridge wings." The wings allow a captain to look down the side of the ship when docking or maneuvering in locks. Most wooden steamers and a few very early steel ships also had a steering station on the pilothouse roof. This open-air station was called a "flying bridge." It served much the same purpose as the upper control stations on modern pleasure boats that have inherited the name.

Like other vessels of its type, the pilothouse of the *Waldo* was so far forward that its wheelsman had difficulty judging the "swing" of the ship as it responded to the helm. The solution was to steal a jib boom from a schooner and mount it on the bow. Called a "steering pole," this pseudo-bowsprit gave the wheelsman a point of reference to judge movement of the bow.

Pilothouses were stepped atop a larger deckhouse known on lake ships as the "texas." The texas raised the pilothouse for better visibility and provided space for living quarters. Inside was the captain's small suite of rooms as well as cabins for the mates and wheelsmen. (A wheelsman on a lake freighter would have been called a "quartermaster" on a 1913 oceangoing ship.) The captain usually enjoyed a private toilet and bathtub, but everyone else in the crew shared facilities. The officers' toilets were separate from those of the deckhands.

Legend holds that the name *texas* came from an early Great Lakes custom of naming passenger cabins after states of the Union. Naturally, the largest cabin was "Texas." Presumably, "Rhode Island" would have been a tiny affair barely large enough for a bunk. Some lake historians have claimed this custom gave rise to the term *stateroom*, which is used to refer to any passenger cabin on a ship. These claims are probably untrue but have been repeated around the lakes so often that no one questions their authenticity.

Larger bulk freighters in 1913 were often equipped with lavish passenger cabins in the texas intended for the ship owners and their guests. In the days before air conditioning, a cruise to Duluth and back aboard an ore freighter was a delightful way to escape the summer heat of Chicago, Detroit, or Cleveland. Although the primary function of these ships remained carrying freight, their passenger cabins were typically furnished with decorative wood paneling and marble bath fixtures similar to first-class cabins on ocean liners. But guest cabins were empty the first week in November. Passengers seldom chose to suffer the rough water and cold winds that accompanied late-season trips.

Beneath the texas was the windlass room. This space was enclosed within the steel hull in what would be the "forecastle" of a saltwater freighter. The triangular windlass room contained steam-powered machinery for handling the anchor chains and mooring cables. Saltwater ships typically left this equipment exposed on the forecastle deck. Windlasses on Great Lakes bulk freighters were not enclosed to protect them from the elements. Rather, this equipment was naturally covered over by the texas and pilothouse during the evolution of the straight decker design.

The men who worked windlasses on the straight deckers were blind to what was taking place outside their triangular steel rooms. The earliest answer to this problem was a simple speaking tube leading from the open deck at the stem down to the windlass control station. Speaking tubes are still seen on conventional straight deckers, although telephones and loudspeakers allow improved communications.

As the *L.C. Waldo* proceeded east the northerly wind was moderate, but the temperature was falling. Captain Duddleson's weather eye warned him that worse was on the way.

St. Clair River — Sarnia, Ontario
REGINA

The gathering gale was still confined to Lake Superior when Captain Edward McConkey steamed his package freighter, *Regina*, up the St. Clair River. He had loaded hay at the farming town of Sombra and was now picking up the rest of his cargo at the larger port city of Sarnia, Ontario. Although they were not heavy, the hay bales took up a large portion of the ship's hold. Their bulk made loading the other items on the manifest more difficult. Goods taken aboard at Sarnia were a mixed lot: a crate of silverware, boxes of bottled ketchup, a case of hand lotion, and buckets of roofing tar. Also on the dock was a case of French champagne for a New Year's Eve party planned for a logging camp in the Canadian wilderness. The champagne sat next to boxes of less elegant but more powerful whiskey. Not all drinking in the Canadian north woods was festive.

First mate Wesley Adams skillfully directed the placement of this strange assortment of cargo in *Regina's* rapidly filling hold. Men wheeled boxes and crates through the large side loading ports typical of a package freighter. These doors led straight into the hold from the pier. Captain McConkey was not worried by the work of loading. Adams was good at his job. What concerned the captain was a stack of iron sewer and gas pipe on the quay beside his tiny ship. The pipe had to be loaded even though it was too long to fit into *Regina's* hold through the ship's hatches. Even if the pipe could have been wedged through the hatches, there was no room inside because of the hay bales. This meant the heavy stack would have to go on deck. The young captain knew that putting so much weight on deck would reduce his ship's stability. He did not want to face a major November gale with a heavy deckload of pipe, but the weather was still pleasant at the foot of Lake Huron. Perhaps they would get lucky on this last trip of the season.

While loading in Sarnia, Captain McConkey welcomed aboard David Renny, manager of the nearby King Milling Company. They had become friends when Renny rode as passenger on the Canadian steamer *Pellet* the previous season while McConkey was filling in as captain. Now the two men undoubtedly spoke of the unusually mild fall weather and of *Regina's* final trip. Renny made plans to see his friend again when McConkey steamed down from Georgian Bay on his way to winter layup.

As the two men spoke there was little hint that the pleasant autumn of 1913 was about to come to an end. The temperature in Sarnia, as reported by the Monthly Meteorological Notes at Detroit, Michigan, was in the 60s with a light southerly wind, but overhead, the sun was surrounded by a faint halo that would soon be obliterated by thickening clouds.

WEATHER OBSERVERS around the lakes had barely finished inking their maps from the Weather Bureau telegraph Friday morning—maps showing no trace of a gale on Superior—when a storm warning from Washington acknowledged that the real weather was different from that displayed on paper. "The course of the storm [over Superior] was watched closely by the Washington [D.C.] bureau and word was flashed here early Friday to prepare for the storm to strike Cleveland," William Alexander would later tell the Cleveland newspapers.

In fact, Washington's warnings were flashed not just to Cleveland but to all stations around Lakes Superior, Michigan, Huron, and Erie. The evidence of a deepening gale over Superior had the Weather Bureau's attention. Storm warning flags were hoisted at 10 A.M. Washington time, their sequence indicating the velocity and direction of the expected wind. Prior to the widespread use of radio communications, flag hoists were the only way to signal ships. At night, red and white lanterns in various combinations served the same purpose.

Friday's signal hoist was a square red flag—8 by 8 feet—with a black center, which a 1913 bureau publication described as predicting "a storm of marked violence." In fact, forecasters expected winds in the 55-mile-per-hour range or higher through Saturday. It was a fairly typical November forecast. A red triangular pennant below the flag signaled that the storm would blow from the southwest. "Hoist southwest storm warning 10:00 A.M.," the directive from Washington had read. "Storm over upper Mississippi valley moving northeast. Brisk to high southwest winds this afternoon and tonight, shifting to northwest Saturday on upper Lakes. Warnings ordered throughout Great Lakes." The warning of a storm moving northeast over Superior suggests that the Weather Bureau believed the low it had mapped south of Duluth that morning was the cause of the Superior gale, when in fact the real cause was the cold front sweeping southeast over the lake, together with a strong area of high pressure over central Canada.

All 112 individual Weather Bureau Signal Stations around the lakes received the same message. Signal stations at Lifesaving Service stations, revenue cutter docks, commercial wharves, and even some yacht clubs hoisted signals in places as diverse as Duluth, Detroit, Port Huron, Cleveland, and Buffalo. Hands at each station pulled the appropriate flags from their bins and hoisted them on signal masts. Lamp wicks were trimmed so that a red lantern could be displayed over a white one after dark—the signal for storm winds out of the west. But although the flags went up and the lanterns were lighted, these signals gave mariners only the most basic information about the deteriorating weather. The 1913 warning system was simply not capable of conveying detailed information about the location of storms or their severity. In effect, captains were being told to duck for cover, but the signals did not tell them what they were ducking from or where to take cover.

"The warning was passed to every port along the Great Lakes and before sunrise Friday morning government storm signals, a red rectangular flag with a black center, was posted in every port," Alexander said later. "The red pennant pointing to the northwest, indicating that the storm was coming from that direction, was posted over each signal flag." But Alexander was wrong when he said the warning came before sunrise. According to the Cleveland station records, he hoisted the warning flags in Cleveland at 9:42 A.M., just 6 minutes after receiving orders from Weather Bureau headquarters in Washington, D.C. His statement about the red pennant was also wrong, or more likely misquoted by the reporter. The red pennant was below, not above, the red flag with a black center (which was square, not rectangular), and it signified winds out of the southwest, not the northwest.

In addition to the official signal flags, the Weather Bureau used wireless telegraph to warn all ships on the Great Lakes equipped with radio. Although this technology was far advanced from red bunting, Alexander's statements indicate the Morse code radio warnings simply echoed the basic information carried by the hoists of flags at each station. "Expect southwest and northwest winds in excess of 55 miles per hour," was the message to those ships that could receive it.

Weather observer Alexander's office in Cleveland was a few blocks from the headquarters of the majority of Great Lakes shipping companies. As a final step, he reached for his telephone. In his Texas drawl he explained the deteriorating weather to company officials. With these phone calls the U.S. Weather Bureau had done everything in its power to alert Great Lakes sailors. Yet despite official warnings, captains on Lake Erie and lower Lakes Michigan and Huron pushed forward on schedule. There was no profit in delay. Bad weather in early November would only get worse later. Writing in 1959, a group of meteorologists would explain in a technical paper:

> November is usually the month of the most frequent severe weather during the season. The energy required for development of large intense storms is released as sharper contrasts between the polar and tropical air over the continent develop. A secondary factor in the intensity of November storms is the heat energy supplied by the relatively warm open waters of the Great Lakes.

Moisture from the lakes explains why Toledo, Ohio, at the western end of Lake Erie, often records more cloudy days than Seattle, Washington, a city famous for its rainy climate. Cloud cover over the lakes can be oppressive. It averages six-tenths of the sky during the winter months. Because of these low-lying clouds, the lower lakes receive less than 60 percent of the total available sunlight.

Evaporation from the lakes produces more than just scudding clouds. It also creates a phenomenon called "lake-effect snow." Winter winds sweeping across the lakes pick up moisture in the form of water vapor. This vapor condenses as it rises into the cold atmosphere. Leaden winter "snow clouds" dump their moisture on any land that lies in the lee of the lakes, but most particularly on areas with high bluffs or ridges. Lake-effect snow is most prevalent on the Upper Peninsula of Michigan, the eastern shore of Lake Michigan, the southeastern shore of Lake Erie near Buffalo, New York, and the Lake Ontario shore south of Watertown, New York.

On Friday, November 7, however, snow was far from the minds of vineyard workers on Lake Erie's Bass Islands as they worked in mid-60-degree temperatures. Pickers welcomed prolonged good weather that fall because it allowed their grapes to develop maximum sugar content. They anticipated 1913 to be a vintage harvest. In nearby Toledo, the wind was from the south and the temperature was 58 degrees when the storm warning was received from Washington. Sailors on ships navigating Lake

Erie also appreciated the comfortable 50-degree weather as they passed north of the islands. It was easier working the decks in shirtsleeves and light jackets than in winter parkas. Cleveland bureau chief Alexander recorded the noon temperature at 66 degrees just as the cloud cover reached 100 percent. Later, he noted that the wind increased slightly that afternoon and there was a trace of rain.

Despite the gloomy skies, summer did not seem to want to end. "Thursday and Friday were the warmest November days in years," the *Cleveland Press* noted on its front page. The headline could have been written about any pleasant summer day: "Warm Weather to End with Rains." In fact, the wind direction, falling barometer, and increasing cloudiness indicated an approaching storm.

At Marquette, Michigan, on Lake Superior, weather observer P. E. Johnson received the storm alert from Washington at 9:50 A.M. He carefully wrote the time in the station's official log using his neat Spencerian hand. Then he stepped outdoors to hoist the appropriate flags on the signal mast warning of storm winds from the southwest. His office was located on the southeast corner of Front and Washington Streets. Thanks to the continuing warm spell, Johnson did not need his heavy winter overcoat. A light 9-mile-per-hour wind from the southeast ruffled his shirtsleeves. The storm that prompted hoisting this warning was still at least a hundred miles to his north and west, not yet affecting Marquette. Back inside the station, he wrote, "Flags displayed at 10:00 A.M."

But a gloom covered Marquette—a dense layer of clouds blocked light from the sun the entire day. There is a particular shade of dark gray to clouds at this time of year over the Great Lakes, resulting from the low angle of the sun's light on the same cloud formations that bring summer rains. Observer Johnson probably could not see the approaching cold front because of the heavy overcast that morning. Maybe that is why his official record book does not contain any mention of a black roll cloud approaching on the northwestern horizon like a celestial steamroller. The water of the lake below it would have been roiling from the turbulent northwest wind. A gray haze of mist and spume must have hugged the base of the roll cloud like dust around a wagon wheel.

Winds churning Lake Superior most of that Friday were no more intense than those of the other ten thousand and more November gales that had swept the Great Lakes since the last Ice Age, so the local weather observer at Duluth was not surprised by the deteriorating conditions. "Local Forecaster Richardson expects the storm to be quite severe, and to cover a large portion of the range and the Northwest," wrote the *Duluth Herald*. "The rain which began this morning, he says, will probably turn to snow this afternoon or tonight."

The range is a local term used by residents to describe the rugged country west of the city where great iron ore deposits were discovered. The most famous of these deposits is the Messabi Range, which has been reduced to huge, gaping pits by a century of open mining. Although forecaster Richards posted a "severe" storm warning, even he did not expect the havoc that actually took place at dinnertime that Friday afternoon.

The southwest winds of the previous day had shifted into the west at 3 A.M. and the northwest at 6 A.M. Temperatures dropped from Thursday's upper 40s to below the freezing mark on Friday. This temperature drop and wind shift marked the passage of the cold front. Duluth and its companion city of Superior, Wisconsin, are ringed by a horseshoe-shaped ridge of hills open only to the lake, which sheltered the cities against the west and northwest winds behind the front until their velocity increased enough to vault the top. Northwest gusts of more than 28 miles per hour rattled windows in Duluth at noon, still nothing particularly unusual for November.

At 5 P.M. actor Walker Whiteside began applying grease paint in preparation for his appearance at Duluth's Lyceum theater. He was the star of a theatrical production aptly titled *The Typhoon*. Just then, a thundering blast of wind from the northwest crested the ring of hills and charged down upon Duluth and Superior at better than 60 miles per hour. Wind thundered through downtown streets like an invading enemy horde. Duluth-Superior was feeling the first real blow of a complex meteorological convergence that would soon encompass all four of the upper lakes.

Store signs, fences, and billboards fell before the blast. At Fourth Avenue and Superior Street in downtown Duluth a newsstand rolled over and newspapers began swirling in the wind. The owner, "Black Eyes" Tompson, watched his entire stock of three hundred newspapers disappear. Unhurt by the upsetting of his business, Tompson remarked to a reporter that he had been able to save the most important thing—his cash register. Not far from the overturned newsstand, patrons of a Chinese restaurant were surprised when the wind smashed a plate glass window.

Shards of glass covered steaming plates of chop suey, but there were no serious injuries.

This blast of wind from the northwest came 12 to 14 hours after the cold front associated with the slow-moving northern Canadian low passed over the city. The barometric pressures ahead of and during the frontal passage were not unusually low, nor do the recorded wind data suggest the presence of a secondary low-pressure center over Superior— at least not yet. Most likely the strong northwesterly gales behind the front were the result of a very strong arctic high-pressure system in central or western Canada. Crews of ships on Lake Superior expected cold winds and towering waves at the end of a sailing season, but they did not expect the wind to suddenly triple its velocity in this manner. It was not a pleasant omen for sailors starting their last trips of the season. There is an odd truth about the Great Lakes: although March and April experience stronger winds, it is the gales of November that prove deadliest.

At the height of Friday's buffeting, the wind helped destroy the Reiss Coal Company's dock 3 at Duluth after a blaze erupted in a boilerhouse. Gale winds quickly whipped the flames out of control. Across the harbor in Superior, Wisconsin, three unloading rigs at the Boston Coal Dock were uprooted and flattened by the same unexpected thundering blast. As if that were not enough excitement for one day, the steamer *H.P. Bope* had started to back out of the Great Northern Ore Dock that morning before all of its steel docking cables had been properly retrieved. One of them became tangled in the ship's propeller, forcing the *Bope* to heave lines back to the ore loading dock and secure itself. A diver from the Union Towing and Wrecking Company put on his hard-hat equipment and went down to cut the cable loose despite the wind and cold. His work was still not finished when the wind reached a maximum sustained velocity of 62 miles per hour, with gusts up to 68 miles per hour.

Ice makes late-season storms like the one now brewing on Lake Superior particularly dangerous. This is not the ice in bergs like the one that had doomed the *Titanic* on the North Atlantic eighteen months earlier. Instead, it is a thin, clear coating that builds layer upon layer on ships' decks and superstructures. Water in the lakes is salt-free and freezes quickly after it splashes on metal chilled by subfreezing winds. Dangerous lake ice first appears as an innocent-looking glaze that makes walking nearly impossible on a pitching deck. Each breaking wave adds a bit more freezing spray until the ship begins to look as though carved from a solid block of ice.

Ice-encrusted ships eerily resemble self-propelled icebergs. Although an ice coating on a ship is strangely beautiful, the heavy covering is a potential death trap. Crews have been imprisoned in their cabins when doors and hatches were locked shut by a coating of ice. Each layer of glaze adds weight to the vessel's superstructure, upsetting its normal stability. Heavy ice has been a contributing factor in capsizes. To prevent their ships from rolling over, crews in 1913 often attacked ice with axes and sledgehammers. Evidence of the work done by these tools remained in the dented metal of superstructures for years afterward. On Saturday, November 8, virtually every ship entering the locks at Sault Ste. Marie from Lake Superior would have an ominous covering of ice.

Lake Michigan — Milwaukee, Wisconsin
LOUISIANA

By Friday afternoon clouds also were thickening over Lake Michigan. A few prudent captains decided to remain in port, but most accepted the deteriorating weather and blustery southwesterly winds as normal for November. They chose to sail on their final voyages of the season simply to get their work done before really nasty winter weather arrived. Other captains departed because of an unpublicized system of bonuses and promotions for shipmasters who made extra trips during the sailing season. These rewards normally went to captains who were willing to sail dangerously late, past fall and into early winter.

One of the vessels that ventured onto Lake Michigan was the twenty-six-year-old wooden steamer *Louisiana*. The 287-foot ship had just carried a cargo of coal from Cleveland to Milwaukee, so its hold was empty for the trip 200 miles north to the iron ore dock at Escanaba, Michigan. Wooden vessels had been plentiful on the lakes during the nineteenth century because of a ready supply of white oak, pine, and other ship-building timber. By the late 1880s, however, the size of Great Lakes ships had grown beyond the capabilities of wooden construction. A 300-foot wooden ship was considered "huge," but iron and steel allowed vessels to grow to double that size. The old *Louisiana* was still earning its keep, but everyone knew that time was growing short for wooden ships.

Lake Superior — Isle Royale, Michigan
WILPEN

Only one ship, the *Alberta*, arrived in Duluth Friday evening and night. Other upbound ships seem to have sought shelter in the lee of Isle Royale, about 190 miles northeast. This island, a rugged chunk of rock and trees, was (and remains) uninhabited except by wolves, moose, and other wildlife. It would later be preserved by the U.S. government. Siskiwit Bay on the island's southeast face became a haven Friday for steamships trying to escape gale-force winds and freezing spray. The bay is shallow, but the northeast-to-southwest orientation of the island gives it ideal protection from northwest winds. According to the captain of the steamer *Wilpen*, the northwest wind gusts that whistled through that makeshift anchorage on Friday exceeded 60 miles per hour.

Directly south across 55 miles of open water lay Michigan's Keweenaw Peninsula, where the Weather Bureau observer at Houghton, Michigan, recorded 68-mile-per-hour blasts. But only 50 miles to the east, at Marquette, the wind was still light from the southeast with temperatures in the mid-50s and the dew point at 46 degrees. This indicates the slow eastward progress of the front on Friday, and as it moved over the warm lake waters, pushing warm, moist air aloft, something else was happening. There does not seem to have been a low embedded in the front early on Friday, but by Friday afternoon an organized low was strengthening, with an associated warm front (which Marquette weather observer P. E. Johnson would have called a "leading line") sweeping out ahead of the cold front and extending eastward across Superior, north of Marquette. As the low intensified, the pressure differential between this center and the large area of high pressure that was by now off the East Coast whipped up stronger south and southwest winds throughout the eastern Great Lakes.

Ships hiding in the lee of Isle Royale were upbound for the twin ports of Duluth and Superior, which shared a large, protected harbor that even today has only two narrow entrances. Trying to run either opening was never desirable during a major storm. Eight years earlier, in 1905, the straight decker *Mataafa* missed an approach to the Duluth entrance during a November gale, and its bow slammed into the north pierhead wall. Before the crew could be rescued, winds and current carried the wounded steamer back into the lake, where it settled on the bottom. People on shore watched Lake Superior tear the wreck into three pieces. Nine men were lost. With that memory still strong, most captains preferred a lumpy night at anchor to running the gauntlet of either narrow entrance.

While the ships at Isle Royale waited for the gale to moderate before attempting the Duluth and Superior harbor entrances, events in the atmosphere were beginning to happen faster than the Weather Bureau could handle. A key mechanism in the formation and steering of surface storms operates high overhead, typically between 25,000 and 35,000 feet, where in 1913 it was unseen and unsuspected. This is the jet stream. A temperature and pressure discontinuity between the warm air near the equator and the cold air over polar regions gives rise to the polar jet, an undulating ribbon of wind that circles the globe. In the summer months it is typically over northern Canada, but in winter the polar jet shifts southward over the United States, and in the autumn it's often at the latitude of the Great Lakes. This ribbon of high-speed, high-altitude wind blows continuously eastward but undulates north and south as it goes, marking the shifting equilibrium between the polar air to its north and the warm air to its south. On a modern weather map the southward undulations, which resemble dips and are called troughs, generally support low pressure at the surface to their east. If there had been an upper-level (500-millibar) weather map available on November 7, 1913, it would probably have shown a pronounced dip from the Hudson Bay region south into the north-central United States—so pronounced, in fact, that the flow may have been traveling a little west of south on the descending limb of the trough. This deep, recurved trough was supporting the low in northern Québec as well as the cold front over Superior.

Unaware of the jet stream, meteorologists in 1913 could only look at surface data as they tried to understand the atmosphere around them. On the surface, the growing storm to the north was the biggest danger. Other than this storm the maps showed no major weather disturbances outside the Great Lakes. In hindsight, however, the forecasters should have been equally concerned by an overlooked disturbance moving east across the southern states. Upper-level data would probably have shown a small, innocent-looking wave moving through Texas on Friday and into the southeastern United States Friday night.

Lake Superior —— Whitefish Bay
E.F. BERRY *and* TURRET CHIEF

Whitefish Bay, at the extreme southeastern end of Lake Superior, has always been a refuge for ships escaping foul weather on the lake. In 1975, the *Edmund Fitzgerald* disappeared while struggling to reach the haven of Whitefish Bay. This semiprotected anchorage remains popular because it is adjacent to the locks at Sault Ste. Marie. Unfortunately, the energy of waves rolling down the open lake can be reflected back into the bay by cliffs along the Canadian shoreline, and the resulting confused seas make anchoring difficult and dangerous.

By Friday evening the bay was anything but a quiet anchorage for the more than twenty ships that had sought shelter there. The southerly winds that had been building over the eastern lakes all day, as the low deepened over Superior, may have been further intensified here by the passage of a warm front Friday afternoon. Confused seas rolling in from the west jerked anchored ships hard against their ground tackle, but off the southeast corner of the bay at Sault Ste. Marie, winds remained stubbornly light and out of the east all day, possibly a result of surrounding topography. Darkness came before nightfall Friday evening due to the heavy overcast, and suddenly, after 9 P.M., the gusty southerly winds in Whitefish Bay veered northwest and increased sharply in velocity. The *E.F. Berry* had anchored behind Whitefish Point after clearing the Soo upbound on Friday evening. When the wind unexpectedly changed to the northwest, the *Berry* slammed hard against its anchor chain. "This was the first time I ever lost an anchor by letting it go," said Captain Balfour of the 480-foot steamer. The anchor carried away even though his ship was using forward power from its propeller to ease the strain on its chains. Nearby, the 586-foot *James A. Farrell* lost not one but two anchors in a similar manner. At least five other steamers also snapped anchor chains as a result of the sudden wind shift.

THE CANADIAN FREIGHTER *Turret Chief* had cleared the Soo locks upbound at 3 P.M. and proceeded through Whitefish Bay and into the open lake against the southwesterly gale that was blowing in the early evening. A "turret" ship had a conventional bow and stern, but amidships the topsides curved inward like the hull of a modern submarine. William

Doxford, an English shipbuilder, sought with the design to create a vessel that would suffer less damage from pounding waves. The design resulted in a marginal improvement in seakeeping, but turret-style ships made cargo handling extremely difficult—especially the bulk cargoes such as grain, iron ore, and coal that are common on the lakes.

At first Superior's south shore provided a lee for the *Turret Chief*, but as Whitefish Bay receded astern the lee disappeared. Captain Paddington must have encountered the cold front about 8 P.M., following which the wind swung into the northwest (dead ahead), paused momentarily, then blew with renewed fury, creating a confusion of seas. As midnight approached, both *L.C. Waldo* and *Turret Chief*—the first downbound and the other upbound—were struggling in the northwesterly storm. Aboard the *L.C. Waldo*, Captain Duddleson was increasingly concerned over his ship's position. He knew he was close to a dangerous shoreline, but how close? Some 170 miles to the south, on Lake Michigan, the wooden *Louisiana* was running north before a southwesterly gale while the crew looked forward to turning into Green Bay and escaping the building waves on the open lake. At Sarnia, at the foot of Lake Huron, Captain Edward McConkey enjoyed the same quiet sleep in his cabin on the *Regina* as former engineer Milton Smith was experiencing in his own bedroom in Port Huron, just across the St. Clair River.

SATURDAY, NOVEMBER 8

BY MIDNIGHT FRIDAY, all Great Lakes shipping was alert to the development of the first November gale of 1913 on Superior. The storm undoubtedly picked up energy from the warm lake water and the warm, moist air overlying it, which surely encouraged the deepening of the low along the cold front late Friday. But other influences were also at work. The more than 60-mile-per-hour winds from the northwest that rattled Duluth late Friday afternoon and swept through Marquette about 10 P.M. Friday evening were likely the result of a southward flow of cold air from a strong high-pressure center in central or western Canada. The cold front advanced southeast, crossing Michigan's Upper Peninsula Friday night and the Big Bay de Noc at the northern end of Lake Michigan just after midnight, and right behind it now came the northwesterly gale. Vacant windows in the ghost mining town of Fayette on the Garden Peninsula must have moaned when the northwest gale roared through those empty stone buildings.

An important duty at U.S. weather stations in 1913 was winding the clockwork mechanisms that drove a variety of recording instruments. One was the barograph that kept track of changes in the barometer throughout the day. Another was a recording thermometer. Windup spring motors of these instruments moved graph paper beneath stationary pen points. This resulted in a permanent record of changes in both temperature and barometric pressure even during the overnight hours, when smaller stations were unmanned.

On Saturday morning, weather observer P. E. Johnson in Marquette easily detected the overnight passage of the cold front (called a "squall line" in 1913) by reading the graphs from his windup instruments. At 8 P.M. on Friday his recording thermometer had indicated a temperature of 52 degrees, the same as the noon high that day. After that, the pen trail plunged steeply downward until midnight, when the temperature was only 31 degrees. Also at 8 P.M., Johnson's wind instruments recorded a sudden shift into the northwest and an increase to more than 30 miles per hour, further evidence that the cold front had reached Marquette a little more than an hour before slamming into the ships in Whitefish Bay, 125 miles to the east. Johnson's instruments showed 26- to 28-mile-per-hour northwest gusts still buffeting his station Saturday morning.

By Saturday morning the low was moving east-northeast toward Québec, while the cold front continued pushing southeast. Evidence of the strong western Canadian high at last began to show on Saturday's U.S. weather map, in the form of a ridge of high pressure building south into the western states.

Lake Michigan — Death's Door
LOUISIANA

The empty wooden bulk freighter *Louisiana* found the trip up Lake Michigan from Milwaukee tolerable despite blustery conditions from the southwest, but things changed as it approached the entrance to Green Bay. In order to head for Escanaba and its final cargo of ore, the ship turned into the northwest. Just before midnight on Friday, as the straight decker slogged its way into Green Bay, the strong southerly winds that had been blowing all evening suddenly went deathly still. "At 12:15 A.M. the brisk wind died out almost completely," recalled *Louisiana*'s first mate, Finley McLean. This was a deeper calm than the one logged 84 miles to the north by the Marquette weather station at 9 P.M. Friday night, a tense interval of disquiet during which the looming shore of Michigan held back the onrushing gale. The atmosphere over Death's Door grew lifeless and still. Calm winds with a full sea running are not a comfortable combination for sailors. Everyone aboard the empty wooden steamer awaited the inevitable.

"In less than half an hour we were fighting for our lives in a 55-mile gale that tore upon us from the nor'west," McLean said. *Louisiana*'s single engine simply could not push the ship through the mounting waves. Captain Fred McDonald decided that anchoring was the only way to ride out the storm. His crew managed to get an anchor down, but even that did not prevent their wooden vessel from drifting backward toward the rocky shoreline of Wisconsin's Door County peninsula. "The wind was too much for us. It blew us back faster and faster and all this time the engines [sic] were going full steam ahead," McLean recalled after the storm.

Louisiana was fetching up near *Porte des Mortes*, the fabled Death's Door passage linking Green Bay to Lake Michigan. Despite its intimidating name, this stretch of water is normally pleasant enough. In the Saturday morning darkness, however, the crew of the wooden steamer faced the stark possibility that the somber appellation would prove devastatingly accurate—at their expense. "By 1:00 A.M. the wind had increased to seventy miles an hour and we were really scared. We were fighting helpless to keep off the beach. We just couldn't do a damned thing," was the way First Mate McLean described that agonizing hour.

Shortly after 2 A.M. the timber keel finally touched near Washington Island, slamming hard onto the rocky coastline. For the next two hours the castaways worked to keep one of their number dry as they put him safely ashore. He was told to seek help from the Plum Island Lifesaving Station, which they believed to be only a few miles away. The rest of the crew intended to remain in the shelter offered by their stranded ship until the rescuers from the Lifesaving Service arrived.

Then someone smelled smoke, and the horror began. Maybe hot coals from a boiler set fire to the aging wooden hull. "How it happened we never knew for certain, but the old *Louisiana* caught fire. Probably the wrecked engines started it, but we never had a chance to find out," McLean told reporters afterward. "The old craft was made of wood and burned like tinder. Fighting the blaze was hopeless." *Louisiana's* crew now faced death not just from freezing in storm waves breaking on the rocks around them but also from being consumed by the raging inferno. They chose to escape the flames by chancing the waves. "We launched a lifeboat into the roaring breakers and floundered through them safely to shore," the first mate recalled. "We were half drowned, two-thirds frozen, and just blamed scared. Fifteen minutes from the start of the blaze, the whole ship was wrapped in flames. She burned clear to the water as we watched. There was nothing left of her but red-hot engines, which hissed like a volcano and set off clouds of steam as the seas rushed over them."

Lake Superior —— Keweenaw Peninsula, Michigan
L.C. WALDO

The storm began picking apart the *L.C. Waldo* shortly after midnight near the Keweenaw Peninsula. The downbound ship, 18 hours out of Two Harbors, Minnesota, was overrun by monster waves out of the northwest. "We were past Keweenaw Point when the wind began to freshen," the *Waldo's* second mate, L. H. Feeger, told reporters later. "We took to the north shore (of the lake). We were about 45 miles northeast of Keweenaw Point when we were hit by a big wave. The wave carried away the front of the pilothouse, both sides and the front of the texas. It tore things loose in the captain's room, bent the steel deck of the compass room, wrecked the compass and swept the wheelsman out of the wheelhouse. That's what one wave did."

Lake Superior is notorious for its "Three Sisters," a trio of so-called rogue waves that appear suddenly, ravage unsuspecting ships, and then disappear. They are common during November gales. The first of the three is said to be half again as big as an ordinary storm wave. The second is bigger still. Old-timers claim the third sister can be three times the size of the wind-driven storm waves from which the deadly trio appeared. It was a rogue wave like the third sister that battered the *Waldo.*

Scientists who study the Great Lakes at first dismissed the Three Sisters as folklore. Sailors who have survived this killer trio, however, have never doubted the Sisters are quite real, and there is at least some reason to believe them. Rocky cliffs around Lake Superior have hard vertical surfaces that do not allow storm waves to "spend" their energy as they do on sandy beaches. When waves crash against rocks, their energy is reflected back into the lake. This reflected energy creates "standing waves." If the reflected waves are out of synchronization with the storm waves, they can have a calming effect, but when the reflected energy happens to be in synch with the storm waves, troughs and peaks of the two wave trains become additive. When reflected energy capable of causing a 20-foot wave is properly synchronized with a 30-foot open lake wave, the result could be a monster "sister" nearly 50 feet tall from trough to crest. A standing wave like that is probably what smashed the *L.C. Waldo's* pilothouse and texas.

"The mate found the injured wheelsman lying on the deck where he had been thrown by the force of the wave. The captain called to him and the mate shouted back, 'everything's smashed forward,' " Mate Feeger recalled of the confused situation aboard the *Waldo*. Captain Duddleson shouted at his mate to take the ship's steering wheel and turn the battered vessel around. The goal now was to reach the shelter behind Keweenaw Point. "The wind sent one gigantic wave after another over parts of the ship," Feeger said. "The snow was so blinding that none of us could see 50 feet ahead."

Lake Superior — East of Keweenaw
CORNELL

A 10-mile-per-hour easterly breeze had been blowing at Sault Ste. Marie when the steamer *Cornell* cleared upbound through the locks behind the *Turret Chief* Friday afternoon. This straight-deck freighter was bound from Conneaut, Ohio, on Lake Erie to the harbor of Duluth-Superior. An hour or so into Saturday and more than 10 hours after departing the Soo, it had put Whitefish Point about 50 miles behind. The steering pole pointed toward the Keweenaw Peninsula when *Cornell's* bow slammed into a massive head sea rolling toward it from the northwest. Shortly after 1 A.M., monster waves like those that struck the *Waldo* seemed to arise from nowhere. The mystery of their origin was not answered until the wind veered into the north with equal suddenness. Waves built by the gale had outraced the storm.

"The wind suddenly shifted to the north, blowing a gale accompanied by blinding snow," said Captain Noble. "The log showed that we were about ninety miles above Whitefish on the Manitou course." *Cornell* was "light" that trip, upbound with no cargo, so it was battered like a cork by the wind and waves. The ship's propeller was regularly thrown clear of the water by the exaggerated pitching.

Not all of the problems encountered by ships that morning were directly caused by the weather. At 2:30 A.M. the mate who had been standing watch in *Cornell's* pilothouse suddenly became ill. "I turned the ship before the wind while the mate was taken down to his room," Captain Noble said. The ship wallowed in the dangerous trough between the waves while the mate was assisted into his bunk. Then, full power was put to the engine, but the bow would not come back into the seas. "She stayed in the trough until 3:30 Saturday afternoon," Captain Noble admitted after the storm. "We couldn't get her out." In the meantime, water rolling over the deck began to build a top-heavy coating of ice on the ship's exposed hull and superstructure.

As the *Cornell* battled Superior, another weather-maker was forming 1,500 miles to the south. The small upper-level wave that had moved across the southern states on Friday—inconspicuous even to the modern forecaster, invisible in 1913—was giving rise to a weak surface low over Georgia, which showed up on the Weather Bureau's Saturday map. In hindsight it seems likely that the deep upper-level trough over the Great Lakes extended southwest into the southern plains by Saturday morning, and its north-flowing ascending limb reached down to catch the surface low in Georgia and steer it northeast. What's more, the interaction of these two mechanisms may have been ideally synchronized to intensify the low as it began to move north.

Lake Superior — Keweenaw Peninsula, Michigan
L.C. WALDO

Aboard the *L.C. Waldo*, deprived of the just-destroyed pilothouse, Captain Duddleson and Second Mate Louis Feeger were exposed to the full fury of the storm as they navigated the *Waldo* through black Lake Superior combers, blinding snow, and winds of more than 60 miles per hour. In the predawn darkness the second mate carefully sheltered an oil lantern from the wind so that its flickering light illuminated a small lifeboat compass, which rested precariously on a stool. The first mate squinted to see the numbers on the dial as he attempted to steer a straight course. "Once or twice, from contact with the lantern, the needle of the compass became magnetized and spun wildly," claimed a news report in the November 14 *Cleveland Plain Dealer*.

Duddleson intended to seek shelter from the northwesterly winds in the lee of the Keweenaw Peninsula. It turned out to be a futile effort. Some reports say that at about 3 A.M. the ship stopped answering its helm. The strain of steering through mountainous waves may have been too much for the fittings holding the single rudder in place. Other reports say that Duddleson and his mates tried to steer their ship to the very end, but the waves were simply too much for the battered ship. Either way, with a rocky shoreline only 30 or so miles to their south, the Waldo's crew could only await the inevitable.

Lake Superior — Copper Harbor, Michigan
TURRET CHIEF

Ships of the so-called turret design were intended to allow waves to wash over the decks. It was thought this would ease the battering from storm waves, which it did to some small extent. However, the turret design did not improve the underwater portions of the hull. Erroneous contemporary news accounts claimed that the Turret Chief's rudder fitting cracked while the ship was within sight of the Canadian shore and that the British-built freighter drifted southward across the full width of Lake Superior toward the rocky shoreline of Michigan's Upper Peninsula.

Later reports from Michigan's Upper Peninsula gave a second, differing account of the Turret Chief's troubles. Captain Thomas Paddington was quoted as saying that after the storm began he could not account for his ship's position. He thought he was well up toward the center of Superior, when in fact his ship had been driven southward by the howling northwest winds, dangerously close to the Keweenaw Peninsula. The truth is that the Turret Chief's steering gear never failed; the ship simply got lost.

Early Saturday morning, the Turret Chief struggled with Lake Superior only a few miles from the rudderless L.C. Waldo. At 4 A.M. the Turret Chief crashed ashore head-on about five miles east of Copper Harbor, Michigan, on the Keweenaw Peninsula. The hull bounced only once before coming to a stop with its bow jammed tightly against a rocky cliff. The ship's rail actually extended over the cliff, making it easy for the crew to climb to dry land and relative safety.

The nature of this stranding belies news reports that the ship was out of control at the time of its accident. Slamming head-on into shore indicates that the vessel was fully under control at the time it struck. It simply steamed onto the land, an action typical of a ship that has become disoriented during a storm. Had it drifted aground, the hull would likely have fetched up broadside to the shoreline and may have been rolled over or broken apart by the plunging breakers.

Fearing the Turret Chief would be pounded to pieces, Captain Paddington ordered his crew of eighteen to escape to shore, where they managed

to build a small hut of underbrush and timbers. In their rush to abandon the wrecked ship they forgot to bring any food, but an attempt to go
back aboard was rebuffed by a coating of ice on the decks and high seas
washing over the ship. It was simply too dangerous to walk back to the
ship's galley for provisions.

Their rude hut was barely enough shelter to keep the men from freezing to death as they awaited rescue. Two days would pass without sight
of another human being. The castaways had only melted snow for sus-
tenance. Finally, on Tuesday, they decided they had been hungry long
enough. The small band of survivors prodded themselves into hiking
inland in search of human habitation, warmth, and a hot meal. Eventually, the hungry sailors found both in the tiny mining town of Mandan,
Michigan.

Lake Michigan—Washington Island
LOUISIANA *and* HALSTEAD

On Washington Island in northern Lake Michigan that Saturday morning,
the soaking wet crew of the *Louisiana* also managed to get themselves
safely ashore. They had escaped the fire but now feared freezing to death
if they waited in the blizzard for rescue. Turning their backs to the ruddy
glow from the steaming wreckage, they set out inland in search of human
habitation—a farmhouse, perhaps. Unfortunately, their ship had fetched
up on a desolate stretch of beach, and the closest occupied home was
miles away. Between the shivering survivors and that oasis of warmth
were hundreds of fresh snowdrifts.

According to First Mate McLean, some of those drifts were half as tall
as the average man. "We turned from *Louisiana*'s graveyard and started to
make our way to shelter," recalled McLean. "We discovered a novel, but
very effective way of getting through the drifts. Since I was the smallest
man in the crew, they chose me for the trail-breaker. The big men would
pick me up, then after a good swing would throw me against a snow
bank. I didn't like this chilly trick too well, you can bet." It seems unlikely
that snow had been falling long enough to build many drifts as high as
McLean described, but true or not, his story made good news copy.

Although the *Cleveland Press* that Saturday reported that by November
20 the movement of iron ore on the Great Lakes would be concluded for

the year, the shipping season had already come to an early and abrupt end for the crew of the *Louisiana*. They were in their third fight against death in one night, this time to survive a blizzard. Stopping was unthinkable. Within minutes their wet clothing would freeze solid, and their bodies would follow within an hour or so. Their only chance for survival was to keep struggling through the drifting snow.

Wet and tired, the nearly frozen survivors finally stumbled upon an occupied farmhouse after an arduous 5-mile trek under blizzard conditions. They were welcomed with dry clothes and hot home cooking. As they enjoyed being warm and well fed, *Louisiana's* survivors could only wonder about the fate of the messenger sent off to find the lifesaving station. As it turned out, that lone member of the *Louisiana's* crew actually reached the Plum Island Lifesaving Station at about the same time that his shipmates found the farmhouse. He quickly told the station commander about the wrecked freighter, and then, despite being cold and exhausted, he volunteered to join the lifesavers as they gathered up their equipment and marched into the blizzard.

The small party trudged its way through the snow, still believing it was heading to rescue the rest of *Louisiana's* survivors from their stranded vessel. None of the would-be rescuers, including the ship's lone crewmember, knew they were headed for a pile of steaming embers, nor did they know that the other members of the ship's crew had already reached safety and were enjoying a farm breakfast. The lifesavers finally pushed their way through the snow to the spot on the shore of Lake Michigan where *Louisiana* had beached itself. No trace of that ship could be seen in the roaring waves. The tired band of men thought they had made their difficult journey for nothing. There was obviously no one to rescue. All they could do was shrug and begin traipsing home.

"Over there," someone shouted over the storm, "a ship!"

Not a hundred yards offshore another vessel was materializing through the blinding snow. The Plum Island lifesavers watched helplessly as the ship drifted toward them and certain doom on the island's rocky shore. There would be work for them yet this morning!

A helpless vessel drew close enough for lifesavers to identify the soon-to-be-shipwrecked vessel as an unpowered barge. That explained why it was drifting to shore. Lake waves seemed to toy with the barge as rescuers waited in the snow, wind, and darkness. The hulk first approached the shore and was then drawn back again until a wave larger than the others picked up the unfortunate vessel and shoved it onto the beach. The bow was driven so far ashore that the rescuers could easily read its name, *Halstead*. There was no need for a dramatic rescue. Men from the Plum Island Station simply put a ladder to the side of the barge and helped its crew of eight climb down to safety on dry land.

Although this rescue was one of the simplest and most effective during the storm, the stranding of the *Halstead* created a minor myth a few days after the storm. Newspaper reports carried florid descriptions of the barge washing ashore with its crew all dead, frozen in the positions they took in life. It wasn't true, but as with Finley McLean's snowdrifts, it made great copy.

Lake Michigan — Northport, Michigan
ILLINOIS

Eighty miles east across Lake Michigan from where the *Louisiana* burned and the *Halstead* came ashore, Captain John A. Stufflebeam headed his passenger ship, *Illinois*, out of the small port of Northport, Michigan, during the early morning hours. Northport is located within Grand Traverse Bay, inside the Leelanau Peninsula, and is further protected from waves on the big lake by Northport Point and Lighthouse Point. The town was founded in 1849 when the schooner *Merrill* was driven ashore in a storm. Today, it is a favorite spot for summer vacationers, but in 1913 lumbering was its primary trade.

Captain Stufflebeam had not considered the gusty southwesterly winds and confused seas to be dangerous while his ship was still protected by the peninsula. Once he steamed beyond the relatively calm bay waters, conditions on Lake Michigan quickly changed his opinion, but he kept on. The cold front swept across the *Illinois* at about 3 A.M., and immediately behind it came the same shift into the northwest and rapid increase in wind velocity that had occurred at Duluth, Marquette, and Death's Door. "After we had been out about two hours, it began to look more serious," the captain admitted afterward in the *Cleveland Plain Dealer*.

Late in the season the *Illinois* seldom carried passengers, and on this last trip of the year its staterooms were empty. Package goods and freight paid the bills in November. The ship had made calls at Mackinac Island and other Lake Michigan cities before starting south to Chicago. "The wind rose higher and the waves became more furious. We stood it well for an hour, then it began to snow and the storm broke all about us," Captain Stufflebeam said, describing the chaotic situation on Lake Michigan.

Although the *Illinois* was heading south, it was considered "upbound" on Lake Michigan. The ship's schedule called for making stops at several more northern Michigan ports. Consequently, the cautious captain was forced to stay closer than he might have liked to Lake Michigan's eastern shoreline. Stufflebeam quickly realized, however, that the northwesterly gale made it too dangerous to enter any of the scheduled ports. Not only that, his ship was going to have trouble staying away from the sandy shoals near the Sleeping Bear sand dunes, south of his position. Fortunately, the Manitou Islands were not far ahead. These islands offered no protected harbors suitable for large ships like the *Illinois*, but Captain Stufflebeam hoped that in their lee he might find a small haven from the gale that roared around him.

Lake Superior — Michipicoten Island
SARNIAN

Having left Jackfish Friday night, the downbound *Sarnian* used the lee of the Canadian shoreline to bash another 75 miles through the gale. "It was blowing hard with snow from the northeast as I came down," Captain Neil Campbell said. "I could see two or three boats trying to make their way up, but I think they came back." When Michipicoten Island loomed up, Campbell decided he had had enough of the storm. "I was forced to find an anchorage behind Michipicoten Island," he said. That heavily wooded island, 100 miles northwest of Whitefish Bay and 8 miles off the Canadian shore, is the second largest in Lake Superior. The *Sarnian* probably sought shelter near what is today called Québec Harbor. The bay is popular with yachts but too small for a steamship, so Captain Campbell must have satisfied himself with anchoring close to the main island, probably north of off-lying Davieaux Island, which would have acted as a natural breakwater.

Lake Superior — Whitefish Bay
JAMES CARRUTHERS, J.H. SHEADLE, *and* HYDRUS

Perhaps as many as twenty ships sheltered in Whitefish Bay early Saturday. One of those was the *J.H. Sheadle*. It had dropped anchor at about 3 A.M. "On arriving at White Fich [sic] Bay it shut in very thick and foggy, which held us there the balance of the night and until about 8:00 o'clock the following morning, November 8th," Captain Lyons wrote to his company headquarters. The fog must have created congestion at the Soo locks. Although the *Sheadle* started down during breakfast Saturday morning, it took another half-day to clear the locks. The traffic jam allowed the American grain hauler to reunite with the *James Carruthers*. This Canadian ship was first of a group of vessels through the Soo locks, followed by the *J.H. Sheadle* and then the *Hydrus*.

The importance of the Soo locks to the industrial development of the United States cannot be overstated. The first iron mines opened at Negaunee and Ishpeming, on Michigan's Keweenaw Peninsula in Lake Superior, in 1846. Great Lakes iron gave General Ulysses S. Grant the unending supply of cannons and shot needed to win the U.S. Civil War. The biggest discovery of iron ore was made at the western end of Lake Superior near Duluth, Minnesota, and Thunder Bay, Ontario. Ore from the Minnesota ranges was pure enough to be fed to furnaces just the way it came from the ground. Unfortunately, that ore was located above the rapids that blocked the head of the St. Marys River at Sault Ste. Marie. With a vertical drop of 19 feet from Superior to Michigan and Huron, ships could not carry iron ore directly to the lower lakes. A wooden tramway with iron banding for rails was constructed in the 1840s to allow transshipment of ore around the rapids, but the demand was still not satisfied until the first canal and lock system was opened in 1855. By 1913, a complex of U.S. and Canadian locks served the Great Lakes fleet. The biggest of the American locks was the 800-foot Poe Lock, completed in 1896. Across the river on their side of the international border, the Canadians operated a single lock 900 feet long. Ships of both nations used either the U.S. or the Canadian locks, as convenient for fastest passages.

Lake Erie — *Ashtabula, Ohio*

CHARLES S. PRICE

Hundreds of miles to the south of the Soo, the *Charles S. Price*, without Assistant Engineer Milton Smith, finally departed Ashtabula Saturday morning and headed west on Lake Erie. After steaming well offshore, Captain Black followed the recommended track toward the Detroit River Light, almost 150 miles away. For a few hours the coal-laden *Price* enjoyed unusually warm November weather as it followed the steamer route to Pelee Passage on the north side of Pelee Island in western Lake Erie. With temperatures in the 50s early in the trip, Arze McIntosh might have opened a pilothouse window when he relieved Wilson McInnes at the ship's wheel, and Steward Herbert Jones may have propped open the galley door when beads of sweat began running down his wife's face as she prepared the noon meal.

At 9:30 A.M. the Washington headquarters of the U.S. Weather Bureau ordered a change in the existing warning to a northwest storm, effective at 10 A.M. The coded telegram said a storm over eastern Lake Superior was moving east-northeast and creating high west to northwest winds. In his office, Marquette weather observer P. E. Johnson prepared to update the storm flags he had hoisted 24 hours earlier. Yesterday, the air temperature had been 52 degrees in Marquette when Johnson put up the southwest warning flags. He had not needed his winter coat then. Today, the temperature was a frigid 27 degrees as he removed one set of flags and connected the revised hoist—a white pennant over the square red flag with black center—to the halyard. A heavy winter overcoat hampered his actions as he raised the new signals for a northwest storm. Washington's change order arrived on the shores of Lake Superior more than 12 hours late. The cold front with its associated shift from southwest to northwest winds had swept through Marquette the prior evening. Johnson could do nothing about the timing of his orders from Washington. All he could do was hoist the required signals as instructed. A northwest wind snapped the cotton bunting, and the new set of flags were sent flying against the heavy overcast of snow clouds. Back inside the warmth of the station, observer Johnson carefully wrote on his *Daily Local Record* sheet that he had hoisted the new storm signals at exactly 10 A.M. He also noted that the wind was averaging 34 miles per hour out of the northwest, with a maximum gust of 37 miles per hour. This was real winter at last: cold temperatures, blustery wind, and the first Upper Peninsula snowfall of the season.

Unlike in localities to the south, the first snow of winter is almost welcomed in Michigan's Upper Peninsula. The waiting is over. Winter is uncompromisingly harsh in the north country, but the anticipation of its arrival is always worse than winter itself. The hearty miners who populated what is now known as the "U-P" learned how to live with snow. They prebuilt rude wooden supports for what would become tunnels through the inevitable snowdrifts, and many houses had "snow doors" on the second floor level or in their roofs. These doors allowed people to come and go even when the ground-floor doors were buried by drifting snow.

The great size of the Great Lakes hides an unsuspected truth—they have almost no drainage basin. Water drains into the lakes from a relatively narrow band of land around their shores. In some places, the ridge marking the limit of the drainage is visible to ships offshore. Water levels in the lakes go down quickly if a dozen or more feet of snow does not fall on northern Michigan, Wisconsin, Minnesota, and Ontario each winter.

St. Clair River — Sarnia, Ontario
REGINA

As the package freighter *Regina* continued loading in Sarnia, Ontario, at the foot of Lake Huron, Captain Edward McConkey remained unaware of the severity of the storm on Lake Superior—partly because of the storm's violence. Telephone and telegraph wires in Wisconsin and Minnesota had snapped in the snow and high winds, and the flow of information to news services was drastically curtailed. According to the November 10, 1913, *Cleveland Press*, the little news that did reach the lower lakes was not entirely accurate. "Fragmentary messages from various stations within radius of the Soo office show no vessels are known to be lost," the newspaper reported. Then it cautioned readers that "many (ships) are unaccounted for, and it can only be hoped that they have reached some obscure port in safety."

Crews of upbound vessels on Lake Erie and the St. Clair River probably heard rumors of weather problems on Lake Superior and Lake Michigan. Ships might be down. No one knew any details. But rumors of vessels in distress caused little concern to sailors on the lakes. Prior to widespread use of marine radio it was common for a Great Lakes ship to be thought sunk, only to have it turn up a few days later. And one or two ships were always lost during November gales on the Great Lakes. It was an accepted, if unpleasant, aspect of the job.

There may have been little news from Lake Superior, but Captain McConkey was undoubtedly familiar with a fatal accident on the Detroit River. The whaleback steamer *Samuel Mather* was downbound at Detroit that Saturday when the mailboat *C.F. Bielman* pulled alongside. First Mate Frank Foster had been using a pole to reach from the stern of the whaleback to the mailboat when he lost his balance and disappeared head first into the Detroit River. The *Mather* immediately anchored while the *Bielman* searched the area, but there was no trace of the thirty-year-old mate.

Several entrepreneurs offered mailboat services at various places around the Great Lakes. These boats kept crews in touch with their families and with events on shore by bringing newspapers and letters from home. Shipping companies forwarded orders to their captains through the mailboats. In return, the captains sent their reports back to headquarters. Today, only the J. W. Westcott Company continues this tradition from its dock on the Detroit River almost beneath the Ambassador Bridge. The Detroit mailboat is the only floating post office in the U.S. postal system and has its own zip code.

Transferring mail and packages between the boats and large ships has always been dangerous. A big freighter never stops as the small mailboat comes alongside. The ship's crew lowers a bucket on a rope to haul up mail and newspapers. Occasionally, a ladder also comes down to the mailboat's deck so that a member of the freighter's crew can leave or join the ship. The two moving vessels are never tied together during these transfers of people, mail, or groceries. Mailboat and freighter remain in contact only because of the skills of their respective operators. Falls and injuries are uncommon, although it is easy to see how it was possible for the *Mather's* mate to lose his life by tumbling overboard. As late as October 2001, a mailboat captain and mate were killed when the *J.W. Westcott II* capsized and sank while transferring pilots to a tanker heading up the Detroit River.

The 1913 sailing season had been remarkably safe on the Great Lakes.

Frank Foster was only the tenth death of a U.S. sailor on the lakes that year. The previous year, in 1912, some thirty-three lives had been lost, and in 1911 the death toll was fifty-one sailors. Foster's was the only death caused by falling overboard. Seven other sailors had been killed in the explosion of the starboard boiler of the *E.M. Peck*. Two other men drowned when the barge *Annabell Wilson* sank in Lake Erie near Dunkirk, New York. There was some celebration in shipping publications over the loss of only ten sailors during a full sailing season. Prior to World War I, it was considered normal for a few vessels to be lost and several dozen sailors killed each season.

Lake Superior — Keweenaw Peninsula
L.C. WALDO

Somewhere east of the Keweenaw Peninsula on Lake Superior, Captain Duddleson faced the inevitable destruction of his disabled ship, the *L.C. Waldo*. During the early afternoon, 10 hours after the rudder failed, the sound of surf pounding on a rocky coastline became loud enough to hear above the howling wind. "My God, Mr. Feeger," he shouted at his second mate. "We're gonners." The *Waldo* was helpless without its rudder. Driven by 70-mile-per-hour winds, it fetched up on Gull Rock near Manitou Island, almost in the shadow of the Keweenaw Peninsula. "Flood the ship," the captain ordered the engine room. He wanted to make sure the broken hull did not wash back off the rocks. With the bottom shredded by the sharp Keweenaw rocks, the ship would have quickly foundered.

Moments after it ran aground the steel hull began to break apart amidships. "All hands forward" was Duddleson's order. The bow was firmly wedged in the rocks, but the stern appeared to be sinking as the result of cracks across the steel deck and down both sides of the hull. As the men began running for the shelter of the forecastle, Steward Price shouted, "Where are the women?" Price's wife and mother-in-law were aboard for this last trip of the season. No one had told the two frightened women to seek safety in the bow, so they were still huddled in the darkness of their cabin, located within the boilerhouse on the twisted stern section.

Joined by engineer Charles Keefer and fireman Adolph Johnson, Price jumped back over the yawning crack in the *Waldo*'s deck. Finding the steward's wife and her mother too frightened to leave their cabin, the three rescuers picked up the women bodily and carried them forward. Pounding waves sent green water across the deck as the piggyback transfer moved forward. Each time a wave washed across them the men used their bodies to shelter the women from the full blast of the icy seas. Only the wire lifelines along the edge of the deck stopped the small knot of human beings from being washed overboard.

Steward Price kept a tight grip on his wife throughout the rescue ordeal, but her mother slipped away from one of the other men as green water swirled around the group and tried to suck them overboard. The mother-in-law's rescuer made a desperate lunge and caught the woman's clothing as she tumbled toward oblivion. In one hand the man held a death grip on the half-inch diameter wire lifeline, and in the other he clutched the woman's dress. Wire rope cut into his fingers, trying to wrench them open. The woman's clothing began slipping through his other hand. The third man reached for a handful of the woman's dress. The two rescuers summoned all their strength to heave her back on deck. In the next instant all five were running for the forecastle.

While the rescue drama played out on deck, Chief Engineer August Lempke (also spelled "Lemke") remained alone in the Waldo's engine room. He was soon joined by two other stokers, who began shoveling coal into the furnaces of the ship's two Scotch boilers. Lempke kept the throttle open, hoping the Waldo's propeller might push the wreck farther onto the shore. He turned the wheel that allowed steam to hammer into the cylinders of the engine. The propeller built a white froth astern, but despite the engine's 1,800 horsepower, nothing moved. Realizing they could do no more, Lempke secured the engine and let the boiler steam vent into the blizzard. The three men climbed out of the warm engine room and raced across the ice-coated deck to the safety of the ship's unheated bow.

Safety was a relative term. In the windlass room the crew was protected from waves crashing over the ship, but from little else. There was no escaping their steel prison. The water around the bow was too deep to wade ashore and too rough for a lifeboat. The forward half of the ship was planted on the bottom, but there was no way to be certain about the stern. It could have been overhanging deep water. If the waves loosened the bow, the whole wreck could slip backward into the abyss. For the moment, though, the crew of the *Waldo* huddled in their triangular sanctuary and tried not to think about their precarious situation.

Lake Superior — Two Hearted River
CORNELL

Somehow the *Cornell* remained upright and afloat despite rolling in the enormous troughs of Lake Superior waves since 2:30 Saturday morning. It drifted like a leaf, driven by the wind to the south-southeast all during those hours. Captain Noble now had to worry about washing up on the Michigan shore between the Two Hearted River and Crisp Point, ironically just a few miles west of Whitefish Point, which he had steamed past some 15 hours before. This coastline is still the pristine wilderness where a youthful Ernest Hemmingway learned to hunt and fish. His family kept a summerhouse on the Two Hearted River, but it would have been shuttered for winter on this stormy November day.

A desperate Captain Noble dropped an anchor on 50 fathoms of chain in deep water, hoping it would catch before the ship was driven onto the looming lee shore. By 3:30 P.M. men in the pilothouse could discern individual trees on shore, yet the single anchor still was not holding. (Some accounts say the first anchor chain parted just after the anchor caught in the bottom.) A second anchor was sent down, this time with 90 fathoms of heavy chain. Still the ship drifted toward shore. In a last-ditch attempt to save themselves, the crew of the *Cornell* began throwing oil over the bow by the bucketful, while more was poured down the anchor hawsepipes. From biblical times the beneficial effects of oil on breaking seas have been known to sailors. Oil changes the surface tension of the water, and a thin film reduces the force of plunging breakers—but does not eliminate them. The *Cornell* continued to drift toward what seemed certain doom.

By 4 P.M. the hand lead showed only 8 fathoms of water, barely enough to float the ship in the rolling waves. Then the motion of the ship palpably changed. The bow began to swing more into the wind and breast the oncoming waves. "She's holding." The words were spoken almost reverently among the crew. "She's holding." It seemed a miracle, but the ship had come to anchor only moments from destruction and not 2 miles from the Deer River. For the next 11 hours the *Cornell* hung precariously at the end of its anchor chains, engine running full speed ahead to ease the strain.

St. Clair River — St. Clair, Michigan
ISABELLA J. BOYCE *and* CONSORT JOHN J. BARLUM

At 2 P.M. on Saturday Captain Walter R. Pringle took advantage of wind gusts to help swing the nose of his wooden steamer, the *Isabella J. Boyce*, into the St. Clair River. "Winding around" was common practice some 50 years before bow thrusters appeared on Great Lakes ships. Conditions in St. Clair were still mild. The frigid gale winds that were just then sending the *L.C. Waldo* crashing onto the Keweenaw rocks had not yet arrived at the southern end of Lake Huron. As Pringle maneuvered to pick up the towline of his consort barge, the 225-foot wooden *John J. Barlum*, he was only dimly aware of the storm on Lake Superior. It really did not seem relevant. Both vessels in his charge were downbound from St. Clair to Cleveland, Ohio.

At first the gale moving down from the north had little impact on the *Boyce* and its tow. Deteriorating weather did not slow their passage until steamer and consort left the protection of the Detroit River and started across the open waters of Lake Erie. An uncomfortable chop from the southwest was building as Pringle chose the northern route above the Lake Erie islands—both the shortest course and the one with the fewest dangers en route to Cleveland. However, the north passage crosses open water that reacts quickly to rising storm winds, and it was on the open water of Lake Erie, sometime after midnight, that the cold front and the gale behind it caught up with Captain Pringle.

> Off the southeast shoals the real fight between crew and storm began. Snow and rain were hurled at the pitching boats by a northwest wind that shot great waves crashing across the decks. For a time it was feared the *Barlum* would be lost and twice it all but stood on end. Capt. Pringle and his crew, however, managed to save their charge.
>
> *Cleveland Press*, NOVEMBER 10, 1913

In good weather, the *Boyce* and its barge should have made Cleveland in 10 to 12 hours. Captain Pringle and his men were beginning an ordeal that lasted nearly twice that long. They eventually battled the storm for almost 24 hours before reaching their destination.

By late Saturday afternoon the cold front had swept onto Lake Huron and was approaching Detroit, even as the low that had been over Superior the day before moved to the northeast. But unknown to the Weather Bureau or the mariners, a new and more deadly weather-maker was approaching. The low-pressure center that had first appeared on weather maps that morning over Georgia—not as the closed circulation it was but as a crudely elongated southward dip of the low pressures around the lakes—was moving north over the Appalachians and intensifying.

Lake Erie — Sandusky, Ohio
JOHN A. McGEAN

About 40 miles directly south of the *Isabella J. Boyce*, Captain Chauncey R. Ney watched dusty black lumps of Appalachian coal tumble into the hold of his ship at Sandusky, Ohio. Before loading was through nearly 6,000 tons of "black gold" were packed into the steel cavern. Ney commanded the five-year-old *John A. McGean*, a 432-foot straight-deck bulk freighter owned by the Pioneer Steamship Company of Cleveland. This coal was to be his last upbound load of the 1913 season. The *McGean* was scheduled to be laid up for the winter after it came down with its final cargo of iron ore. Captain Ney looked forward to spending time with his school-age son, Paul. The morning's mild weather rapidly deteriorated as Ney headed out Mosely Channel, leading from Sandusky's coal docks to Lake Erie.

Chauncey Ney had quite a reputation as a ballroom dancer. It was said that he arranged his ship's schedule so that he could be in certain ports on Saturday night in order to attend local dances. It is doubtful, however, that he had any fancy footwork on his mind as he guided the *McGean* out of Sandusky Bay. Anyone looking at the sky to the west and north could tell that unpleasant weather was brewing.

The land surrounding Sandusky Bay had been flattened more than a hundred centuries earlier by the Laurentide glacier. Scraped smooth by the ice, the terrain of northwest Ohio still displays the effects of glaciation. Indeed, the Lake Erie shoreline is still springing back from the weight of the glacier. The land is rising a fraction of an inch each year, particularly along the Canadian shoreline.

Southwesterly wind gusts made it difficult to keep the loaded *McGean* within the confined channel. Sandusky Bay is mostly shallow, and Saturday's winds drove much of that water out of the bay and into Lake Erie, making navigation all the more tedious. Due to shallow water in its bay, the port of Sandusky had been unable to accommodate large ships until deep channels in the floor of the bay were discovered by a local high school science teacher. These natural channels in the underlying limestone rock were created by the flow of water out of Lake Erie during the melting of the last ice age. Captain Ney followed buoys and range lights to stay in this twisting natural channel.

As the *McGean* worked its way out of Sandusky Bay it passed south of tiny Johnsons Island, site of a Civil War prison camp. Confederate officers as well as northern dissidents had been held there in rude wooden barracks. The prison had closed a half-century earlier, and in 1913 its few remaining traces were invisible from the water. Another turn of the channel took the ship past the popular summer bathing beach at Cedar Point. Today the skyline of this point is studded with roller coasters, but Captain Ney saw only glimpses of a few white buildings through the black and bare branches of trees on the point. The thousands of bathers who visited this spot during the hot summer months were gone, and the park was silent.

Chauncey Ney had negotiated Sandusky's Mosely Channel many times before. He knew when to look backward out the back windows of his pilothouse to line up his ship's masts with the range markers. It was a simple task, but there was little room for error. Bay Point to his west was a low sandbar that shifted with every storm. Shoals extended almost to the edge of the shipping channel. Ney was undoubtedly relieved when the *McGean* finally reached the deep water of the lake.

The *McGean* was not the only vessel on Lake Erie expecting to end the 1913 sailing season during the second week of November. Two barges owned by the Pittsburgh Steamship Company fleet arrived in Cleveland on Saturday to be unloaded prior to their final voyages of the year. Instead, the crews were told to secure their ships and go ashore. The men were not happy about starting their winter layup earlier than planned, because it meant the loss of a week's pay.

Detroit River — Detroit, Michigan
Charles S. Price

By dinnertime, the *Charles S. Price* was passing the Detroit River Light, and both the galley door and the pilothouse windows were shut tight. Ever since late morning the air temperature had been dropping, and heavy snow clouds were beginning to press down on the lake waters. After passing the Detroit Light, Captain Black turned the bow north to head up the Detroit River. Current in the river slowed the ship's progress from perhaps 8 or 9 miles an hour to 4 or 5.

Wilson McInnes carefully placed the wheelsman's chair in a back corner of the pilothouse. By custom, the man at the wheel of a Great Lakes freighter never sits while steering in the Detroit or St. Clair Rivers (or in the St. Marys River below the Soo locks), because of their strong currents. Elsewhere on the lakes, wheelsmen are allowed to use high "pilot's chairs" to make the task more comfortable. Neither McInnes nor Arze McIntosh expected to enjoy the comfort of the tall wooden armchair again until the *Price* reached the open waters of Lake Huron.

Just downriver from the city of Detroit, the mailboat *J.W. Westcott* came alongside with packages and letters from home. At 11:30 P.M. a bend in the river forced the ship to turn east, and for a few minutes the crew amused themselves by looking south into Canada and north into the United States. Just before midnight, as the cold front swept through Detroit, the coal-laden *Price* crossed shallow Lake St. Clair before heading up the St. Clair River to Lake Huron. The water journey would take the *Price* more than 30 hours of steaming to accomplish what former engineer Smith, traveling by train three days before, had done in half the time. Had Smith been watching the river from Port Huron in the dead of night, he might have seen the *Price* steaming northward into the lake.

In the narrow St. Clair River Arze McIntosh experienced a phenomenon called "bow cushion" or "stern suction." By either name it was the same. The ship's movement created low pressure in the water between the *Price's* stern and the nearby riverbank. This pulled the stern toward the bank, giving the impression that the bow was being pushed away by an invisible cushion. McIntosh instinctively gave the ship a touch of right rudder to keep the stern away from the Canadian shoreline. His experienced eye used the steering pole to judge the ship's progress. Performing this task in open water was relatively simple, but in the fast-flowing rivers steering was a tedious business that required full attention. McIntosh could not afford to watch the lights of St. Clair, his hometown, sliding by to port.

Sault Ste. Marie — St. Marys River
JAMES CARRUTHERS, J.H. SHEADLE, *and* HYDRUS

Saturday night, more than 12 hours after lining up for the locks at the Soo, the *Hydrus*, the *Carruthers*, and the *Sheadle* were finally below the rapids. Crowded conditions at the locks can be inferred from this unusual delay. A typical locking usually took less than an hour. After the locks, the three ships faced the rocky and twisting St. Marys River below the Soo. This stretch of water is still one of the biggest dangers faced by Great Lakes ships. The river channel was much narrower in 1913, with rock outcroppings along the way. Its bottom also is solid bedrock that resists dredging except with explosives. A moment of inattention while navigating the St. Marys River can put a ship hard aground.

Had Saturday's high winds been blowing across the river from either east or west, the captains of the *Hydrus*, *Carruthers*, and *Sheadle* might not have attempted the river passage in the darkness. But the wind was in the north, blowing roughly parallel with the river. It was a wild ride down, but by 1:55 A.M. on Sunday the ships had successfully passed DeTour Village and were on northern Lake Huron.

Lake Huron — Port Huron, Michigan
HURLBUT W. SMITH *and* J.F. DURSTON

Though Lakes Superior, Michigan, Huron, and Erie were all buffeted by howling winds and snow early Sunday morning, most sailors expected the weather to improve west to east as the day wore on because the storm was into its third day, about the limit for a November gale. So traffic on the lakes continued its normal pace. If the storm had been caused by the passage of a single low, they would have been right.

The 421-foot straight decker *Hurlbut W. Smith* cleared the St. Clair River upbound on Lake Huron at 1 A.M., bound for Milwaukee. In the *Smith*'s hold was a cargo of coal loaded the previous day at Buffalo.

Although the weather was deteriorating, Captain Thomas W. Carney was not overly concerned. After all, it was November. Snow, ice, and gusty wind were normal on the lakes late in the year. He expected this storm to be no better or worse than others he had weathered.

Shortly after 9 P.M. Saturday night, the steamer *J.F. Durston* had preceded the *Hurlbut W. Smith* out of the St. Clair River. The Port Huron lightship was right on station as the *J.F. Durston* passed in the darkness. Captain James B. Watts saw the flash from the anchored beacon. He pitied the men who lived aboard the tiny craft that bobbed beneath the flashing light. A brisk wind was riling the lake, and the tiny light from the ship seemed to thrash in agony. The crew would have to have cast-iron stomachs not to be seasick.

By 2:30 A.M. on Sunday, almost six hours after passing the lightship, the *Durston* had managed to bash its way no more than 50 miles north and was now about opposite Harbor Beach, Michigan. "The wind was north-northwest and quite a sea was running," Captain Watts later recalled. His thirty years of sailing the lakes told him this last trip of 1913 was going to be a long one.

SUNDAY MORNING AND MIDDAY

NOVEMBER 9

GOVERNMENT FORECASTERS did their best to track storms in 1913, but they simply did not have enough data or knowledge of the atmosphere to understand the complexity of what took place on November 9. Surface weather observations were collected only twice daily from the local stations around the country. The collected data were then painstakingly plotted by hand on outline maps in the Washington central office. Five different maps were created simultaneously. One contained the barometric pressures, temperatures, and wind directions for all reporting stations. Another made a comparison map of current temperatures and those of the previous day. The remaining maps showed the 24-hour changes in barometric pressure, regional changes in humidity, and the type of precipitation. Information from these five maps was then used to prepare the national forecast.

Simplified data from the master maps in Washington were then transmitted back to the reporting stations using the special telegraphic code to reduce the time and cost of transmission. The local offices created their own national maps by decoding the data and repeating the hand plotting done in Washington. The maps drawn by local observers contained less information than those created in Washington and were always hours behind the actual weather patterns.

On Sunday morning, the Weather Bureau centered the southern low that had been traveling north all night over Washington, D.C. It had continued to intensify and was now lashing the Weather Bureau's headquarter offices with wind and rain. More ominously, it was entraining the cold air that had moved down across the lakes behind the now-weakening arctic cold front—which had passed over Toledo at 1 A.M. and Cleveland at 3 A.M.—and that cold air was giving the low stronger vertical motions and a lower central pressure as it continued spinning north, now turning slightly west. In the databank of storm tracks proposed by chief forecaster Edward Garriott in 1901, there was no precedent for what this storm was doing. The Weather Bureau could not have predicted it. The low had not even existed as a discrete, closed circulation on the previous day's map.

Lake Michigan — South Manitou Island
Illinois

At 7:30 A.M. Sunday on northern Lake Michigan, Captain John A. Stufflebeam and the *Illinois* found the minuscule shelter the captain had been seeking behind South Manitou Island. It had taken the ship more than four hours to cover less than 30 miles. Now the captain's problem was coming up with a way to make use of the tiny lee created by the island. The quiet patch of water was hardly larger than the ship. Without hesitation, Stufflebeam carefully nosed his vessel right up to the shore. "There were no docks at which to land. Nor was it possible to anchor safely," he was quoted as saying in the *Cleveland Plain Dealer*. His description of what happened next is an account of creative seamanship combined with more than a dash of good luck. The captain sent men ashore to secure a mooring line from the ship. Stufflebeam tied his ship to a tree much like an American cowboy might tie up his horse.

> I saw only one safe solution. We drove into the land and forced the nose of the boat up on the beach. Then I kept the engines going slowly for forty-nine hours with the bow of the boat up on the beach. Thus we were able to ride the water, which continued to come against us with great fury. In that position we were in less danger.
>
> After forty-nine hours of battling the waves with the engines we were able to throw a line ashore and this we fastened to a large tree.
>
> Then I stopped the engines and we rested there, fastened to the tree, for twenty-three hours more.

The *Illinois* was one of the few lake ships then equipped with wireless communications. Captain Stufflebeam used his radio to learn when it was safe to resume his trip. The cove he used on the southern side of South Manitou is still a popular anchorage for pleasure boats seeking protection from northerly gales. Known locally as Crescent Bay, it is called South Manitou Harbor on official government publications.

Lake Superior — Keweenaw Peninsula
L.C. WALDO *and* GEORGE STEPHENSON

Dawn Sunday allowed the crew of the *L.C. Waldo* to better assess their precarious situation. Their drifting ship had somehow managed to clear the Keweenaw Peninsula. If they had fetched up on that rockbound point of land, the crew probably would have been doomed within minutes. Instead, the *Waldo* came to grief on a ledge extending out from Lake Superior's Manitou Island, which lies to the east of the Keweenaw. This ridge ends at Gull Rock, where water depths as little as 12 feet are found well offshore. Almost bolt upright, the *Waldo's* appearance from a distance gave little hint of trouble except that the broken hulk was sitting in water too shallow to float a fully loaded ship.

Although the Keweenaw Ship Canal was in regular use by commercial vessels, traffic to and from this artery did not normally pass within sight of Gull Rock, nor did the ships following the regular steamer tracks that ran well offshore on Lake Superior. Without a radio, the crew's only hope of rescue from their predicament was to attract the attention of a passing freighter. For any chance of survival they had to stay inside the protection of their broken and ice-covered ship, where they were invisible to sailors on the lake. Yet if no survivors were seen on deck, anyone passing close enough to spot the *Waldo* would likely think it was an abandoned derelict.

Unlikely as it seemed, Captain Mosher of the bulk freighter *George Stephenson* somehow came close enough to spot the broken *Waldo* on the rocks. The experienced sailor's curiosity also forced him to investigate. At first he assumed the hulk was abandoned because of its desolate and broken appearance. "On Sunday morning at daylight, I saw a steamer ashore . . . she seemed to be abandoned. There were no lights on her and no smoke was coming from her stack. Her decks were out of the water and big seas were breaking over her," he said.

For a moment Captain Mosher thought no one remained alive on the wreck. "I knew there must be men aboard her, but I wasn't sure. We first knew definitely when we saw a distress signal go up on her foremast at 7:00 A.M.," he said. The *Waldo* was stranded in water too shallow for the *Stephenson* to approach. High waves and howling winds prevented him from attempting a rescue using his freighter's lifeboats. All Captain Mosher could do was hoist a red-and-white-striped answering pennant. The sailors aboard the wrecked *Waldo* understood the meaning of that flag and gained renewed vigor from the hope of rescue.

Mosher immediately abandoned his voyage and began what turned into a three-day marathon effort to bring help to the stranded sailors. He headed the *Stephenson* under Keweenaw Point and toward a small fishing port inside Bete Grise Bay on the southern side of the peninsula. This tiny port served only small local boats and was not on the regular shipping routes, and its docks were too small to accommodate a freighter. Instead of tying up, the *Stephenson* found good holding ground for its anchor in the larger part of the bay, well protected from west, northwest, and north winds. Captain Mosher needed that lee, as he would be spending a lot of time anchored there.

One of the ship's lifeboats was hastily lowered to take news of the *Waldo*'s predicament to shore. "I sent the mate ashore to find a telephone and notify the lifesavers," said Captain Mosher. Early news reports from the Keweenaw Peninsula claimed the *Stephenson* had dropped a message in a bottle to a local commercial fishing boat. Confusion over how the world learned of the stranded ship probably began when the mate hired a fishing boat to cross Lac La Belle and then used a horse-drawn sleigh to reach the Eagle Harbor Lifesaving Station.

Aboard the *Stephenson*, Captain Mosher expected to resume his last voyage of the 1913 season in a few hours after a rescue mission to the *Waldo* was underway. But ashore on the Keweenaw Peninsula, the *Stephenson*'s mate finally reached the lifesaving station only to find Eagle Harbor's large motorized lifeboat, the *Success*, broken down. Station chief Charles A. Tucker knew his smaller surfboat, with its 8-horsepower gasoline engine, lacked the mechanical muscle to push through the seas running on Lake Superior, but duty required him to try anyway. After only a mile or so, Tucker and his crew were forced to admit defeat and return to the safety of their station.

Men from the Eagle Harbor station realized that if they were going to rescue the *Waldo*'s crew, they would have to finish repairing their larger lifeboat. Tucker turned the work over to two surfmen, Anthony F. Glaza and Thomas F. Bennett. The men worked through the night turning wrenches and making adjustments. By 3 A.M. on Monday the two impromptu mechanics were rewarded when the repaired engine started and ran smoothly. The 34-foot motorized lifeboat *Success* was ready for duty once again.

Meanwhile, comfort of sorts had been found in the *Waldo*'s windlass room, despite its clutter of large steam-powered machinery. If the ship had been intact, this room could have been toasty warm with heat from the ship's boilers. The break in the deck meant the windlasses were no longer connected to the engine room. Even if they had been, the boilers were cold now, flooded in the sunken stern section of the broken ship. Without steam, the windlass room was little more than a cold steel tomb in which the survivors clung to life.

Scrounging through the wreckage of the forward deckhouse, the crew found hundreds of dollars in cash lying about from the ship's broken safe. They let the money lie and instead seized upon the captain's bathtub, which Chief Engineer August Lempke quickly turned into a makeshift fireplace. Bottoms of tin fire buckets were punched out to make a crude chimney. The crew demolished what remained of the ship's wooden cabins to feed their fire. Their improvised fireplace did not completely take the chill out of the windlass room, but at least they would not freeze until the supply of wood ran out.

Hunger was a different story. No amount of ingenuity could create a hot meal from nothing. In the mad rush to abandon the stern, nobody had thought to bring a supply of food forward. One man had picked up three cans from a counter in the galley, but they were hardly a meal. One can contained tomatoes and two held peaches. All three combined were hardly enough to serve as an appetizer to the men and women huddled together for warmth in the windlass room. After that meager supply of food was gone, there was no more.

For the moment, however, the hungry crew of the *Waldo* were safe from the fury of the gale raging outside. Several men lit cigars as they awaited their fate, and the aromatic smoke curled upward in the quiet air of the windlass room. All around them the atmosphere had been whipped into a frenzy. No one could hazard a guess as to how long they would remain marooned in the wreckage of their ship or how long that wreckage would hold together.

Lake Erie — Cleveland, Ohio
State of Ohio *and* Alexander Holley

Waking up in cold Cleveland, Ohio, that Sunday morning was a sobering experience. Throughout the city, snow driven by 45-mile-per-hour northwesterly wind gusts piled into growing drifts. If that was not enough, the seemingly endless downpour of white flakes showed no sign of quitting, and the wind was actually increasing. The precipitation had started as wet sleet at 4 A.M., then turned to wet slush and finally to snow by 7 A.M. as the temperature dropped to the freezing point. There was nothing unusual in this progression of precipitation from rain and sleet to ice and snow, nothing except its amount.

The changing nature of the precipitation suggests that even in these early stages it was influenced by the warm, moist air in the cyclonic circulation of the southern storm that was now moving north. A lake-effect snow resulting entirely from the northwesterly gales would have been relatively dry and fluffy. The enormous weight of ice, slush, and snow was too much for the myriad electric and telephone lines connecting the city. Stout wooden utility poles snapped like saplings in the storm. City streets were so ice covered that more than one hundred automobile accidents were recorded.

At East 9th Street on the city's waterfront, the passenger steamer *State of Ohio* parted its lines sometime during the night so that at first light it was riding diagonally between two piers. The large ship caught and smashed to pieces several good-sized pleasure boats. Gone in a twinkling were *Vim*, *Bertha*, *U-and-I*, and *Anna Joe*. The unruly passenger ship also tore the upperworks off the tug *Kitty Downs*. All that havoc did not leave the *State of Ohio* undamaged. It sustained several large holes that were fortunately located above the waterline.

The barges that the Pittsburgh Steamship Company had sent into early layup on Saturday also broke loose overnight and began drifting inside the Cleveland harbor breakwater. Just back from their last trips of the season, they were not fully secured for the winter. Ordinarily, there would have been deckhands aboard each barge to handle emergencies like snapping docklines. But because they had been paid off a week early, the men were home in their beds when the winds began to howl. The whaleback barge *Alexander Holley* crashed into the East 40th Street pier with more damage to the pier than the barge. Nearby, the barges *Jenny* and *Thomas* also were driven ashore.

The anemometer at Cleveland's weather station showed northerly wind in the 20- to 30-mile-per-hour range during the overnight and early morning periods. Reports from ship captains indicated that winds on the water exceeded those readings, but even vessels moored some distance up Cleveland's normally well-protected Cuyahoga River found themselves in grave danger. Steamers tied up along Cleveland's crooked river were "swept loose," according to news reports. Several stacks of lumber were blown into the river and washed out into Lake Erie. Overhead, as witnesses later told the *Cleveland Plain Dealer*, the Main Avenue Bridge "swayed to and fro, seemingly ready to collapse."

At the Cleveland weather office, observer Alexander watched his barometer reading drop before his eyes. "Sent 10:40 A.M. special observation to central office, the barometer having fallen .15 inch in two hours," he wrote in the official *Daily Local Record* book. "The barometer fell quite rapidly after the midnight hour and unusually rapid after the morning observation." When he sent that special observation to Washington, the station pressure in Cleveland read 28.64 inches of mercury (29.34 inches corrected to sea level). That was the second lowest station pressure in history, the lowest being 28.28 on February 21, 1912. Winds were gusting through the city streets at more than 30 miles per hour. The snow was continuous.

Lake Erie — Lorain, Ohio
G.J. GRAMMER

The 418-foot steamer *G.J. Grammer* successfully departed Cleveland in Sunday's predawn twilight despite snow and high winds. Carrying a partial cargo of only 2,000 tons of coal, the straight decker was bound 25 miles west to Lorain, Ohio, where it expected to complete its load. Captain John Burus had been able to see well enough to pass through the main entrance to the Cleveland breakwall, but the blizzard completely obscured the entrance to Lorain's Black River. Rather than tempt fate, Burus decided to anchor off Lorain and wait out the storm. About 10:30 A.M., the fish tug *Seawing* hailed the freighter and offered to guide it into the harbor. Captain Burus declined, saying his ship would be safe enough until the snow let up.

But this was not just another November gale. Slowly, the *Grammer's* anchors began dragging. Captain Burus made an unsuccessful attempt to steam into deeper water, but the ship's steady drift toward the beach could not be halted. The single engine was overwhelmed by the combined forces of wind and waves, and the hapless vessel was thrown onto a small beach below the cliffs. As groundings go, it was a soft event that seemed to have done no harm to the ship's steel bottom.

Men from the Lorain Lifesaving Station quickly arrived with their breeches buoy and other equipment to rescue the *Grammer's* crew. Following the commands of Captain William Griesser, the lifesavers set up the line-throwing gun. Their first shot sent a line across the ship's bow. Soon, the breeches buoy was rigged. Instead of sending a member of his crew to shore, Captain Burns surprised the lifesavers by sending only a message in the buoy, reported in the *Cleveland Press*: "All safe. Our ship is not damaged. Do not know how soon we may need assistance."

There was little the lifesavers could do if the crew of the stranded ship refused to be rescued. So, they stood by the stranded ship in the blinding snow and waited for developments. In the meantime, they also advised the U.S. Revenue Service of the ship's plight. That agency had large steam-powered cutters on the lakes, one of which might prove useful in pulling the *Grammer* off the sand and into deep water.

Lake Huron —— Sarnia, Ontario
REGINA

Overnight the bulk freighters *Matoa*, *John A. McGean*, and *Howard M. Hanna Jr.* passed through the St. Clair River upbound onto the lake. In the predawn darkness before *Regina* sailed, Captain McConkey may have been comforted when he saw the new 534-foot strait decker *Charles S. Price* also heading northward onto Lake Huron. The sight of that ship leaving the river reassured McConkey that he was not the only captain

willing to face the season's first November gale. Despite the wind
whistling around the pilothouse, *Regina* departed at 7:30 A.M. on Sunday.

A solitary figure standing on shore took note of *Regina's* passage out
of the St. Clair River. Denny Lynn of the Lynn Marine Reporting Company had the job of spotting ships and reporting them to their respective companies. Ship spotting was a service that became obsolete after
the adoption of ship-to-shore radio by the Great Lakes fleet. In 1913,
however, Lynn could make a good living watching vessels entering and
leaving the river. He received a small payment for reporting each ship to
its owners.

The *Regina's* appearance bothered him. Lynn noted its top-heavy load
of sewer and gas pipe that rose above the ship's rail. "It didn't look good
to me at the time. I was afraid there would be trouble," he told the *Port
Huron Times-Herald* later. "I don't believe it is intended that boats of that
description should be loaded in that manner." Lynn must have been shivering inside his overcoat as he watched the package freighter depart.
Instead of the mild temperatures of 24 hours before, the mercury had
tumbled to the upper 20s and was still falling as the wind gusts increased.

Captain McConkey was bound for the north shore of Georgian Bay,
where he was to make deliveries at ten different lumber ports. Cargo
stowed in *Regina's* hold contained both the necessities and the niceties of
life for lumberjacks who would spend the winter logging in the Canadian woods. In addition to safety razors and ketchup, the two most critical items on the manifest were wooden kitchen matches and whiskey.

Lake Erie — Port Colborne, Ontario
CITY OF HAMILTON

Just past noon on Sunday, a combination package freight and passenger
ship passed through the last lock of the Welland Canal at Port Colborne,
Ontario, on eastern Lake Erie. The *City of Hamilton* was a wooden Canadian vessel that made regular runs from Lake Ontario to ports along the
northern shore of Lake Erie. "We left Port Colborne at the end of the
Welland Canal at 1:45 P.M.," said Captain J. L. Baxter. "I had noticed storm
signals at Kingston, but didn't think the storm was bad." While in the
canal Baxter had been shielded from the northwesterly gale, a fact he soon
discovered. "Two miles out in the lake [Lake Erie], I saw what I was up

against. The snow made it impossible to see half a length of the boat ahead," he said later. The *City of Hamilton* steamed southwest, its course almost 90 degrees to the 70-mile-per-hour northwesterly flow of air sweeping down from Canada. Captain Baxter found scant protection from the low-lying Canadian coastline to his north. "I hugged the shore as tight as I could to get shelter," he said. "Snow covered the windows so that you couldn't see. Outside the sleet mixed with the snow stung one's face like tacks."

With his wooden ship battered by the waves, a worried Captain Baxter dismissed any thought of returning to the safety of the Welland Canal. "Things looked bad. I didn't think I could get back into Port Colborne, so I continued on." Normally, the run to his next destination of Port Stanley, Ontario, would have taken well under 8 hours. The captain faced 14 straight hours of fighting the gale.

Between Port Colborne and Port Stanley lies a sandy point of land that crooks into Lake Erie like a beckoning finger. This is Long Point, reputed to be the single most dangerous hazard on the Great Lakes. It is really just a narrow sandbar more than 18 miles long and rising only a few feet above the surface of the surrounding water. Much of the point is marshy, and shoals extend outward in all directions for some distance. LaSalle and his band of adventurers nearly came to grief there aboard *Le Griffon*. Even today, Long Point does not show up well on radar screens. It is virtually invisible in foul weather, a fact that bedeviled Captain Baxter as he attempted to navigate through the blinding snow.

Because the *City of Hamilton* was a passenger ship, its superstructure had a tall profile to contain its staterooms. Hurricane-force winds on Lake Erie found the ship an inviting target. "The big house and upper decks were just like sails before the wind. I don't believe we went half a mile without the boat listed away from the wind at such an angle that our lower deck was in the water," the captain recalled.

Despite it all, Captain Baxter's dead reckoning was right on target. He brought the ship to harbor without incident. "When we did reach Port Stanley, the first thing I saw was the lighthouse a few feet in front of us, about a dozen feet to our starboard," he said proudly. During the entire ordeal Baxter had stayed in his pilothouse, sustained only by an occasional cup of coffee.

Lake Erie — Cleveland, Ohio
ISABELLA J. BOYCE *and* CONSORT JOHN J. BARLUM

Fifty-four miles directly south of Captain Baxter, the steamer *Isabella J. Boyce* struggled to enter Cleveland's harbor early Sunday afternoon. Slipping through the city's breakwall would have been difficult enough if the small wooden freighter had been on its own, but the *Boyce* was towing the barge *John J. Barlum*. Until after World War I it was common on the Great Lakes for ships to have a "consort" in the form of an engineless barge. Parsimonious shipping lines adopted this practice to get double use out of a single expensive steam engine. Unfortunately, steamships doing the towing were seldom, if ever, given enough additional horsepower to make up for the drag of the consort.

The *Barlum* was a hybrid vessel, not quite a schooner and not quite a barge. Its wooden hull had the traditional shape of a schooner and two masts, one in front of the long hold and the other aft. Both were rigged to carry a gaff sail, although photos of the vessel hint that sail power was seldom employed. The *Barlum* did not have a pilothouse or texas on its forecastle. Although it had an afterdeck cabin similar to a boilerhouse on a steamboat, it was not self-propelled.

Exhausted from a long night of battling the storm, Captain Walter R. Pringle could almost see his home on Woodland Avenue as he lined up his ship and consort with the Cleveland harbor entrance. One try was not enough. The *Boyce* simply did not have enough power to bull its way through the narrow entrance. Several times Pringle was forced to slew away and seek open water before both vessels made it through the 500-foot-wide opening in the breakwater. As soon as they were inside, tugs swarmed around the *Boyce* and its consort to assist them.

PRINGLE AND OTHER CAPTAINS of ships caught on Lakes Superior, Michigan, Huron, and Erie could not imagine what was happening in the atmosphere above the lakes during that Sunday afternoon. The southern low was moving north-northwest now, over Maryland and into Pennsylvania. As it entrained cold arctic air, and with the jet stream drawing off or "exhausting" the rising air above, vertical accelerations within the low continued to intensify. It was becoming more dangerous by the hour. There had been record snowfalls in West Virginia overnight. Now the blizzard was burying Zanesville and Columbus, in central Ohio, and still heading north toward Cleveland.

But the captains could not see the jet stream blowing away the air aloft like a planet-sized leaf blower. They could not see the warm, moist, south-flowing air north and west of the advancing low begin to merge in a vast and ghostly pas de deux with the southeast-flowing arctic air blasting down from Canada. The tighter, faster-turning, more organized circulation emerging from this chaos—had it been visible—would have been mesmerizing, perhaps even beautiful, but no captain privileged to see it would have left port ahead of it. In fact, no Great Lakes captain, mate, or deckhand in 1913 had ever experienced a weather event like this, nor has anyone since. By early Sunday afternoon, the growing weather cataclysm had achieved unprecedented size and strength, the result of an atmospheric throw of dice that hasn't been repeated. "Today's snow and windstorm combined was more severe than any other previous one at this station," noted the weather observer at Toledo, Ohio. His thoughts were echoed by the public press. "What vesselmen seem unanimous in declaring the worst storm in the history of the lakes," wrote the *Port Huron Times-Herald*, "swept down and fastened its grip on Port Huron and the Thumb district Sunday afternoon."

"All lake traffic has been abandoned for the last 48 hours," the *Cleveland Press* would declare, inaccurately, on Monday. "The storm on Superior started Saturday afternoon [sic] and has increased in violence ever since," the article went on to say, "and from information gathered at various weather stations it has not yet reached its height."

In fact, western Lake Superior was into its third full day of northwesterly gales, each hour seemingly worse than the preceding. The most violent weather of a typical Great Lakes gale lasts only a day or so, and most storms are over in three days. Years of experience told captains to expect better weather Sunday, but this time experience was not the best teacher. The polar air from the strong and sprawling high to the west continued to blast southeast over the lakes, rushing "downhill" toward the deepening low that was now approaching western Pennsylvania.

SUNDAY AFTERNOON

NOVEMBER 9

AS LATE AS LUNCHTIME Sunday, conditions on lower Lake Huron had been what might be called dangerous but normal for a November gale. Work went on for crews of the freighters making their last runs of the season. The low that had swept over Superior was moving off to the north and east, and in some locations barometric pressures were reassuringly on the rise again. The familiar pattern of a three-day blow followed by improving conditions seemed to be repeating. This time, however, the lakes were not experiencing just a single gale.

Instead, what was about to happen from Lake Superior down to Lake Erie was a sort of weather explosion. It came at a bad time of day for the Weather Bureau, shortly after noon. That was four hours after the morning reports had been forwarded to Washington. Another round of reports was not due for 8 more hours. This gave the storm the entire afternoon and early evening to build its hurricane-force winds and seas before the bureau's Washington headquarters would learn the full extent of the deadly situation on the Great Lakes. By the next round of reports at 8 P.M. the storm would become the uniquely destructive cataclysm that mariners would dub the "White Hurricane."

Lake Huron —— Thunder Bay, Michigan

JAMES CARRUTHERS, J.H. SHEADLE, J.F. DURSTON, *and* HURLBUT W. SMITH

Horsepower is needed to push loaded freighters through storm waves. Stokers had had to sling a lot of coal into the boilers of their ships on Saturday and Sunday to provide enough steam for the engines. Captain

Wright of the *Carruthers* and Captain Lyons of the *Sheadle* prudently took on fuel Sunday morning, even though they did not know the extent to which the storm would intensify. They put their downbound ships into the Pickands & Mather fuel dock at Alpena, Michigan, inside Thunder Bay on Lake Huron, shortly after 8 A.M. The Canadian *Carruthers* loaded first and departed slightly ahead of the American vessel. Skeins of snow had been flying all morning, but visibility was good. The barometer was low but stationary. At 10:15 A.M. weather forecasters in Washington continued the northwest storm warnings. One new sentence was added to yesterday's warning, "Storm over Virginia moving northeast." In fact the storm was farther north by late Sunday morning and traveling just west of north.

South of Thunder Bay the steamer *J.F. Durston* continued its battle with huge seas that cascaded over its deck studded with dozens of vulnerable hatches. "The engineer, Edward Sampson, was throttling the engine because of racing," Captain James B. Watts recalled. "We soon had a lively time of it."

Shipmasters on the lakes customarily sounded a special passing signal with their whistles called "captain's salutes"—a long blast followed by two short blasts. This signal originated during the earliest days of steam on the lakes, just after the Civil War, and continues today, even though the one-long-and-two-short pattern of whistle blasts is now reserved under the Inland Rules of the Road as a fog signal.

"Just before she [the storm] settled down to some real blowing, we passed the steamer *Hydrus* and exchanged passing signals," Captain Watts of the *Durston* recalled sadly to a *Detroit Free Press* reporter after the storm. "They were the last she ever blew, for she went down with her whole crew a few hours later."

Not far south of the *Durston*, the coal-laden *Hurlbut W. Smith* had managed to thrash its way north past the opening to Saginaw Bay. Captain Thomas W. Carney intended to throttle back the *H.W. Smith*'s engine and wait out the storm with his bow to the waves. He did not want to chance capsizing his steamer by turning it around in a wave trough. The pounding from steaming head-on into the waves eventually became too much when a particularly large wave swept over the ship and crushed the pilothouse.

Carney concluded that his only hope of survival was to turn around and run before the waves. The ship's 1,480-horsepower, triple-expansion steam engine struggled for more than an hour to bring the *H.W. Smith* through the dangerous troughs between the waves. During most of that time the hull rolled on its beam ends, constantly threatening to capsize. Wooden doors on the superstructure collapsed under the weight of water pouring across the decks. Windows shattered, and the furnishings were washed about inside the cabins.

At the height of the gale, porter Paul Becker made the mistake of going on deck for a scuttle of coal. A huge sea knocked him off his feet and carried him toward the *H.W. Smith's* fantail like a piece of debris. Other members of the crew plucked the helpless sailor from the wash and kept him from going overboard. They hustled him back into the relative safety of the boilerhouse, where it was discovered that one of Becker's legs had been injured in the mishap and the other appeared to be broken. The husband-wife team in the *H.W. Smith's* crew were also injured by storm-tossed debris. Both steward John F. Sweeney and his spouse required hospitalization after the storm.

"I am fearful for the safety of two boats which were trying to cross Saginaw Bay with us," Captain Carney said afterward. "I am particularly anxious for the Pickands, Mather & Company steamer. We evidently all were swept around at the same time. I am afraid that the captain went just a little too far." Although Carney could not identify the vessel, the only Pickands, Mather & Company ship on that portion of Lake Huron was the *Hydrus*, a ship that was never seen afloat again.

Lake Erie — Toledo, Ohio
OPEN MOTORBOAT

A storm that was strong enough to threaten huge steel ships would hardly seem a place for small wooden boats. Yet around the lakes Sunday duck hunters, sport anglers, and other adventurers braved the elements without regard to personal safety. Near Toledo on Lake Erie that afternoon F. F. Goodaite, Clarence Warner, and Leon Baldwin decided to take a spin on Lake Erie in a small motorboat. The men apparently took no heed of the building gale. Even though the trio remained in protected water near the Toledo entrance, the waves were too much for their small craft. Rather than return to their home dock, the hapless navigators headed for Guard Island near the mouth of the Maumee River, where they spent a miserably cold afternoon, evening, and night.

Lake St. Clair —— St. Clair Flats, Michigan
Open Boat

At 3:30 p.m. a judge from Detroit, Michigan, and two companions boarded an open boat to cross what is known as the "middle channel" of the St. Clair River in the St. Clair Flats. They were heading for Muscamoot Bay, where the judge was to catch a steamboat for Detroit. Judge James Phelan was due in court on Monday morning to preside over a trial. The three men had reached the midpoint of their short trip when the boat's gasoline engine popped, sputtered, and stopped. It was obvious that the craft was hard aground. Two of the men, wearing hip boots, jumped into the river and carried the boat's anchor to shore, where they drove it into the ground. They attempted to free their craft by hauling on the rope, but the scheme failed. With darkness falling, the trio's only recourse was to make themselves as comfortable as possible in the bottom of the boat.

They arranged life preservers into makeshift bunks. For shelter from the blizzard they had only a single oilskin coat, which they used to cover their heads. The single source of heat in the boat was the tiny gasoline engine. The men managed to start this engine from time to time during the night to gain a few minutes of warmth from its exhaust pipe. Starting the engine also caused the propeller to wash out the mud beneath their boat. By 4:30 in the morning the craft was free, and they could have resumed their journey. Instead, Judge Phelan and his companions turned back toward the cottage they had departed 13 hours previously. Shortly after dawn they staggered ashore and headed for the warmth of their bunks. According to an account in the *Detroit Free Press*, none of the three showed any lasting effects from the ordeal. The court session was postponed due to "bad weather."

Lake Superior —— Marquette, Michigan
Henry B. Smith

At Marquette, Michigan, on Lake Superior, Captain James Owen was uncharacteristically anxious to be underway despite rapidly deteriorating weather. His straight decker, the *Henry B. Smith*, was loading nearly 10,000 tons of iron ore. Immediately after loading, Jimmy (as Owen was known) intended to start down for Cleveland on his last trip of the year. The normally mild captain was upset by the blizzard conditions interfering with the loading of ore and threatening to delay the departure of his ship.

Allegedly, Captain Owen was uneasy because of an ultimatum given to him by the ship's owners: deliver this last cargo on time, or he would not return as the ship's captain in 1914. Supposedly, the *H.B. Smith* had been late on its runs numerous times. News accounts said these delays were seldom the captain's fault, but no matter what their cause, they resulted in higher port costs and fewer trips for the ship. That meant lower profits for the owners, who allegedly gave Owen a none-too-subtle hint not to be late on this final voyage. Jimmy Owen had been the *H.B. Smith*'s master from the day it was launched.

Captain Owen demanded that his ship be loaded despite howling winds and blizzard conditions. It was an unreasonable request, and not typical of this popular captain. Cold temperatures and snow caused iron ore to freeze in the loading chutes. The only way to make it flow was for a man to crawl down the chute on his hands and knees and knock the clog loose with a sledgehammer. Loading ore in freezing weather was so difficult and dangerous that dockworkers avoided it whenever possible. Men working the ore dock were not pleased with Owen.

"I'll clear [port] as soon as the ore is loaded," Captain Owen told the superintendent of the dock Sunday morning, according to the *Duluth Herald*. He was true to his word. "Wire the company that I am coming," he announced late in the afternoon.

Northwest seas were crashing over Marquette's breakwater at 4 P.M. when Captain Owen nosed the *H.B. Smith* out of the harbor. As he left, Captain Owen reportedly said, "I will go down the lake with the wind and make up lost time." A slight rise in barometric pressure was reason enough for him to depart even before his ship was ready for sea. Even after nearly ninety years, news accounts of his departure are hard to believe:

> Before leaving he said it was up to him to make the Soo and that he would run down the lake before the gale. He had absolute confidence in his boat, and with 10,000 tons of ore to steady him, he is said to have joked over suggestions of disaster.
>
> So confident was he that his ship could weather any storm, that it is alleged he left the harbor without first battening down his hatches and

that as the boat cleared the breakwater, sailors on the *Denmark* and *Choctaw*, which lay near by, say they saw men endeavoring to make the ship watertight.

Cleveland Plain Dealer, NOVEMBER 14, 1913

The cargo hold of a Great Lakes bulk freighter has never been particularly watertight because of the hatches needed to ease the problem of handling bulk cargoes. The simplest way to carry materials such as iron ore or coal is in open hopper barges like those used on rivers and other protected inland waterways. However, open vessels on the Great Lakes would be swamped almost instantly by storm waves. Designers of Great Lakes ships solved this problem by covering the cargo with a large number of hatches separated by narrow strips of deck. An ocean freighter of 1913 might have had six or eight hatches, whereas a straight decker had two or three dozen.

This number of hatches was necessary to give several pieces of unloading equipment simultaneous access to the entire cargo hold. Each hatch on a Great Lakes bulk freighter crossed almost the full width of the deck. Narrow strips of steel deck between hatches were balanced on the internal transverse framing that maintained the structural integrity of the hull. Although these ships were called "straight deckers," they actually exposed far more square feet of hatches to storm waves than they did solid steel deck.

Hatches have always been the weakest point in the traditional Great Lakes bulk freighter. The system of wooden covers with tarpaulins used on ocean ships proved impractical. Steel covers were the obvious answer, but covers made out of a single sheet of metal were too heavy for deck gangs of four and five sailors to manhandle. The newest solution in 1913 was telescoping covers made of several pieces of steel that slid beneath one another. Deckhands muscled these telescoping covers open and closed with the help of a multipart block and tackle. Canvas weather cloths might be lashed over the steel covers if unusually rough weather was expected.

Leaking hatches were a problem even after telescoping covers were properly dogged down, because of the low coamings typical of the era. Hatch coamings in 1913 were often only a foot high and never more than 18 inches. Coaming height was slightly increased on ships built after

1913. Even so, the coamings of modern straight deckers are still less than 3 feet high, and hatches continue to be a weakness of bulk freighter design.

Claims that the hatches of the *H.B. Smith* were not fastened are probably true. Regardless, it was hardly prudent to depart from any Lake Superior port on that particular Sunday. The local Marquette newspaper carried an interview with several ship captains about Jimmy Owen and his sailing into a storm with open hatches.

> It was felt at the time that he was pursuing a rash and foolhardy course, and marine men freely predicted that he would be compelled to put about and make for shelter. Captain Cleary prophesied that the *Smith* would be back in Marquette harbor within a few hours.
>
> . . . Captain Smith of the *Choctaw*, which was in port with coal during the storm asserts that the *Smith* put about less than half an hour after leaving the harbor. It is generally believed that he realized the danger of trying to make the Soo with the weather so heavy and decided to seek the shelter of the east shore of Keweenaw Point.
>
> *Marquette Daily Mining Journal*, NOVEMBER 14, 1913

According to news accounts, Captain Owen then headed north from Marquette and disappeared into swirling snow. The *Daily Mining Journal* reported that winds "howled so fiercely on Sunday night that many believed a hurricane was in progress." Local weather observer P. E. Johnson's instruments recorded the velocity each hour through the night. His notebook shows that the wind on land averaged only 35 to 37 miles per hour from the northwest. That is less than half of hurricane velocity. The maximum gust Johnson recorded was 46 miles per hour at 8:25 P.M. However, the weather station recorded wind speeds a short distance inland. Gusts on the open waters of Lake Superior could have been considerably stronger.

The temperature at Marquette dropped to 18 degrees that night. Snowdrifts of 6 to 9 feet were reported overnight in nearby Ishpeming, Michigan. The tracks of the South Shore railroad on the Keweenaw Peninsula were nearly washed out by high waves at a place known locally as "Carp Furnace." Workmen had spent much of the previous summer reinforcing a trestle there with lake sand and waste mine rock. "When this work was finished, it was believed that the fill had been made secure against any storm that was likely to occur," the *Daily Mining Journal* reported. "The water found its way between the rock and the sand and washed it out. The rock that was used to cover the sea face of the fill now lies in a pile on the beach." The paper claimed the trestle was still sound despite the battering from storm waves.

An unidentified captain of a lumber hooker for the Edward Haines Lumber Company was quoted as saying, "It was the worst storm that I ever experienced, and I have seen a few bad ones. We were approaching Point Aba when the blow struck. It was the most peculiar storm that I have ever seen. The wind, snow and waves all came at the same time. If we had been 25 miles out, I am afraid it would have been a toss of the coin whether we would have weathered the blow."

Lake Superior — Whitefish Bay, Michigan
MARICOPA

Captain Owen's course should have taken him to Whitefish Bay at the Soo, also the destination of the 406-foot steamer *Maricopa*. Captain Storey of that ship described conditions during his trip down Lake Superior from Duluth to a *Port Huron Times-Herald* reporter: "We never had a let-up from the time we left Duluth. The gale blew fifty miles an hour all the way down Superior. . . . Ice gathered fast on our boat. It was necessary at times to thaw it away from the front of our wheelhouse in order to see. The furious wind, coupled with the freezing temperature, made it the fiercest trip I have made for years." The *Maricopa* arrived at the Soo more than 10 hours late and finally locked through at 5:30 P.M., on its way down to Lake Huron.

Lake Huron — Sturgeon Point, Michigan
MATOA

The coal-laden *Matoa* made heavy weather of its trip up Lake Huron all day. The ship was nearing Sturgeon Point, south of Thunder Bay, when the biggest of the seas slammed over its straight deck. "Before we knew what happened," recalled Captain McLeod in the *Cleveland Plain Dealer*, "they stove in part of the after cabin, flooded the messroom and let a mountain of water into the engine room." None of that damage was as serious as what happened on deck, where three hatch strongbacks were swept away. Captain McLeod decided his only option was to turn and run before the storm.

Reversing course was necessary to put the ship's stern into the waves. Instead of knifing into the swells, McLeod intended to allow the *Matoa* to run ahead of them. The elliptical "schooner" stern would lift the hull as the waves roared past. He hoped this would free the decks of the constant deluge of water that was tearing open the hatches and destroying the cabins. The problem was that all of those benefits could only be obtained by putting the ship broadside to the wind and waves during the turn.

"We dreaded the thought of attempting the turn," the Captain McLeod recalled. To ease the strain on the hull he ordered two barrels of oil poured into the waves, one over each bow. "I believe that saved us from shipping a deadly mass of water during the four minutes it took us to turn," he said. His ship began moving back down the length of Lake Huron with its engine turning a slow 26 revolutions per minute. Outside the pilothouse, Captain McLeod noted the temperature had dropped well below freezing to 15 degrees, accounting for the ship's heavy accumulation of ice.

Lake Huron — Harbor Beach, Michigan
H.A. HAWGOOD

Battered by Lake Huron waves, many upbound captains appear to have decided to reverse course and return to the relative calm of the St. Clair River at Port Huron that afternoon. This would turn out to be a mistake, but during the afternoon of November 9 it seemed sensible. The gales of Friday and Saturday were giving signs of "blowing themselves out." If things went the way they always had in past years, the strong northwesterly winds would be gone by Monday morning. Rather than smash pilothouses and snap rivets, captains thought it prudent to return to calmer water where they could wait out the waning storm.

Early that afternoon, Captain A. C. May turned around his upbound freighter, *H.A. Hawgood* somewhere north of Saginaw Bay and not far to the south of the *Matoa*. He intended to return to Port Huron and the safety of the St. Clair River by running ahead of the waves that were rising higher than his pilothouse windows. About opposite Harbor Beach, Michigan, he caught a glimpse of the *Charles S. Price* struggling to make headway up the lake. A few minutes later he spotted *Regina* also making heavy weather on its way north with its heavy deckload of pipe, but Captain May had little time to think of other ships. Driven southward by huge following seas, the *Hawgood* found itself running out of room near the bottom of Lake Huron later in the afternoon.

"The wind and seas kept increasing and the snow got thicker," Captain May admitted to reporters after the storm. When darkness fell he was sure he knew his ship's position within a mile or so, but that wasn't good enough. "After a while it got so thick we couldn't see the smokestack. The seas went right over the pilothouse."

Lake Huron ——— Saginaw Bay, Michigan
REGINA

Aboard *Regina*, Captain McConkey's optimism for an easy upbound trip was quickly checked. A chill gale from the northwest was building steadily, and the barometer was dropping again. The largest waves of his career were already rolling down Lake Huron as his small package freighter bashed its way up the lake. By 1:30 P.M. Sunday, *Regina* had struggled as far north as the notoriously roughest patch of water on Lake Huron: the mouth of Saginaw Bay. It was then that the wind, which had been less than 50 miles per hour from the northwest, suddenly veered into the northeast. With that wind shift came an equally sudden increase in velocity to 70 miles per hour with higher gusts.

Regina's pilothouse windows must have rattled and moaned like the windows of other ships caught in the rising wind. Against this eerie backdrop of sound, Captain McConkey considered the wisdom of turning around and heading back down Lake Huron for the apparent safety of the St. Clair River. He may have caught a glimpse of another straight decker attempting to reverse course at about that time. It would likely have been the *Charles S. Price*, the ship that had preceded the Canadian freighter out of the river earlier that morning. A brief sighting of another vessel making the turn may have confirmed the young Canadian captain's intuition that returning to Sarnia was the prudent thing to do. Unlike the master of a bulk freighter with its cargo safely stowed below in the hold,

McConkey had to worry about that top-heavy load of iron pipe frozen to the deck. Turning around meant putting *Regina* sideways to the waves for several minutes. He could imagine his small ship rolling over like a log in the huge combers that were marching down the lake.

Regina's chief engineer, C. J. McSorley, managed to squeeze every ounce of power out of the ship's single "up-and-down" steam engine during the daring maneuver. Somehow, the package freighter climbed out of the trough and began retracing its course down Lake Huron. Keeping up steam for the engine must have been increasingly difficult throughout the afternoon. Ice would have covered *Regina's* fiddley grates located in the roof of the boilerhouse, restricting the flow of fresh air into the boiler room. Burning coal to produce steam would have consumed oxygen from the air more quickly than it could have been replenished through the partially blocked ventilators. Despite constant raking and prodding, the glowing coal would have grown colder, resulting in lower boiler pressure. Chopping ice away from the fiddleys was out of the question. No one could have survived such a foolhardy errand to the top of the after deckhouse.

Ice-covered ventilators were not the only problem faced by ships like the Canadian package freighter. As the result of swirling snow and flying spray, visibility on Lake Huron during the afternoon and evening was effectively zero. Deprived of the familiar landmarks he normally used to judge his ship's position, Captain McConkey had only a compass and his intuition to guide him. An accurate dead reckoning plot was out of the question. Immense waves pushed his ship forward. There was no way to calculate *Regina's* true speed over the bottom accurately. Worse, he had nothing against which to judge the ship's slide to leeward. From a safety point of view, McConkey was effectively lost, even though he probably knew his exact position within a mile or less.

Lake Huron — Sulphur Island, Thunder Bay, Michigan
ACADIAN

One of Captain McConkey's fellow Canadian skippers, Robert McIntyre, was also battling Lake Huron Sunday. Both men worked for the Merchants Mutual Line of Toronto. McIntyre's ship, the *Acadian*, was upbound to Fort William, Ontario, with a cargo of dry cement and wire in its hold and iron billets on deck. The ship was making for the St. Marys River on his way to the Soo when the weather rapidly deteriorated. Captain McIntyre decided to seek shelter in Thunder Bay near Alpena, Michigan. More than twenty other ships were attempting to ride out the storm by anchoring as deeply as possible into that bay.

In the swirling winds and snow the *Acadian* came too close to Sulphur Island and struck a reef. It was an honest mistake in navigation caused by the impossible sea, wind, and snow conditions. The two-year-old, 300-foot ship came to a halt almost 7 miles from Alpena, fully exposed to the wind and waves. Captain McIntyre immediately ordered his crew to fire distress rockets. The distress signals were invisible from shore because of the blizzard. Like the other crews of stranded ships, the men on the *Acadian* resigned themselves to a long, cold wait for rescue.

Lake Huron — Thunder Bay Isle, Michigan
J.F. Durston

Aboard the *Durston*, Captain Watts made the opposite choice to Captains McConkey and Carney. Instead of turning around, he continued smashing his way north—almost directly into the raging wind. The nearness of the Canadian shoreline on the north shore of Lake Huron required him to do something unusual for a ship in a gale of hurricane strength: to "check back," or slow down. Watts was doing his best not to run out of lake. "By 1:30 Sunday afternoon we were off Thunder Bay Isle, which is about 150 miles from Port Huron," he recalled. "We were under check and not making much headway. The sea was too heavy for me to try to make a lee of Thunder Bay, so I kept the *Durston* heading into it, steering north. The sea was increasing all the time and our decks and hatches were coated with huge masses of ice."

Captain Watts made the wisest choice. Although he appeared to be heading into the gale, heading north actually took the *Durston* out of the worst conditions and into the fringes of the maelstrom then developing over the southern end of the lake. In addition, the *Durston* eventually found a measure of protection from wind and waves in the lee of the Canadian shoreline at the top of the lake.

Captains who headed south toward Port Huron that day took their ships into grave danger. Going south was a popular decision because it seemed to be the best way to outrun the howling wind and waves rolling down the lake. South was the course chosen by the masters of the *Hydrus, John A. McGean, Argus, James Carruthers, Wexford,* and *H.A. Hawgood.* Unknown to them, the most violent winds and blinding snow awaited them in southern Lake Huron, the very shape of which created the biggest danger for southbound ships. By steaming south, ships entered the closed toe of the lake, where land converged around them. All of this land was to leeward of their vessels, hence the nautical term *lee shore.* Prior to the invention of modern rescue helicopters, being driven aground in a gale often meant certain death for a ship's crew. Plunging breakers made it unlikely that anyone aboard a stranded ship could escape in lifeboats. For the same reason, rescuers in surfboats could not reach trapped sailors. The ultimate cruelty was that the same waves isolating survivors from rescue also tore apart what remained of their ship. Piece by piece, the vessels were destroyed as crews clung to what shelter remained, until one last wave claimed all for the sea.

Storm tactics on the open ocean allow captains to "run off" before a gale. Running before an ocean storm often takes ships several hundred miles off course, but it's a scant price to pay for survival. Captains of ships on the Great Lakes have no such luxury. They constantly navigate within a few miles of rocky cliffs or low-lying sandy shores. A relatively minor deviation from course sends an unwary skipper running onto a rocky shoal or crashing ashore.

Lake Huron — Positions Doubtful

HYDRUS, JAMES CARRUTHERS, *and* J.H. SHEADLE

The full fury of what was now a full-blown storm caught three ships—the *Hydrus, Carruthers,* and *Sheadle*—in central Lake Huron just past noon on Sunday. They were not operating together; their proximity is simply an indication of the crowded Great Lakes shipping lanes even so late in the season. "The sea kept on increasing, and the wind changed to due north, blowing a gale," wrote Captain Lyons of the *Sheadle.* "At 11:30 A.M., the course was changed to south by east one-half east in order to bring the ship more before the sea, and we continued to shift as the sea increased from a half to a point so as to keep the ship running practically dead before it; also to keep the ship from rolling and the sea from breaking over the decks."

Lake Huron — Off Thunder Bay, Michigan
J.F. DURSTON

As afternoon passed to evening, the *J.F. Durston* continued pushing north, the one ship to do so. "About 5:00 P.M. Sunday, the storm doors throughout the ship washed away and the shutters on the windows started to cave in," recalled Captain Watts. "It was snowing heavy and freezing hard. I had the engineer check the propeller down to 55 turns a minute. By 6:00 P.M., it wasn't safe for a man to try to get from forward aft or from aft forward. The lifeline was covered with solid ice, which made it as thick around as a man's body and absolutely useless."

The 440-foot *Durston* took a terrific pounding from smashing headlong into the seas. The point of the bow parted the waves, only to have the billows join back together on top of the ship's deck for a headlong rush against the after deckhouse. None aboard could remember seas as angry as those on Lake Huron that afternoon. "No man could have lived in them," Captain Watts said ruefully. "All the lifeboats, liferafts and life belts in the world wouldn't have been worth a tinker's dam. In that black seething water these so-called safety aids couldn't have lasted a minute."

Ice coating the forward walls of the *Durston*'s cabins was credited with helping save the ship. Captain Watts said he thought the thick coating helped armor the pilothouse and texas against the force of the waves. He also gave credit to a full coal bunker for protecting the after deckhouse. It was filled above the spar deck to nearly the roof of the boilerhouse. Coal in the bunker provided mass to help the lightweight structure of the forward wall of the deckhouse absorb the energy of waves crashing against its flat vertical surface. As long as that wall held, the vital boiler and engine rooms were safe.

An unexpected reason the *Durston* survived was checking down its speed. Slowing down allowed the ship to keep its bow into the waves throughout the killing hours on Lake Huron. "Checking her down was the answer," Captain Watts said. "It gave the ship a chance to rise with the sea. Lake steamers when loaded deeper than two-thirds of the molded depth, are loggy [sic] and lift with difficulty."

Lake Huron — North of Port Huron, Michigan
J.H. Sheadle

Just before 6 P.M. the steward on the southbound *Sheadle* prepared to serve the evening meal. His ship was nearing the closed lower end of Lake Huron and running with the waves. One wave larger and more massive than the others climbed over the fantail and slammed against the after wall of the boilerhouse. Water sloshed through the galley, washing provisions out of the ship's refrigerator. Flour in the cook's storage bin instantly turned to paste. The crew's supper, which had been on the table, sloshed to the deck, where it mixed with broken dishes, spilled jars of spice, galley knives, cooking oil, and silverware. Onions and potatoes bobbed in the water draining over the galley doorsill. Only a single ham and a few potatoes survived.

"It was blowing about 70 miles an hour at this time, with high seas, one wave following another very closely," Captain Lyons of the *Sheadle* wrote in his report. "Owing to the sudden force of the wind the seas had not lengthened out as they usually do when the wind increases in the ordinary way. In about four hours the wind had come up from 25 to 70 miles an hour."

Lake Michigan — Chicago, Illinois
The Boy *and* J.G. Boyce

Lake Michigan was far enough west to be spared the full fury of the developing storm. Even more than Lake Huron, however, it has a north–south orientation. All of its waters were open to the full effect of the northwest winds of more than 30 miles per hour that blew without letup all Sunday. Huge waves rolling down the lake were particularly destructive at Chicago and Milwaukee, where harbor improvements had been underway the previous summer.

Chicago residents were treated to startling sights that afternoon. During the summer of 1913 the city had completed a large landfill breakwall intended to protect the Lincoln Park basin from Lake Michigan storms. Six months of work worth more than $100,000 went into the project. It was all swept away in just a few hours. As people watched helplessly from shore, Lake Michigan combers scooped up whole sections of the protective wall and washed it out to sea.

Hundreds of thousands of persons lined the lakeshore and chatted in the cold all day watching the great waves that washed over the Lake Shore drive, made the outer driveway in Lincoln Park unsafe, left the German Building in Jackson Park and the new Convent of La Rabida surrounded by newly formed lakes, swept over a twelve-foot pier in Jackson Park, smashed pleasure boats and imperiled even the rock-ballasted Illinois Central tracks.

Chicago Record Herald, NOVEMBER 10, 1913

Anyone with binoculars might have been fascinated by the sight of waves crashing against Chicago's water intake crib. Solid green water smashed the heavy plate glass windows in the living quarters for the crib tenders. Unseen from shore, the men on the crib dodged their furniture as rampaging waves surged through the living quarters.

Captain W. Schlosser and the seven-man crew of the lumber hooker *The Boy* were growing weary of fighting Lake Michigan off Chicago harbor. They had successfully brought their wooden schooner from Marinette, Wisconsin, to Chicago despite the storm, but waves breaking across the harbor entrance now formed an almost impenetrable barrier to the relatively calm water inside. It was then that the schooner's deckload of lumber started to break loose. Rough-sawn flitches began washing overboard as the crew scrambled to avoid the flying wood. The steam tugs *Waukegan* and *Kenosha* went to the aid of the struggling schooner. Each tried several times to pass a towline to the drifting ship. There was nothing more the tugs could do. They would have to stand by overnight and wait for calmer weather.

Chicago lived up to its nickname "the Windy City" that Sunday. (The name actually came from the long-winded speeches allegedly given by the city's politicians, not the local weather.) Electric and telephone wires were blown down by blasts of winter wind roaring through the streets. One pole with nearly three hundred wires of various kinds fell on Devon Avenue near Clark Street. That caused a string of poles to tumble like dominoes as far as Sheridan Road. Police battled frostbite as they stood guard on the arcing wires. Damaged insulation of wires along Winnemac Avenue allowed the wires to come into contact with one another, resulting in a shower of electric sparks mixed with blowing snowflakes in a pyrotechnic display of ice and fire.

The gusty wind buffeting Michigan Avenue and Wacker Drive proved deadly for Antonio Zupsyus. He was walking along the Chicago River at the height of the storm when a sudden gust knocked him off his feet. Blown like a falling leaf, he tumbled into the black water of the river, where his head quickly disappeared beneath the swirling water.

People on shore were watching Chicago's Lincoln Park breakwall disappear when the lumber schooner *J.G. Boyce* hove into view on Lake Michigan, flying distress signals. The wooden sailing vessel was taking a pounding from waves just off the harbor entrance. "The storm struck us about 10 o'clock Sunday morning," recalled Captain N. G. Norlem. "The wind was from the north and we were obliged to strip off everything but the headsails and run before the gale."

Running before the storm eased the strain on the aging *Boyce*, but eventually the wooden schooner simply ran out of lake. The crew had no choice but to attempt to force their way through the breakers blocking the harbor entrance. That meant hoisting stiff, wet canvas into the howling gale. "Off the Chicago harbor entrance we vainly tried to get sail on her to bring her in," said Captain Norlem. "I was forced to send up distress signals."

Rescuers from the city's lifesaving station managed to reach the battered sailing vessel in their motorized lifeboat. "The lifesavers responded," Captain Norlem told reporters, "but were unable to do anything for us. I would not abandon her. We got two anchors over and tried to ride it out." There the wooden ship was left to its own devices.

Seventy miles to the north at Milwaukee, a new breakwall had been under construction all summer. According to news reports, the entire south section of that new wall was torn out by the storm waves. The contractor, a Mr. Hathaway, estimated the loss at $20,000. Several thousand people gathered on Milwaukee's shoreline to watch the destruction of the new wall. Once that occurred, the seas were then free to begin attacking South Park along the city's beach.

At the foot of Lake Michigan, the steamer *Clarence S. Black* was driven against a concrete wall in the Gary, Indiana, harbor. The force of the impact was enough to open seams in the plating and cause the ship to sink at its dock.

Lake Superior — Whitefish Bay

Sylvania

Darkness was falling on Lake Superior when Captain Warren C. Jones decided to take the *Sylvania* out from the shelter of Whitefish Bay. At that moment, weather observer Alexander G. Burns was recording 34-mile-per-hour winds out of the north at his station inside the Soo canal grounds. Because winds blow stronger over the water, it is reasonable to assume the *Sylvania* faced at least 50-mile-per-hour gusts once it reached open water. "We left Whitefish Point at 5 o'clock Sunday and within an hour were right in the midst of the storm," he said, according to the *Duluth Herald*. "Waves twice as high as the boat dashed over us while the wind and snow blew with such terrific violence that it was impossible to get out on deck." Captain Jones had no way of knowing that he had departed during the time when the northern and southern weather systems were coming into phase with one another, resulting in the rapid strengthening of the low over Lake Erie. When that happened, the *Sylvania* felt the impact 400 miles to the northwest.

Thirty men, two women, and several children were aboard the *Sylvania* during its battle with Lake Superior. Captain Jones was rethinking his options when the storm stole control of his vessel away from him. "Our boat was turned completely around and we did everything in our power to keep the vessel from being dashed against the rocks," he said afterward. This unplanned reversal of course meant that the ship was now being driven headfirst toward Lake Superior's rocky southern coastline. "It was then that I was compelled to back the boat, hoping in this way to keep away from the shore." The ship's propeller beat the lake into a froth, and the fantail literally jumped up and down several feet from the exertion of the engines. Worried engineers tried to coax a bit more out of their equipment, but iron and steam could only do so much against the fury of the weather.

"The wind drove us on and that experience, waiting as it were for the final crash, will never be forgotten by myself or the crew," Captain Jones said. The wheelsman held the ship's steering wheel hard against its stop, as if pushing harder on the spokes would help the bow come around. In the boiler room stokers abandoned their wheelbarrow used for the task of moving coal from the bunker. Instead, they heaved the black lumps onto the steel deck and shoved them with the backs of their shovels to the open mouths of the ship's furnaces.

One of *Sylvania*'s mates, A. Mussman, echoed his captain's report about conditions on the ship as it rolled in the Lake Superior billows. "We never expected to get out of it alive. Everyone on the boat expected the vessel to crash against the rocks or turn over on account of the heavy winds," he said. "The gale seemed to play with our boat at will, for we couldn't do a thing."

A desperate Captain Jones ordered *Sylvania*'s anchor lowered. "When I realized that a crash was almost imminent, I threw out the anchor, allowing it to drag behind the boat. There was about 200 feet of the chain out. In this way I hoped to avoid a crash on the rocks," he said. It was a dangerous bit of seamanship. The *Sylvania* was heading bow first toward the beach with its anchor trailing beneath its spinning propeller. Jones took this risk because if the anchor did not catch, the ship would surely have been driven to its doom on the rocky coastline. But survival was not certain even if the dangling anchor caught. The ship faced the uncertain prospect of rounding up into the wind, which would cause the hull to rotate broadside to the waves. Once in the trough, it might capsize almost without warning.

"My plan turned out favorably and soon we found we were stuck fast, the anchor having caught," was Captain Jones' simple explanation of what happened. The men, women, and children aboard the anchored ship settled down for a long, uncomfortable night on Lake Superior.

Weather observer Burns dutifully kept a record of the gale as it roared around his office at the Soo. After the storm ended he dispassionately cataloged the damage in his official report for the month of November 1913.

> The storms of 7, 8, 9, and 10 were the most severe experienced on the lakes for many years. A large fleet anchored in the upper river and the lower part of White Fish [sic] bay. The wind and sea sweeping down the bay, into the river caused the steamers *J. T. Hutchinson* and *Fred G. Hartwell* to drag their anchors and strike shoals, sinking both vessels and causing very heavy damage. . . . While the wind at this station only reached a maximum velocity of 37-NW at 6:55 P.M. on the 9th, Vessel masters report that on the lakes it was 60 to 80 miles per hour.

Sunday Evening, November 9

Lake Huron

Pennsylvania should not have a port on the Great Lakes. The state's northern boundary lies below the southern shoreline of Lake Erie. This was rectified by extending the state boundary northward in a 40-mile-wide strip known as "the chimney" because of the way it rises on a map like the chimney of a log cabin. This land puts the city of Erie inside Pennsylvania. On the afternoon of November 9, 1913, it was out of this "chimney" that the powerful southern storm rose toward the waters of Lake Erie. Its path can be tracked by the records kept by observers William Alexander in Cleveland and David Cuthbertson in Buffalo. Cleveland's winds remained northwest during the day, building steadily. By 5 P.M. they shifted into the west at a sustained speed in the mid-50-mile-per-hour range. In Buffalo, only 180 miles to the northeast, the morning northwest wind went north and northeast before noon, shifting to the east and southeast at the 5 o'clock hour. The differences in wind direction between the two lakeport cities are explained by the counterclockwise rotation of wind around the low that passed between them. Buffalo's highest gust of 80 miles per hour came between 1 and 2 P.M. that day, while Cleveland's 79-mile-per-hour gust did not occur until 4:40 P.M.

The depth of the storm is illustrated by the dramatic drop in barometric pressure at Buffalo between the 8 A.M. and 8 P.M. readings Sunday. In the morning, the pressure was recorded at 29.52 inches, corrected to sea level. That evening, Buffalo recorded 28.77 inches of mercury, a dramatic 0.75-inch drop in barometric pressure that is one measure of the power behind the winds that howled down Lake Huron.

The low-pressure center probably picked up some energy from the warm lake before making a Canadian landfall near Port Dover. This northward movement during the afternoon and evening hours Sunday brought the counterclockwise winds circling the low ever more tightly into phase with the cold northwesterly winds howling down Lakes Superior and Huron. The result was an explosive increase in both the northerly winds and the swirling snow. Driven by rising wind, huge waves marched southward the length of Lake Huron toward the St. Clair River. Vessels lucky enough to be north of Alpena, Michigan, escaped. Those caught in the lower part of the lake near Harbor Beach, Goderich, Port Huron, or Sarnia found themselves in a ship-killing zone.

Viewed from inside the pilothouses of ships caught on Lake Huron that day, the storm seemed to be a single, continuous event. In reality, however, those ships were caught by the rapidly strengthening low to the east beginning about noon, when the wind shifted suddenly into the northeast over southern Lake Huron. During the four hours from 8 P.M. to midnight this monster weather event became what modern forecasters often call a "weather bomb" because of its destructive power. Deadly northerly winds increased to hurricane speeds. Winds on the four upper lakes did not simply increase; they exploded out of the north at sustained speeds of 70 miles per hour and more. The worst of these blasts roared down the length of Lake Huron toward its closed southern end, where so many ships were running for shelter.

There is still some question as to why the winds at the toe of Lake Huron reached hurricane velocity on Sunday evening. In a 1959 Weather Bureau briefing paper for saltwater captains who were about to enter the lakes for the first time via the new St. Lawrence Seaway, meteorologists suggested that the southern low combined with the low that had moved over Superior on Friday. In reality, however, the Superior low was well off to the north and east when conditions reached their worst on Lake Huron. Meteorologist Robert Shiels of WTOL-TV in Toledo has suggested another alternative. Based on his experiences with Great Lakes weather, he thinks the surface low that moved up from the south managed to get in phase with a much larger, more powerful low aloft in the jet stream. At the same time, cold wind began pouring down from high pressure over Canada "that would have caused killer winds out of the north, just like we saw on the night of November 9th," he says.

Often overlooked is the shape of Lake Huron. It is perfectly oriented to be raked by northerly winds, and the closed "toe" of the lake offers ships no protection. The Canadian shoreline east of the entrance to the St. Clair River is sandy, with shoals extending well offshore. Kettle Point near Port Franks offers no protection because it is surrounded by dangerous rocky shoals. On the west side of the lake, the Michigan shore is rocky and inhospitable all the way to the river. Hurricane-force winds had a fetch of nearly 200 miles over which to build the waves that rolled down Lake Huron Sunday night. As with many storms, the worst of the waves did not appear until near midnight, a few hours after the wind had peaked and started to diminish.

Wind speeds increase over water because there is less surface friction than over land. This increase can be up to 30 percent or more. One ship off Harbor Beach, Michigan, reported wind gusts of 90 miles per hour, a believable number considering that gusts of 75 to 80 miles per hour were recorded by a land station at Port Sanilac, Michigan. Wind also "steers" to follow the long axis of a body of water. The 1913 gale seems to have done this on Lake Huron. It "steered" down the lake, taking dead aim at the entrance to the St. Clair River, where so many ships were heading for safety.

Lower Lake Huron
GEORGE C. CRAWFORD *and* ARGUS

Darkness came early on Sunday, as heavy clouds and swirling snow obliterated the twilight. Day simply became night. Before that happened, however, the crew of one ship had enough daylight to witness the destruction of another ship. The steamer *George C. Crawford* had departed the St. Clair River earlier that morning in ballast, headed up the lake. Captain Walter C. Iler expected foul weather, but nothing like what he encountered. He described the winds as "blowing great guns" as his bulk freighter bashed its way north of Point Aux Barques on the Michigan shore.

Waves parted by the bow rejoined on the *Crawford's* straight deck and then made a rush for the boilerhouse. Green water roared over the roof and plunged through a broken skylight into the engine room. The ship's galley was smashed, and the crew's sleeping rooms were turned into a soggy shambles. Captain Iler decided to turn around and head back south toward the foot of Lake Huron—where conditions had been better during the early morning hours.

It was still just light enough to see other ships through the swirling snow. Captain Paul Gutch in the pilothouse of the steamer *Argus* watched the *Crawford* making heavy weather as it lumbered down the lake. Both vessels were struggling in the mountainous seas. Aboard the *Crawford*, Captain Iler was also able to make out the upbound *Argus* as it smashed headlong into the seas. Both men were too busy fighting the storm to do more than note the other ship's presence. There wasn't time for the friendly passing signals that would have been exchanged on a quiet mid-summer day. In fact, something happened just before the two ships lost sight of each other that haunted Walter Iler the rest of his days. "The *Argus* seemed to crumple like an eggshell," he said. "Then, she was gone." It was that simple. One minute the other ship was struggling to stay out of the deadly trough, and the next it was gone with twenty-four sailors. Nobody spoke in the *Crawford's* wheelhouse. There was nothing to say.

The indelible image of a modern steel freighter simply folding up and sinking could not be erased from the minds of the men who witnessed it. The storm, however, created enough work to take their minds off even such a horror. Captain Iler studied the reading of his depth-sounding machine for signs that the bottom was shoaling. The *Crawford* was headed for the closed southern end of the lake. Soon he would have to either turn around through the deadly troughs or try to find the entrance to the St. Clair River. Neither prospect was good.

"It snowed for a solid twenty-six hours," Captain Iler recalled later. "We hadn't seen a thing, but we were guided by the sounding machine. It gave us excellent service." He elected to turn upwind. During the maneuver he attempted to signal the engine room with the chadburn tele-graph. The bending and twisting of the hull in the waves had stretched the cables that linked the pilothouse instrument to the one in the engine room. The telegraph handles would not budge because the cables were stretched so taut.

Unable to climb out of the troughs, and running out of sea room as he approached the southern end of Lake Huron, Captain Iler had no other alternative than to attempt to anchor. He put down first one and then the other bower on their full lengths of chain. Both anchors dug into the bottom and the ship came head to the seas, but not for long. The strain was too strong for the port chain, which parted not far from the anchor. The starboard chain was not up to taking all of the strain. A few minutes later it parted near the ship. The *Crawford* was once again at the storm's mercy.

Hindsight shows that the safest course for the *Crawford* on Lake Huron during that deadly period would have been to follow the *Durston* north toward Great Duck Island and then west into the Straits of Mackinac. Winds roared at 70 to 90 miles per hour on lower Lake Huron. At Mackinaw City, the strongest gusts reported during the storm were half that velocity, about 36 miles per hour. At 10:30 P.M., during the height of the storm, the saltwater freighter *Ogdensburg* passed through the Straits without incident. According to the November 10, 1913, *Port Huron Times-Herald*, it was the only vessel reported in the straits all day.

Lake Huron — Kettle Point, Ontario
H.A. HAWGOOD

With the coming of darkness, Captain May aboard the *H.A. Hawgood* began to realize that his decision to head south had been wrong. Hurricane-force winds and mountainous seas were pushing his freighter toward the low-lying Ontario shoreline he knew was not far ahead but could not see through the snow. The *Hawgood* was dangerously near a lee shore fronted by extensive sandy shoals.

Peering through the ice-rimmed pilothouse windows, Captain May managed to catch sight of the steamer *Isaac M. Scott* trying to make headway upbound. "I thought the captain was a fool to leave the [St. Clair] river. I would have given my head to have been inside," May said following the storm. Men in the *Hawgood*'s pilothouse shared the same unspoken worry: Would they spot the entrance to the St. Clair River in time? Or would they be driven ashore?

Lake Huron — Port Franks, Ontario
NORTHERN QUEEN

Most navigation on the Great Lakes is properly called "pilotage." A successful captain must have a working knowledge of every underwater danger along his route. The 833-mile journey from Duluth, Minnesota, on Lake Superior, down to Cleveland, Ohio, on Lake Erie, never takes an ore freighter more than 30 to 50 miles from land, and that short distance offshore is reached for only a few hours of the voyage. Much of the time, heavily laden cargo vessels navigate the snakelike bends of the St. Marys River. During the crossing of shallow Lake St. Clair a ship can go aground while out of sight of land. It has been said that a lakes captain can wake in the dead of night, peer at the dark silhouette of a nearby shoreline, and announce, "We're about a quarter mile off Wobbleshanks." He'll not be wrong by more than 300 feet.

But being a skilled pilot did no good Sunday evening on Lake Huron. The shoreline was hidden by darkness, blinding snow, flying spume, and ice frozen on pilothouse windows. Navigation on southern Lake Huron had become no more than a deadly game of blindman's buff, and nobody knew that better than Captain Crawford of the steamer *Northern Queen*. He had departed Port Huron, Michigan, on an upbound trip at 9:30 that morning. His ship slogged about 45 miles north on Lake Huron before the storm became more powerful than the vessel's single engine and all headway disappeared.

Captain Crawford wondered aloud if turning around and running ahead of the waves might be safer. His line of thought ended abruptly when a single wave picked up the ship, turned it end over end, and sent it scurrying back toward the St. Clair River. The decision to head south had been made for him. The job now was to successfully work down Lake Huron with huge, breaking waves coming up astern. By 4:30 P.M. the men in the pilothouse thought they could see the lights of Port Huron, which at that hour still burned brightly. Those shore lights would shortly be extinguished by a boilerhouse flood, but for now they served the critical function of marking the southern limit of the lake.

Afterward, Charles McKay of the *Northern Queen's* crew regaled reporters with a story that the moan of the Port Huron foghorn caused Captain Crawford to order the ship turned around again. This was another of those sea stories that made wonderful news copy in 1913 but probably was not true. At the time when *Northern Queen* turned around, the wind was roaring at nearly 70 miles per hour from the wrong direction to hear a foghorn situated to the south of the ship. It is doubtful that any horn or whistle could have penetrated that gale.

More likely, Captain Crawford saw the lights of Port Huron on the nearby shoreline, realized he was running out of lake, and decided to go back north to open water. Whatever his reasons, the fact remains that the ship was turned around and it did head north on Lake Huron once again. After bashing another 30 miles up the lake, the beleaguered captain decided they had fought the storm long enough. He decided to anchor the *Northern Queen* off Port Franks, Ontario.

Lake Huron —— Off Port Huron, Michigan
LIGHTSHIP 26

Lightship 26 was anchored just off Port Huron to guide downbound vessels to the entrance of the St. Clair River. Despite the ship's huge mushroom anchor, however, wind and waves simply carried it off station Sunday night. The crew paid out every link of anchor chain, but the ship continued drifting through the night. Yard by yard, it moved closer to the Canadian shoreline. At times the waves washed completely over the small vessel while the crew huddled inside.

With the lightship off station, ships seeking the safety of the St. Clair River had only one remaining beacon: the Fort Gratiot Lighthouse on the Michigan side of the river. The keepers of the light, Captain Kimball and his wife, stayed at their posts despite waves crashing against the brick tower. Although they did not know it, storm surge was actually washing away the beach at the base of the lighthouse.

> For many years the Kimballs have been in charge of the lighthouse and have witnessed many storms, but never in the history of their service have they witnessed such a raging blizzard as swept Lake Huron Sunday and Sunday night. From the tower of the lighthouse they could see the small twinkling lights of the storm tossed ships that were trying to make port through the narrow mouth of the St. Clair river. The fog horns were kept busy sending out weird, wild blasts across the storm swept lake to warn the mariners that they were approaching the river's mouth and the heavy powered light shot its rays through the blinding snow storm to guide the few steamers that were trying to make port, while the waves almost engulfed them.
>
> *Port Huron Times-Herald*, NOVEMBER 10, 1913

Lake Huron—Harbor Beach, Michigan
HOWARD M. HANNA JR.

At Harbor Beach on the shore of Lake Huron, a large "casino" had entertained generations of Michiganders. That tradition ended Sunday night when the storm demolished the building containing bowling alleys, pool and billiard halls, and boathouses. Waves picked up the building, smashed it like a child's toy, and scattered the remains for hundreds of yards along the beach.

On southern Lake Huron, Captain William Hagan of the 480-foot *Howard M. Hanna Jr.* was still plunging his way upbound with some 9,200 tons of soft coal destined for the Lake Superior port of Fort William, Ontario, piled in the hold of his five-year-old ship. He had departed Lorain, Ohio, Saturday morning while the weather on Lake Erie remained mild, and the ship's Cleveland-built hull and engine had seemed equal to the building storm as the *Hanna* had pushed onto Lake Huron that morning. Things went well until the "weather bomb" started exploding after lunch.

Exposed to the full force of the blast in the middle of the lake, the *Hanna* took a fearful beating. Windows on the starboard side of the pilot-house were blown in by crashing waves that soaked Captain Hagan and wheelsmen Albert Curtis and George Winters as they struggled to keep the ship on course. Late that afternoon, the *Hanna* seemed to stand still despite full thrust from its 1,600-horsepower, triple-expansion steam engine. It was impossible for the ship to make headway against gale-force winds and mountainous seas.

In the *Hanna's* engine room, Chief Engineer Charles Mayberry was astounded by the power of the storm. "About 6:30 P.M. the bloody destruction began," Mayberry recalled. "The oiler's door on the starboard side was the first to get smashed in. Shortly afterward the two engine room doors and windows went. It was terrible. Tons of icy water poured into the engine room. The whole place was a damn mess. We stood knee deep in the swirling ice water."

Mayberry had taken precautions. Even before the first signs of destruction he had ordered the ship's electric dynamos covered with tarpaulins to keep them dry. He also inspected the bilge pumps and had them operating from the beginning.

"I kept in contact with the captain by telephone. 'We mustn't yield to the weather,' he said. We needed all the power we could possibly get to keep the ship headed into the wind," Mayberry explained to reporters after the storm. "The next bloody break came when the windows and doors of the engineer's room went at 7:30 P.M. After that it seemed as if everything else went in order. The cook's room and dining room went. The woodwork was carried away, part coming into the engine room to add to the wreckage already piling up there, and part going overboard."

The after deckhouse of a straight decker like the *Hanna* was called the boilerhouse because it was located over the engine room at the stern. Originally, it enclosed the boilers. Later, cabins were added around its perimeter. By 1913, these additional rooms contained the ship's galley and dining facilities as well as sleeping quarters for engineers and stewards. Separate dining facilities were always provided for the crew and officers. The boilerhouse roof offered the only flat space large enough to stow the two lifeboats carried by most Great Lakes ships.

All but one of the crew berths on Great Lakes ships were single bunks. The chief steward was customarily supplied with a double berth because it was typical in 1913 for the steward's wife to sail as a cook. It was usual for a husband-and-wife team to prepare meals for freighter crew. There might be one other double bed aboard some ships, for the captain. Shipmasters were provided a double bed if there was room in the texas. Captain's wives occasionally accompanied their husbands on trips to escape the hot summers ashore.

When the boilerhouse collapsed, among the debris that fell into the *Hanna*'s engine room was Sadie Black, who served as the ship's second cook while her husband, Clarence, sailed as the *Hanna*'s steward. The same wave that demolished much of the boilerhouse also drove the unfortunate woman down a companionway and into the engine room. Somehow she emerged from the wreckage thoroughly soaked and slightly bruised but otherwise unhurt.

Lake Huron — Off Port Sanilac, Michigan
J.H. Sheadle

Driving any ship in front of the 35-foot waves rolling down Lake Huron took the coordinated efforts of sailors in both the pilothouse and the engine room. Men at the throttles monitored shaft revolutions to prevent overracing the engine when the propeller heaved out of the water. "From 2:30 P.M. until 5:00 P.M., the engines raced, requiring the greatest care and judgment," wrote Captain Lyons of the *J.H. Sheadle*. "At times the ship was so heavily burdened with seas coming over her decks that her revolutions were decreased from 75 to 35 turns per minute."

From Captain Lyons' description, life in the pilothouse was equally difficult. "The heavy rolling tore adrift the binnacle on top of the pilothouse. After that it was extremely dangerous to be in the house, as this heavy object was hurled back and forth across the deck as the ship labored and rolled in the heavy sea," he wrote. "The way the ship was behaving we had every confidence in her."

Although the *Sheadle* was heading downbound, it was taking much the same beating as the upbound *Hanna*. Water poured down into the *Sheadle*'s engine room through broken skylights. Men at the throttle were constantly drenched by the icy downpour until canvas protection could be rigged over their heads. Crew cabins and dining areas around the boilerhouse were a soggy shambles. One of the lifeboats stored on top of the boilerhouse was smashed to kindling, and the chadburn at the emergency steering station was carried away.

"I ordered the boatswain to take sufficient men and shutters to close all the windows in the after cabin," Captain Lyons recalled. "They forced their way aft, braving the wind, sleet and seas, one hand grasping the life rail and the other the shutters. Reaching the after cabin in safety, they began securing the shutters only to have another tremendous sea sweep over the vessel. The bulky shutters were stolen from the men's hands as they clung to whatever was nearest to keep from being washed overboard. Immediately a third sea, equally as large, boarded the vessel and again flooded the fantail and hurricane deck."

Men who had gone aft as a group to save their ship were now caught in one-on-one battles with Lake Huron for their personal survival. Water surged around inside the steel bulwarks of the *Sheadle*'s fantail. One wheelsman struggling to reach the door of the crew's dining room was knocked off his feet. He tumbled into a cataract running along the deck beside the boilerhouse and was sluiced toward the fantail like a scrap of dirt in the blast from a fire hose. With nothing to grab but the smooth steel deck, the wheelsman expected to be washed over the waist-high steel bulwark. Then, the toe of one boot caught in a bulwark brace. It was a slender attachment, but enough to stop his slide.

There was no time for the sputtering wheelsman to savor his good fortune. Another monster wave surged over the fantail and swept everything in its path. The unfortunate man was once again sliding toward oblivion. His fortunes turned for the better a second time when he became tangled in the coils of the ship's towline. This hawser had been washed loose by one of the earlier waves, and it now served as a makeshift safety net to catch the terrified wheelsman. He scrambled to his feet and tried again.

"One of the oilers stood watch at the dining room door," Captain Lyons recalled, "closing it when the boat shipped a sea and opening it when the decks were clear to let the water out of the cabins." The door swung open just as the wheelsman approached, and in another instant he reached the relative protection of the deckhouse. What he entered, however, was hardly a quiet haven from the storm. The *Sheadle's* steward and his wife were standing knee-deep in icy water while the remnants of the galley stores sloshed across the room with the rolling of the ship. Underfoot was an odd collection of silverware, broken china, cooked ham, potatoes, and canned goods.

Lake Huron — Port Austin, Michigan
HOWARD M. HANNA JR.

The evolution of straight deckers resulted in curious difficulties for their crews. The captain, mates, and wheelsmen were traditionally quartered forward in the texas beneath the pilothouse. The galley was always located aft, as were the separate dining rooms for officers and crew. Anyone working in the pilothouse had to walk the full length of the open main deck to the stern for meals, even during storms. Curiously, those straight deckers with passenger accommodations made no special provisions for their high-ranking guests. Passengers quartered in the texas were forced to walk the full length of the open deck to obtain their meals in a private dining room located adjacent to the galley.

The long walk from galley to pilothouse meant that men working forward never enjoyed hot coffee. They would draw a "cup o' joe" into a white china mug and start forward, but the steaming liquid would be tepid by the time they reached the ladder to the texas. Coffee mugs that

migrated forward from the galley seemed to have great difficulty in returning, especially at night. Stewards found themselves ordering replacement
coffee cups almost as often as they replenished the supply of coffee beans.
One retired steward has noted, "You can probably follow the steamer
tracks on the bottoms of the lakes by the trail of white china mugs."

The fore-and-aft split of living and dining often resulted in captains,
mates, and wheelsmen going without hot food for a day or more during
foul weather. Worse than the lack of food was the distance from pilothouse to lifeboats. Crew in the bow were virtually cut off from that vital
lifesaving equipment. If it became necessary for someone to cross from
bow to stern while storm waves were washing over the midsection, a steel
cable called a "jackline" was rigged from the texas to the boilerhouse.
The 1913 sailor donned a special harness much like those later worn by
parachutists. A safety tether attached to the harness would be snapped
to the jackline and the perilous walk would begin. If the sailor was lucky,
he would only get wet. Often, a wave would carry him over the side with
the tether his only connection to the ship.

"Ratways," or tunnels beneath the weather deck, could have been
installed on 1913-era ships, but that would have required extensive
reengineering of the large web frames that braced the hull. Such a modification would have increased construction costs with no offsetting increase
in the revenue generated by the ship. Since crew comfort (not to mention
safety) did not earn the shipping companies additional profits, no thought
was given to installing protected walkways from texas to boilerhouse.

By 8 P.M. it was snowing so hard on Lake Huron that the crew of the
Hanna could not see from one end of their ship to the other. Although
he had no way of judging his position, Captain Hagan thought he was
15 miles off Point Aux Barques at the entrance to Saginaw Bay. A 70-
mile-per-hour gust of wind twisted the ship into the trough between two
waves. "After she got into the trough, she commenced to roll and tumble. The mountainous seas smashed over her," Chief Engineer Charles
Mayberry said (*Cleveland Plain Dealer*). "The propeller wheel was out of
the water and it was impossible for us to bring the ship back to head
into the sea. In spite of our every effort, we lay in the trough rolling heavily with the seas washing over us."

The *Hanna's* situation was desperate, but fate had one more cruelty in
store. Captain Hagan noticed a flash of light outside the ice-coated

windows of his rolling pilothouse. It was the Port Austin lighthouse on Point Aux Barques, just a few hundred yards to the southwest of the ship's port bow. Without hesitation, Hagan ordered his first mate to drop both bow anchors. The full lengths of the two anchor chains rattled out of the hawsepipes, but the ship continued its inexorable drift toward the low-lying shore.

"In a short time the great waves rode her to destruction," said Captain Hagan as he quietly described the stranding of his ship to reporters. "She drifted broadside into the reef at 10:00 P.M. The port side fetched up on the rocks first and the seas and wind pounded her the rest of the way onto the reef." The *Hanna* came ashore not 500 feet from the lighthouse that marked a dangerous spit of land jutting into Lake Huron.

The *Hanna's* crew was now divided into two groups. One huddled in the stern, while the other sought refuge in the bow. There was no longer any telephone communication between them. The ship's survivors watched massive waves tear off the smokestack and then rip away portions of the roof covering the boilerhouse. Steel could only stand this much pounding for so long. A crack developed amidships, and the *Hanna* seemed ready to split in two. The crew knew they were in for a long, cold night before anyone could come to their rescue.

Lake Huron — Georgian Bay
SOPHIE

Although the Great Lakes are immense, their waters were too confined for the large, square-rigged ocean sailing vessels of the nineteenth and early twentieth centuries. There was simply not enough room for them to maneuver. Schooners with fore-and-aft rigs were handier on the lakes and appeared in large numbers. But even schooners could not solve the long, windless doldrums of summer. Faced with the inadequacy of sail for their purposes, the major shipping companies on the Great Lakes quickly adopted steam power. In the aftermath of the Civil War, the single-screw propeller ship became the preferred bulk freighter on the lakes almost a generation before a similar transition to steam was completed on the oceans.

Wooden schooners, however, remained a common sight on the lakes through World War I. Most were owned by their captains, and many were a family enterprise. Wives often served as cooks and business agents, while sons helped with the sails. These small trading windships made a living hauling lumber and other cargoes not profitable enough to attract the attention of the larger shipping companies. Eventually, paved highways and large trucks took most of their business, and working schooners disappeared. One of the dwindling number of sailing vessels still employed on that deadly Sunday was a Canadian lumber "hooker," the *Sophie*.

Around noon, Captain Hugh McKinnon was working his lumber schooner through Georgian Bay when the wind shifted into the north and increased to hurricane strength. Georgian Bay lies northeast of the shore of Michigan's Lower Peninsula where the *Hanna* fetched up. Entirely in Canada, Georgian Bay is almost a separate lake, cut off from Lake Huron by Manitoulin Island and the Bruce Peninsula. Captain McKinnon sought shelter behind Cape Smith, but the schooner's two anchors would not hold. Rather than have his ship pounded apart, McKinnon deliberately ordered it flooded. He and his crew successfully escaped their scuttled vessel in the yawlboat.

Deliberately sinking the schooner actually saved it from serious damage. Several days after the storm abated, it was possible to refloat the ship by pumping water out of its hold. After a thorough cleaning, the *Sophie* returned to service, little the worse for its ordeal.

Lake Huron ⎯ Port Sanilac, Michigan
REGINA

Running before the storm down Lake Huron, Captain McConkey of the *Regina* experienced the "thump" that all sailors dread. Felt through the feet rather than heard, it told the crew their ship had touched bottom somewhere along the Michigan side of Lake Huron. The ship touched once again before surging forward. Even before McConkey could blurt out an order the wheelsman must have turned the bow to the left, back toward deep water. Once again all of the motion of the ship came from wind and waves. The men in the pilothouse looked at one another, their eyes asking the unspoken question, "How big is the hole?"

It didn't take long for the engineers to report water coming from somewhere in the middle cargo hold. They could not tell exactly where. As darkness fell, a sagging *Regina* was still bashing its way down the lake while its crew struggled to keep the ship afloat. The men knew they had to "pump or drown." There could be no thought of rescue in the storm that now enveloped them. There was no choice but to keep the pumps working until they reached safety.

As the small package freighter drew opposite the Michigan town of Port Sanilac, it became obvious that *Regina* was losing its battle. Captain McConkey decided to anchor, perhaps to preserve the ship's remaining steam pressure for the sole purpose of running the bilge pumps. Second Mate Bert Dasome probably took two or three other sailors down to the windlass room located beneath the pilothouse. One of them managed to knock the keeper loose from the anchor chain. Instantly, it came alive like an iron snake as the anchor plunged into the depths of Lake Michigan. Miraculously, the flukes of the anchor caught on the rocky bottom and held. The chain went bar-taut. *Regina's* engine stopped turning.

Lake Huron — Near Kettle Point, Ontario
H.A. HAWGOOD

At almost the same instant as *Regina's* anchor chain went taut, Captain May aboard the *Hawgood* also decided that anchoring was his only hope for survival. Wind and waves on southern Lake Huron were now beyond survival conditions. "I actually had to crawl the few feet from one side of the pilothouse to the other," May said. "By God, that wind blew fully 75 miles an hour." He ordered one anchor down, then both bowers. Even at full scope the two were not enough. "She dragged steadily for eight miles," he said. There was nothing to be done but resume steaming for the safety of the St. Clair River—if they could find it.

Lake Huron — Off Saginaw Bay
MATOA

No Great Lakes sailor has ever stood watch in a storm worse than the one that tore at the *Matoa*. Thirty-five-foot waves and subfreezing temperatures combined with 70-mile-per-hour winds. "At about 10 P.M. we received a vague sensation of impending disaster," recalled Captain McLeod. After 16 hours of battering by the storm, his ship began to come apart around him. "She started to crack up before our eyes. A spar deck plate just forward of the boilerhouse split open." The crack quickly ripped its way across the full width of the deck. With the storm raging around them, the crew of *Matoa* could only turn to prayer. For a while, it appeared their prayers were being answered. No new cracks appeared in the inch-thick plates.

A cracked deck meant that the hull was in danger of breaking in half at that spot. The deck of a straight decker was part of what naval architects call the "hull girder" that gave the ship strength. Once *Matoa's* deck cracked, this box-shaped girder was compromised. The crack could start to extend down the sides. If that happened, the crew knew it would only be a matter of seconds before their ship split in two. Given the large holds of bulk freighters, neither end could have floated for long, and the crew did not need to be told they would perish. One thing that may have saved the ship was its construction. *Matoa* was built of individual steel plates held together by rivets. A crack in one plate did not automatically migrate into another of the inch-thick slabs of steel, as sometimes happens in more modern ships in which plates are welded together.

Lake Huron — Port Huron, Michigan, and Sarnia, Ontario
CHARLES CHAMBERLAIN, CITY OF ALPENA II, *and* CITY OF DETROIT II

Port Huron, Michigan, and Sarnia, Ontario, are companion cities located directly across the St. Clair River from each other at the toe of Lake Huron. As darkness fell on Sunday, both communities were smothered under a howling blizzard. "Toward evening the wind grew in velocity and a blizzard raged so that all traffic was put out of commission," reported the November 10, 1913, *Port Huron Times-Herald*. "Pedestrians caught in the blinding snow turned into the nearest houses for shelter. Automobiles, loaded with human freight, skidded and whirled about the pavements, unable to make progress and, after fighting for hours, remained abandoned alongside or in the middle of the road."

The wooden schooner *Charles Chamberlain* had been securely tied up in the Black River at Port Huron. The ship was out of service and laid up for the winter. Despite stout winter mooring lines, the schooner heeled over in the arctic blast that clobbered the city. With no one aboard to prevent catastrophe, the *Chamberlain* slowly rolled on beam ends and sank at its dock.

The raging gale convinced several captains to stay holed up in Port Huron. The master of the D&C Line's *City of Alpena II* elected to remain tied up as the blizzard gripped the southern end of Lake Huron. His ship had been scheduled to depart for Toledo, Ohio, where it was due at 2 A.M. Monday. Remaining in Port Huron proved a wise decision. The gale blew the water out of the Toledo harbor to the extent that yachts docked at the entrance of the Maumee River found themselves dry. According to the *Toledo Blade* on November 11, the river at Jefferson Avenue in downtown Toledo dropped to 6 feet below normal. Captain Fred Simpson of the passenger ship *City of Detroit II* also decided to remain in port rather than risk the gale. Simpson's ship had been scheduled to depart Detroit, Michigan, for Cleveland, Ohio, on Sunday afternoon.

Lake Huron — Port Sanilac, Michigan
REGINA

Ships in the grasp of the storm were on their own, beyond human aid. No matter what happened, they were cut off from potential rescue by the fierceness of the winds and the height of the waves. Even though their anchor held, *Regina's* crew recognized their perilous situation. The pumps were no longer controlling the flooding, and their ship was becoming waterlogged. It would be only a matter of time before the small freighter succumbed to Lake Huron. Staying aboard a sinking ship was certain doom. If they were to survive, the crew realized they were going to have to rescue themselves.

Regina was becoming visibly waterlogged. Somebody suggested the unthinkable: abandon ship. As risky as launching a lifeboat into hurricane-force winds and waves sounded, there was really little other choice for survival. The crew hoped a small lifeboat scudding ahead of the hissing surf would have a better chance of staying afloat than the ship's sagging steel hull. The men who struggled to launch the lifeboat left no record as to why they chose to escape their ship. However, the evidence is inescapable that they were successful in getting away. At least one lifeboat with some of *Regina's* crew pulled away from the sinking freighter.

Lifeboats are clumsy at best, their oars heavy and cumbersome. An enormous effort was required at the oars of *Regina's* lifeboat to move it clear of the plunging ship and orient the tiny craft so that it rode the waves properly. Men in the boat were probably too busy to notice their ship disappear into the blizzard. Once on its own, however, the lifeboat must have given its crew a sense that they had done the right thing. The looms of the oars extending outward from the sides of the boat actually gave it stability that a powerboat of the same size would not have. For the moment, rowing provided the men with body heat to fight their soaking wet clothing that whipped in the fierce winds.

Captain McConkey chose not to leave his first independent command. His hand reached for the whistle pull as his crew boarded their tiny rescue craft. With a jerk, he jammed open the four-foot-tall brass handle to keep the ship's sonorous steam voice screaming from its perch near the top of the lone smokestack. The steady shriek of a whistle was, and still is, an accepted distress call. McConkey probably hoped that someone on shore would hear it and respond by ringing a church bell to guide the lifeboat to safety.

People on shore did hear *Regina*'s whistle screaming for aid, but they were helpless to do anything about it. A man could hardly walk against the wind, and if he tried, he would not have been able to see where he was going through the swirling and drifting snow. With massive storm waves crashing ashore, launching a surfboat from the rocky coastline was impossible. Local residents would later recall how *Regina*'s whistle moaned in the wind for at least an hour that night. It was heard, and it was understood. Men ashore listened and shook their heads knowingly. The whistle meant the doom of a ship and its crew, but there was nothing anyone on shore could do about it. Nobody thought to ring a bell or blow a factory whistle.

Lake Huron — Point Edward, Ontario
H.A. HAWGOOD

About 10 P.M. that night, eighteen-year-old Edward Kanaby took his turn at the *Hawgood*'s wheel. Hand steering the 414-foot straight decker in a gale was taxing work, so wheelsmen were spelling one another at short intervals. As the young sailor struggled with the ship's wheel, Captain May pressed his face to the glass of the pilothouse, trying to pick out any sign of the Canadian shoreline. He knew they were running out of lake, but the low-lying sandy beach would be extremely hard to spot through the swirling snow.

"Turn!" Captain May shouted. "Those are breakers on the beach."

Young Kanaby strained to make out the patch of beach that his captain had seen, but it was invisible through the snow. Instinctively, the youthful wheelsman turned the wheel, but there was no open water to be found. As the ship fought to respond to its rudder the men in the pilothouse could sense breaking waves all around. The motion of the deck was different beneath their feet. An instant later the ship's forefoot struck the bottom, bounced once, then again. Suddenly, the violent motion of the storm disappeared. The *Hawgood* was hard aground.

Until he died, Edward Kanaby always told the story that he disobeyed his captain's last helm command. Kanaby said he turned toward the beach in a young man's frightened effort to escape the gale. Perhaps he did. It probably mattered little. The *Hawgood* was too close to shore to have been steered to safety. The ship was hard on the beach before the rudder could have had any effect.

In the morning, the imposing sight of the *Hawgood* startled people at the Lake Huron Hotel near the town of Lake Huron Beach, just north of Point Edward, Ontario. The ship's bow came to rest within a hundred feet or so of the hotel building. After the waves subsided it was possible to walk from the wooden hotel to the steel bow of the *Hawgood* on dry sand.

"But for the crash on the beach just in time, there would have been another missing ship," Captain May admitted after the storm. Of course, coming ashore did not immediately end the danger for his crew. They still had to spend a frightening night aboard their stranded ship at the height of the storm. "We struck so hard I was almost thrown out of the pilothouse," he said. "Although she was light, the seas broke over her and the crew was in constant danger of being swept overboard."

Lake Huron —— Near Port Huron, Michigan
J.H. SHEADLE

The *Hawgood* was slammed ashore and *Regina's* crew launched its lifeboat at almost the same moment that Captain Lyons aboard the *J.H Sheadle*—based on depth soundings he had been taking with a mechanical sounding machine—decided that he, too, had just about run out of lake. "At 9 o'clock had soundings of 18 fathoms. This carried us well off the west shore. I called the engineer up at this time and told him that at 10 o'clock I was going to turn around head to sea unless I could locate the land or Fort Gratiot light," the captain wrote after the storm.

Turning the *Sheadle* around so it could steam back to the north was not going to be any easier than turning any of the other straight-deck freighters on the lake that night. Captain Lyons was well aware that for most of the turn his ship would lie broadside to the waves with the possibility of being capsized in the trough. With that in mind, he asked his engineer to "increase the speed up to the ship . . . so as to enable me to bring the boat around head to on account of the sea running behind us." The *Sheadle's* triple-expansion steam engine began pounding as the ship built up momentum for the risky maneuver.

"At 10 o'clock we turned heading north haft [sic] east; the vessel rolled very heavily, but came around all right head to," the captain recalled. His one-sentence description of the maneuver made it seem matter-of-fact, but it took a full 10 minutes to get the *Sheadle* through the trough and onto a reciprocal course upbound on Lake Huron. All during that time the ship rolled deeply and was always in danger of a fatal shift of its iron ore cargo. Immediately after making the turn, Captain Lyons asked a mate to inspect the steering quadrant to make sure it had not been damaged by the strain.

"I started back on a vice-versa course, which would be north half east for 6 hours, following my soundings back from 10 to 22 fathoms," Lyons said. He dismissed the hunger the pilothouse crew must have been feeling after so many hours of battling the storm. "During this time one of the wheelsmen got aft, securing a few pieces of bread, and came forward again," was all Lyons said about it.

Lake Huron — Off Port Huron, Michigan
MATTHEW ANDREWS

Few ships survived by anchoring at the height of the storm, although many tried. One that succeeded was the bulk freighter *Matthew Andrews*. Downbound on Lake Huron, Captain John Lampoh held his course for Port Huron until late Sunday evening. The snow- and ice-covered windows of his pilothouse made it impossible to find the entrance to the St.

Clair River. The only safe thing to do, the captain thought, was to anchor. Lampoh did not want to slam into the unseen Michigan shoreline that lay in front of him.

Storms are noisy. Wind howling at more than a mile a minute roars in the outer channels of human ears. Waves tumbling and crashing create a nonstop thunder. It is an unending cacophony that ranges from the low rumble of the combers to the high-frequency hiss of the surf and the whistle of wind in the rigging. No one who experiences this overpowering pressure of sound ever forgets it. Commands bellowed by the heartiest lungs are lost in the maelstrom. The human voice is inadequate. Communication is reduced to hand signals and gestures.

No matter how loud the gale, however, it never silences a sailor's inner voice. Each man or woman can still hear the sounds of personal fears. Perhaps that's why the height of a storm, when life is most in jeopardy, is also a quiet time for personal reflection. The sounds of human activity that interrupt personal thoughts are washed away by the roar of the gale. Ruminations heard by the mind's ear above the constant thrumming of the wind sometimes have a narcotic effect. They have been known to freeze sailors into inaction. The only antidote is to divert thoughts of personal danger by keeping busy with the routine work of the ship.

On the *Matthew Andrews* the roar of Lake Huron was so loud that orders could not be passed to the windlass room in the usual fashion down the speaking tube. Instead, crewmembers stood shoulder-to-shoulder shouting Captain Lampoh's orders down the line to the windlass operator. "Let go". . . "Let go". . . "Let go". . . the word went man to man until it reached the operator of the brake on the chain. He pushed the lever and watched the links of anchor chain fly out the hawsepipe. The normally deafening metallic rattle of the chain was lost in the shriek of the wind.

A few miles from the spot where the *Andrews* dropped anchor is the city of Port Huron, Michigan. One reason Captain Lampoh could not find the Michigan coastline was that Port Huron had lost electric power. None of the city's lights were burning, so the maritime community was virtually invisible from Lake Huron. The power outage resulted from a surge of high water caused by the storm. Water from the St. Clair River flooded a tributary, the Black River, which escaped its banks to extinguish the fires in the city's lighting plant. Without steam, the municipal dynamos rolled to a halt and lights throughout Port Huron flickered and then faded. The

Michigan shoreline became a dark line against a black sky.

THE FOUR MOST DEADLY HOURS in Great Lakes history saw waves on the open waters of Lake Huron crest well above pilothouse windows. Sailors who survived Sunday night on Lake Huron came back with reports of unbelievable 35-foot wave heights. Scientific wave height tables support these observations. Although published for saltwater waves, the tables show that it would take 40 hours for a 45-knot wind to raise waves that high. By Sunday night, Lake Huron had experienced more than 36 hours of northerly winds in the upper 40s, and that was before the 80- to 90-mile-per-hour White Hurricane began racing down the lake. Adding to the force of the wind was the tendency for waves to grow taller as they touched bottom at the southern end of Lake Huron.

The monster waves that marched down Lake Huron Sunday evening and night were not the smooth swells of the ocean. These were freshwater billows roaring through shallow water. The size, shape, and depth of Lake Huron combined to give its waves unusually steep sides and plunging crests. Water tumbling off the fronts of the waves crashed down onto the decks and superstructures of the struggling ships. The power behind waves like these is enormous. In a 1966 test, strain gauges placed on the 730-foot *Edward L. Ryerson* during a much smaller storm recorded forces of 23,000 pounds per square inch.

Great Lakes bulk freighters have always been somewhat limber in rough seas. They bend and twist even when moving through ordinary storm waves. Sailors often claim that the stern of a straight decker will lean to port in a storm while the bow leans to starboard. Such twisting placed enormous strain on the millions of rivets that held 1913-era ships together. Conditions during the White Hurricane generated racking forces strong enough to snap steel fasteners an inch in diameter.

> The captain of a leviathan, after battling with a storm on Lake Huron found . . . that the working of her plates had cut thousands of the steel rivets fastening the plates together, and several hundred pounds of the rivet-heads were taken from her hold.
>
> JAMES COOKE MILLS, *Our Inland Seas*

The snapping of an inch-diameter rivet should have produced a report similar to a shotgun blast. Hundreds of rivets popping during a single storm should have released a rattle resembling nothing less than a military firefight. If sailors heard such sounds, nobody bothered to mention the popping and snapping of rivets to reporters. But storms are noisy places. The roar of the wind and the hiss of the surf may have drowned out the sounds made by the tormented ships as they were torn apart by the waves.

Fifteen steel ships, some the newest and strongest on the lakes, were lost that night. Luckier ships were driven ashore.

Lake Huron — Near Port Sanilac, Michigan
REGINA

By 11 P.M. it must have been bitterly cold for Captain McConkey, who was now the sole human being aboard *Regina*. The waterlogged ship still rode to its anchor not far south from the wrecked Harbor Beach casino building. The last steam from its boiler had long since been vented through the screaming whistle, which was now cold and silent. With steam gone, there was nothing to heat the cabins.

Regina's lone occupant was bone-tired after 18 straight hours fighting the storm. Wind whipped his clothing as he closed the pilothouse door and went down the narrow, ice-covered outside ladder from the bridge wing to the forecastle deck. Once inside his familiar cabin, he instinctively reached for the light switch. There was a quiet "snap" but no blaze of light. The ship's electrical system no longer functioned because the dynamo did not have steam to drive it.

Yet another ship was fighting to stay off the beach a few miles north of McConkey's cold cabin. The *D.O. Mills* had been upbound in ballast when it was caught by the sudden wind shift just after lunch. A 532-foot steel straight decker, the *Mills* eventually lost its struggle with Lake Huron around 11 P.M. and was thrown ashore just above the small port of Harbor Beach, Michigan. Captain James Jackson immediately ordered his ship's hold flooded to prevent the *Mills* from being lifted by the waves and pounded to pieces against the lake bottom.

Captain McConkey had no way of knowing that around him seven modern steel freighters were being slammed to the bottom of Lake Huron by the power of wind and waves. In four hours the lake would claim eight ships—an average of one every half-hour. With those ships went the lives of at least 178 sailors. Most of the dead were men, but a few wives of stewards found watery graves as well.

It was a massive blow to the combined U.S. and Canadian Great Lakes fleet. It would not be until the darkest days of war that commercial shipping would suffer such a huge 4-hour loss. Even German U-boat wolf packs during two world wars rarely matched the carnage the 1913 storm created on Lake Huron that night.

Pulling a blanket around him in the darkness, the lone man aboard *Regina* knew nothing of the other ships and shipwrecks around him. His world consisted of one tiny, dark cabin in the middle of the maelstrom. He had nothing else to do but listen to his private thoughts. No longer Captain McConkey, he was just Edward, a frightened thirty-four-year-old husband with a toddler daughter, Aileen. She would probably not remember him, but he would remember her tiny warm fingers and bright eyes for the rest of his life.

SUNDAY EVENING, NOVEMBER 9

LAKE ERIE

NOT EVERYONE BATTLING THE STORM that Sunday was aboard a large steel straight decker. Commercial fishermen based in Port Clinton, Ohio, at the western end of Lake Erie, watched helplessly from shore as mountainous waves tore apart their nets. Permanent pound nets that had been built just offshore were uprooted, stakes and all. There would be weeks of work ahead fixing the storm damage, but for the moment all the fishermen could do was check the mooring lines and adjust the woven rope fenders protecting their wooden fishing boats moored along the Portage River. They might as well tend to the boats because the nets were beyond reach. There was no sense losing everything to the storm. While they worked, the roads in Port Clinton became impassable because of snowdrifts 6 feet deep in the main intersections.

A few miles to the east, the larger port city of Sandusky was hit by the same high winds and blinding snow that were crippling Port Clinton. One gust of wind created several days of uneasiness for city residents. At the height of the gale a thousand-pound box of dynamite was blown into the slip at the coal dock where the *McGean* had loaded only hours earlier. The case of explosives disappeared almost instantly into the black water, where it remained for several days until weather conditions permitted workers to retrieve it.

For sailors, however, the most disturbing news in Sandusky was that the telephone wire to the nearby Marblehead Lifesaving Station had broken. The Marblehead Station was the primary source of aid for ships stranded on the Lake Erie coastline. Without a phone, word of sailors in peril would have to come by foot through snowdrifts as tall as the average man. Valuable time would be lost.

Locomotive engineers on the New York Central, Pennsylvania, and Nickel Plate main lines that paralleled the shore of Lake Erie were as stymied by the snow as the fishermen in Port Clinton or the dynamite workers in Sandusky. Drifts at Elyria Junction near Lorain finally grew too high for the trains to push aside. Traffic on one of the busiest tracks in the country was forced to a standstill. Railroads in Ohio lacked the huge snowplows that kept the lines open through the Rocky Mountain states. As a result of the blockage at Elyria, westbound passenger trains from Cleveland to Toledo were running more than 10 hours late.

> More snow fell between 12 noon yesterday and 9:00 A.M. today than in any 24 hours in any November for the past 28 years or longer, and there was much damage to electric wires and delay to traffic of all kinds on account of the wind and snowfall.
>
> *Daily Local Record*, NOVEMBER 10, 1913

At the far eastern end of Lake Erie, the city of Buffalo was rocked by 70-mile-per-hour westerly winds that carried stinging sleet and drifting snow. Buffalo is situated at the apex of lake-effect snow caused by lake storms. Over a typical winter, residents there routinely expect up to a dozen feet of snow. In some places on this Sunday the drifts were equal to half a normal winter's snowfall. Pedestrians walking against the wind found the icy streets extremely treacherous. Trains arriving in the city were 7 to 10 hours late and covered with ice.

No ships were sighted entering or leaving Buffalo harbor on Sunday. Local weather observer F. A. Math gave credit to himself and the Weather Bureau for this lack of ship traffic at the eastern end of Lake Erie: "Everything was snug and tight in the harbor this day in anticipation of the storm and as a result of the timely warning of the Bureau, local shipping suffered practically no damage."

Starting on Sunday and all through Monday, Buffalo endured what Math termed "a heavy and blinding snowstorm." He wrote in the station records that "it caused havoc to pedestrians and traffic in general. . . . Street cars could not run on many lines and railroad trains were delayed. A wreck occurred on the Erie R.R. killing one man."

Lake Erie — Buffalo, New York
LIGHTSHIP 82

There comes a point in a storm when everything has been done that can be done. The pumps are working, and the hatches are dogged. But what if the very fabric of the ship starts to disintegrate? What do men think about at a time like that? Time must seem eternally long in those moments, giving opportunity for a sailor to realize that by morning he will no longer be a part of his family. Captain Hugh M. Williams could not have avoided mulling such thoughts on Sunday aboard the disintegrating *Lightship 82*, which had been anchored near Buffalo until the storm carried her off station. The lightship was supposed to guide ships from Lake Erie into the harbor at Buffalo.

The almost-new steel hull of the lightship was holding up to the waves. What bothered Captain Williams was the wooden superstructure, which was breaking apart under the constant pounding. At first there were a few leaks where none should have been. Then, skylights and windows caved under tons of water cascading over the top of the ship. That was the beginning of the destruction. In a topsy-turvy repeat of the *Walk-In-The-Water* disaster on the same stretch of water almost a century earlier, Lake Erie poured into the tiny hull faster than the pumps could remove it. Just when the floating beacon's anchor broke loose is uncertain. *Lightship 82* was not reported missing until Tuesday, when the ore carrier *Champlain* noted the beacon vessel was nowhere to be found.

Lake Erie — Cleveland, Ohio
JOHN P. REISS

The straight-deck freighter *John P. Reiss* first approached the Cleveland harbor about midafternoon Sunday, not long after Captain Walter Pringle had arrived in the *Isabella J. Boyce*, but chaotic waves and high northwest winds made entering the city's breakwater too dangerous. Men in the pilothouse had trouble enough seeing the ship's steering pole, let alone the narrow main harbor entrance. So, the 504-foot straight decker headed back offshore to the relative safety of open water. During the next 6 hours, the *Reiss* made a large circle that took it almost 50 miles north to the

Canadian shoreline of Lake Erie before it returned to the Cleveland harbor entrance.

> For nine hours on Sunday, from 3 P.M. until midnight the wind tore through the city at sixty miles an hour. At one period a velocity of sixty-two miles an hour was attained.
>
> Cleveland Plain Dealer, NOVEMBER 11, 1913

The waves battering Cleveland's breakwater were enormous. They picked stone blocks larger than automobiles out of the protective wall and cast them aside like pebbles. Two large openings were breached in the artificial wall designed to protect the city's port from lake storms. Warning signal flags cracking in the wind at the Cleveland Lifesaving Station suddenly disappeared in the storm. Surging waves undermined the tower that held the flags, and everything collapsed into the harbor. "The worst storm in my twenty-two years of experience on the lakes," said Captain Hans Hansen, who commanded the station.

The wind on western Lake Erie now gusted into the mid-40-mile-per-hour range. The snow that had begun overnight continued falling through the afternoon and into the next night. This combination of wind and snow was powerful enough to blow apart the anemometer at the weather station in Toledo, Ohio. "Wind velocity circuit out of order and wind velocity approximated from 5:00 P.M. to 6:16 P.M. and from 8:49 P.M. to 12 midnight," said the station's official daily log. "Today's snow and wind storm combined was more severe than any previous one at this season for many years. The snow was badly drifted in places." By midnight, Toledo had 27 inches of snow on the ground, and it was still falling.

MONDAY, NOVEMBER 10

THE MORNING OF NOVEMBER 10 found the low-pressure center of the White Hurricane northeast of London, Ontario. It may have slowed for a while over the flat strip of glaciated land that separates Lake Huron from Lake Erie, then begun moving quickly northeast across Ontario and into Québec. But even as the weakening storm was leaving the region, its back side hit Cleveland with a blizzard of lake-effect snow. Seventeen more inches fell that day. This additional snow knocked down even more electric lines. City streets that had been shoveled open were clogged with new drifts more than 6 feet high.

The city's electric streetcars were trapped by the drifts and the lack of electric power. Some streetcars were abandoned, but many motormen loyally waited out the storm aboard their stalled machines. They slept two nights on the hard seats of the cars and ate what food local residents were willing to supply. Pedestrians staggered along Cleveland's Euclid Avenue as they tried to force their way through the blizzard. Many people caught away from home had no choice but to find shelter and wait out the storm.

Unlike the citizens of Cleveland, Minnesotans have plenty of experience with harsh winter weather. They know how to dress for low temperatures and how to get around when falling snow reduces visibility to a few yards. The storm of 1913, however, was more than just an early Minnesota winter storm. In Duluth, the temperature dropped to 6 degrees overnight. At 3 A.M. winds at the city's weather station were still gusting to 48 miles per hour. In the November 10, 1913, *Duluth Herald*, Duluth's weather observer, H. W. Richardson, estimated the snow-laden winds on Lake Superior must have been at least 60 miles per hour.

Lake Huron——Harbor Beach, Michigan
GEORGE C. CRAWFORD

An hour into Monday, the situation aboard the *George C. Crawford* had not improved. Both anchors had carried away, and the ship was being blown toward the unseen lee shore at the foot of Lake Huron. There was nothing for Captain Iler to do but attempt once more to turn his ship into the wind and seas. A lull in the wind at about 2 A.M. gave him the break he needed to force the bow around. The ship started back toward deep water on its original upbound course for the Soo.

Lake Huron——Point Aux Barques, Michigan
MATOA

The new day found the crew of the *Matoa* still nursing their disintegrating ship through the monster waves. They carefully studied the ominous crack across the deck just in front of the boilerhouse that had appeared two hours earlier, at the height of the weather bomb. No one needed to be told that an opening like that could suddenly "run" around the hull and split the ship in two. If that fear was not enough, sometime around midnight a wave bigger than the others climbed over the ship's fantail and swept everything before it. For a terrifying moment the crew was certain the wave would collapse the ship. Instead, the water buckled the quarter-inch-thick steel of the after boilerhouse wall inward about 3 feet, but the wall held. If that wall had collapsed, the result could have been fatal to the ship.

"I guess we're lucky to have stranded at 12:30 A.M. on Monday," admitted Captain McLeod to a *Cleveland Plain Dealer* reporter. Waves threw his ship hard aground on Point Aux Barques at the mouth of Saginaw Bay. The battered hull bounced once and then surged ahead several ship lengths before striking again harder. The bow swung into the west as the hull came to a halt. Although the *Matoa* was hard aground, it was still almost 2 miles off the beach. McLeod reached for the whistle pull and began sounding the continuous blast that indicated distress. *Matoa's* whistle was carried by the wind.

Lifesavers from the Point Aux Barques Lifesaving Station immediately answered by firing a pyrotechnic Coston flare to acknowledge the wrecked ship. That was as much as they could do for the time being. Storm surge had raised the level of Lake Huron almost 5 feet, and waves surged back and forth inside the station's boathouse. The front doors had been knocked off their hinges, and nothing remained of the launching rails for the power surfboat. It would take hours of work to clean up the rubble before one of the boats could be launched. Sailors aboard the *Matoa* found themselves facing the same uncomfortable wait for rescue as the crews of the *L.C. Waldo*, on Superior, and the *Howard M. Hanna Jr.*, which lay broken on the beach at Port Austin just a few miles to the east.

The situation was a little less grim aboard *Matoa* than on the *Waldo* or *H.M. Hanna* because engineers had been able to carry an oil heater with them when they abandoned the stern section of the ship. The crew moved to the forward section because they feared the crack in the deck would open and allow the stern to be washed away. By morning, what remained of their ship was coated in ice, but the crew remained warm in the windlass room. "With our heaters we were fairly comfortable," said Captain McLeod.

Lake Huron — *Off Saginaw Bay, Michigan*
J.H. SHEADLE

By 4:15 A.M. on Monday, Captain Lyons on the *Sheadle* had decided his ship was far enough north on Lake Huron and it was time to reverse course again. This time, he would turn south and put the waves on his stern as he headed back for the St. Clair River. From pilothouse to engine room, the crew thought they knew what to expect on their second time through the deadly trough. They were wrong.

"I turned again," the captain wrote. "This time we experienced much difficulty in turning, the ship remaining longer in the trough of the sea on account of not getting so much way and running head into it, but she behaved well, handled well in every way and steered well."

Even though the *Sheadle* successfully reversed its direction, Captain Lyons candidly admitted this second turn had its frightening moments. "The rolling was very bad—I was lifted right off my feet. Only by the greatest effort were the second mate and myself able to hold onto the stanchions on the top house, our legs being parallel with the deck most of the time." Barrels of paint and oil broke loose inside the paint locker and smashed their way on deck. "I never have seen seas form as they did at this time; they were large and seemed to run in series, one mounting the other like a mighty barrier," Lyons wrote.

Running before a following sea, as the *Sheadle* was now doing, is extremely difficult at any time. During the White Hurricane, running with the 35-foot-tall waves seems to have been the key to disaster for vessels on Lake Huron. Monster waves overtook the ships and canceled the effectiveness of their steering, because rudders only work in a stream of flowing water. As waves passed, the motion of the water was opposite to the discharge currents from the propellers. The result was virtually motionless water around the rudders, rendering the steering gear useless. At the same time, energy from the waves pushed the sterns sideways so that the vessels tumbled into the deadly troughs. Only through a combination of opening and closing the throttle, careful steering, and a large dose of good luck could a ship be kept under control.

Another effect of the following sea was to speed up a ship's forward progress. Water moves forward with each passing wave. This movement pushes the vessel faster over the bottom than if the ship had been operating in quiet water. The converse is also true. Bashing into a head sea slows down a ship's forward progress. Captain Lyons reported these effects on the *Sheadle's* speed during the storm. "Running back, we decreased our speed from 'full' to 55 turns," he wrote. "We came back in two hours where it took us 6 to face the sea."

By 6:30 A.M. Captain Lyons was once again worried by the depths he was obtaining with his sounding machine. It was time to put the *Sheadle* about and head north once again. "I called the engineer and told him . . . to be prepared at any moment to give me full power to turn the ship again. We could see nothing on account of the heavy fall of snow," the captain wrote. "At 6:45 A.M., we turned for the third time, heading north by west. This time the sea had decreased, and the wind had gone to the northwest in the meantime so there was practically no sea to bother us."

Lake Huron——Harbor Beach, Michigan
D.O. MILLS

At full daylight, lifesavers from the Harbor Beach, Michigan, lifesaving station launched their motorized rescue boat and headed toward a ship stranded on the beach. There they found the straight decker *D.O. Mills* hard on the bottom and apparently full of water. They cruised around the steel hulk shouting and trying to attract the attention of anyone alive inside the ship. Silence. If the crew had survived the storm, they certainly were not eager for rescue. There were no answering shouts. In fact, there was no sign of life aboard the ship. The lifesavers could only shrug and head back to their station. In truth, the crew of the *D.O. Mills* were alive and quite well. Why they failed to notice the rescue boat or hear the shouts of the lifesavers remains one of the mysteries of the storm.

The *Mills* was not seriously damaged by going aground. When it first touched bottom at 11 P.M. Sunday night the crew flooded the hold to keep the ship from pounding itself to pieces. After the storm subsided on Monday afternoon, the crew pumped the water out of the hold and used wave action on the lake to help them back their ship into deep water. Although the *D.O. Mills* was able to extricate itself, the ship received enough damage that it spent much of the winter dry-docked for repairs.

Lake Huron — Port Huron, Michigan
HURLBUT W. SMITH

A misshapen lump of ice entered the St. Clair River during the early hours of Monday morning. At first glance, it could have been an iceberg broken off the face of some phantom glacier. In reality, the apparition was the battered *H.W. Smith*, which had survived 24 terrible hours on Lake Huron. Before receiving its coating of ice, the forward superstructure had taken a terrible beating. "I have seen many storms on the Great Lakes," said Captain Thomas W. Carney, "but never in my life as a sailor have I witnessed such a one as Sunday."

Lake Huron — Off Port Huron, Michigan
MATTHEW ANDREWS

North of Port Huron, Captain John Lampoh was also dead tired after surviving the worst night of his career. His skillful seamanship brought the 532-foot straight decker *Matthew Andrews* and its cargo of iron ore safely through the worst of the storm. "We had been swept by the heavy seas and windows in the pilothouse were broken," Captain Lampoh told reporters later that day. "Things were upset in general, but aside from that everything was alright." With the storm moderating, Lampoh was feeling optimistic that his ship had survived this last trip of the 1913 season.

At 9 A.M. Lampoh expected to see the distinctive silhouette of *Lightship 26* off Port Huron, Michigan. Southbound ships like the *Andrews* used the lightship to help locate the entrance to the St. Clair River. Monday morning, however, the horizon was empty. The tired captain had no way to know that the lightship had been blown off station by the storm. All he knew for certain was that this familiar beacon was not floating in its customary location. So, Lampoh steered the *Andrews* through swirling snow toward the spot where he reckoned the lightship should be anchored.

From the pilothouse of the salvage tug *Sarnia City*, Captain Tom Reid caught the dark silhouette of the *Andrews* as it approached from the north. Reid was attending the Port Huron lightship, where his offer of assistance had just been rebuffed. His offer to tow the government ship and aid to navigation back to its regular station for a modest fee was met with a thoroughly bureaucratic response. The officer-in-charge of the lightship said he could not hire the tug without authorization from Chicago and would have to wait until the storm-damaged telegraph wires were restored to get that authorization.

Just as this unsuccessful negotiation concluded, Captain Reid noticed the *Andrews* coming down the lake. The straight decker appeared to be heading for the dangerous water surrounding Corsica Shoal. Reid started toward it in an attempt to warn the freighter, but the unsuspecting *Andrews* slammed to a stop on the shoal. "This was my first accident, and it was a bitter disappointment to have brought my ship safely through the storm only to wind up on the shoal," a frustrated Captain Lampoh told reporters after the incident.

Lake Huron — Port Austin, Michigan
HOWARD M. HANNA JR.

Monday morning found Captain Hagan and twenty-three other members of his crew still trapped aboard the wrecked *Howard M. Hanna Jr.* near Port Austin. Half of the crew remained in the stern, while the rest found shelter in the bow. Their dire situation had not gone unnoticed. Having worked all night to clear his launching rails of rubble, Captain Frahm of the Point Aux Barques Lifesaving Station bravely responded to the *Hanna's* distress by ordering a lifeboat launched into the surf. The lifesavers strained to reach deep water, but their sturdy rescue craft was unceremoniously flung back upon the beach, where the boat filled with sand. Luckily, the crew escaped with their lives. For the moment, lifesavers had their own mini-wreck to clean up before they could assist the *Hanna*.

Deprived of their boat, the Point Aux Barques crew telephoned two nearby lifesaving stations for assistance. Both were involved with wrecks of their own. There was nothing for the Point Aux Barques men to do but go back to their swamped surfboat and dig it out. The tiring work of shoveling sand out of the wooden hull was a labor of Sisyphus. As fast as they shoveled, the pounding surf threw more sand back into the boat. To make matters worse, the breaking waves continuously soaked the workers with freezing water. Persistence eventually paid off. By midday the boat was free of the sand.

The would-be rescuers of the *Hanna* then discovered the serious damage that had occurred when the lightly built craft was slammed onto the beach by the storm. Five breaks were found in the gunwale, and several holes had been punched through the boat's wooden bottom. Even though repairs were slapdash, the work took until well after sundown, when darkness made it unwise to begin a rescue. The *Hanna* survivors had to endure another freezing night in the wreckage of their ship.

A few miles inside Saginaw Bay from where the *Hanna* washed ashore lies the small Michigan fishing port of Sebewaing. Seven duck hunters had arisen there before dawn Monday, checked their shotguns and shells, and headed for the shallow waters known as the "Middle Ground." This partly submerged spot was covered by rushes and known to be a favorite habitat of several species of ducks. Monday night, searchers on the beach found only an empty duckboat and no other sign of the hunters.

Lake Huron — Off Port Huron, Michigan
J.H. Sheadle

A break in the snow on Lake Huron about 8:30 a.m. let Captain Lyons aboard the *Sheadle* glimpse a few prominent landmarks. He also spotted wreckage on the water, giving him a hint of what was happening to other ships around him. Lyons noted the Port Huron lightship was off station and even managed to spot it off in the distance before another flurry of snow blocked his vision. Rather than tempt fate, the always prudent captain dropped anchor to await better weather. The *Sheadle* remained at anchor almost 4 hours, until noon. By then, visibility cleared sufficiently to allow Lyons to get underway again. Just after lunchtime the battered ship found sanctuary in the confines of the St. Clair River.

"After entering the river the steward served dinner in the galley, which was the first regular meal since Sunday noon, and which consisted of beef and potatoes," Lyons recorded in his memoirs. With nothing else left in the galley to eat, the *Sheadle* was forced to stop at Smith's Coal Dock in Port Huron for provisions.

Lake Huron — Off Port Huron, Michigan
SARNIA CITY *and* "MYSTERY SHIP"

On Monday afternoon the salvage tug *Sarnia City* headed out of the St. Clair River once again. Captain Ely was now in command of the tug while his boss, Tom Reid, remained ashore to take care of office paperwork. It had not been a successful morning for Reid, who was still stung by the lightship's refusal to accept a tow. The tug had not been scheduled to depart again so soon, but men at the Lakeview Lifesaving Station near Port Huron had sighted what they thought was the hull of a freighter awash in the seas. As reported by the *Detroit Free Press* on November 11, Captain Plough of the Lakeview Station had been unable to launch any of his surfboats because the storm had collapsed the boathouse in which they were stored.

"It certainly is tough to be handicapped in this way," Captain Plough told a reporter. "I sighted the vessel this afternoon, but of course my boats are just a crumpled mess. I have had my men at work all day trying to rig up some kind of a temporary boat and by morning I expect that we will be able to get to the steamer."

Captain Plough untangled the wreckage of his boathouse while the *Sarnia City* conducted a careful search for the ship. No distressed ships were sighted, so the tug headed for home. Minutes later the salvage vessel came upon perhaps the most startling sight ever seen on the Great Lakes: lolling in the waves was the upside-down bow of a large steel freighter. For a few seconds, Captain Ely and his crew thought it was a small ship lying awash, but they quickly recognized it as the overturned bottom of a full-size freighter. Numerals marking the ship's upright 20-foot draft were just out of the water, with about 100 feet of the hull showing.

Captain Ely quickly returned to Sarnia with news of the overturned ship. The *Sarnia City* was only minutes in port before it headed back to the overturned hull. This time, it was under the command of owner Tom Reid. After viewing the wreck, Reid said, "I think it is one of the big fellows. That's the way it looks to me. I think she was headed back toward the river, running for shelter, when she must have been caught in the trough of the sea and bowled over." Recognizing that the overturned hulk was a danger to navigation, Reid agreed to warn away ships that otherwise might have smashed into the unfortunate vessel. The name of the capsized freighter was hidden beneath the waves, causing the most famous mystery in the history of the Great Lakes. What was the identity of the floating wreck?

Lake Huron — Port Franks, Ontario
Northern Queen

Salvor Tom Reid spent too much time marveling at the overturned hull that day. He should have steamed a few miles north to where the steamer *Northern Queen* was drifting onto the Canadian shore of Lake Huron. He might have earned a fine commission for helping keep that straight decker from grief. The *Northern Queen* almost succeeded in riding out the gale at anchor. For more than 19 hours its two anchors kept the vessel from disaster. Luck ran out about 7 P.M. Monday when the ship slammed ashore bow first not far from Port Franks, Ontario.

> Some distance from the beach stood the battered *Northern Queen* tossed about by the heavy waves. On her decks stood 22 men and from the evident condition of the *Northern Queen* there was not much chance for them unless the storm abated.
>
> . . . There was no help that could be rendered by the men on shore and the sailors on the *Northern Queen* had to work out their own salvation. It was a terrible situation. In the bow of the *Northern Queen* were

clustered 22 men. Around them tossed the angry waves and as the heavy
seas buffeted the steamer she shook and shivered from stem to stern.

Port Huron Times-Herald, NOVEMBER 11, 1913

Lake Huron —— Sulphur Island, Thunder Bay, Michigan
ACADIAN

As the storm abated on Monday, the crew of the *Acadian* considered themselves lucky to be alive. They hoped that another ship or a Lifesaving
Service surfboat would come to their aid in the morning, but the horizon was empty. It was not until late Monday afternoon that the tug *Ralph*
happened past the derelict. The tug was cruising Thunder Bay looking for
a stranded or wrecked ship. While the stout little vessel was able to rescue
the crew, it was not large enough to salvage the cargo ship. In fact, there
wasn't a tugboat in Alpena big enough for the job. Captain McIntyre
would have to seek help from the *Success*, one of many specialized salvage
ships that served the Great Lakes. Salvage was profitable that November.

Lake Superior —— Whitefish Point
J.T. HUTCHINSON

At 1:30 A.M. Monday on Lake Superior, a tired Captain H. J. Yacques
stared red-eyed out of the pilothouse windows of the bulk freighter *J.T.
Hutchinson*. He had managed to bring his ship down the lake from Isle
Royale during the height of Sunday's gale. "We shipped water and
expected to see our hatches go at any minute," he wrote to his wife, in a
letter reproduced in the *Detroit News*. "No breakfast or dinner. The coal
bunker hatch had been torn away. . . . All wet, clothes frozen and my
rubber boots full of water. . . . Ship log broke, lost all track of distance
and don't know where we are."

Hours of fighting the storm had robbed both Captain Yacques and
his crew of sleep, so he decided to seek shelter. Yacques first tried the lee
of Caribou Island. A wind shift forced him to abandon this location so the
Hutchinson headed for the popular anchorage behind Whitefish Point.
"We have a hard run all the way," he wrote to his wife about his ordeal
during the storm. "Nobody can sleep and everybody wet and hungry."

Lake Superior—Keweenaw Peninsula
George Stephenson *and* L.C. Waldo

By early Monday morning, Captain Mosher of the *George Stephenson* was extremely frustrated with the Eagle River Lifesaving Station. Rescuers there were still unable to launch a boat to rescue the *Waldo's* trapped crew. Mosher had seen the survivors wave and signal with his own eyes, but his freighter was not suitable for a rescue attempt near the Keweenaw rocks. Having seen them, he was duty bound not to abandon his fellow sailors. Now, almost another full day had passed. No one could say for sure that the wreck of the *Waldo* was still wedged on the rocks. It could have washed to sea in the meantime. Even if it remained on the rocks, had anyone survived?

Considering the weather, Captain Mosher's only recourse was to send his mate ashore a second time to find out what was happening. Once on land, the mate quickly confirmed that it would be some time before the Eagle River station could repair its primary motorboat and head to the *Waldo*. Acting on his own initiative, the mate telephoned a second lifesaving station at Portage Canal on the Keweenaw Peninsula at Hancock, Michigan. Lifesavers there immediately agreed to launch their lifeboat for the dangerous 65-mile passage to the stranded and broken freighter.

During their first hour of motoring, the men from the Portage station made only a scant mile. Boat commander Collin Westrope recognized the futility of battling with the storm. After returning to his station he described the wet, cold boat ride in his official report:

> The waves smashed against the bow and shook us like a dog shaking water off his back. . . . In the troughs, the boat stood on her nose with the propeller out of the water, racing in the air.
>
> As quoted in T. Michael O'Brien, *Guardians of the Eighth Sea*

Portage Station Keeper Thomas H. McCormick decided to take a much longer but less dangerous route to the *Waldo*. Instead of fighting the open lake the entire way, he ordered his lifeboat to cross the Keweenaw Peninsula by using the Portage Canal. Despite their fatigue, the men put their lifeboat on a railroad flatcar to transport it to Lac La Belle. McCormick also requested the tug *Daniel Hebard* to stand by to assist his men near the wreck.

Lake Superior — Whitefish Point
SYLVANIA *and* EDENBORN

The failure of the Portage lifeboat to reach the *Waldo* was not surprising. Conditions on Lake Superior Monday morning were still far too rough for a small wooden boat. In fact, they were still dangerous for large steel ships. At Whitefish Point, near the eastern end of the lake, Captain Warren C. Jones was slightly surprised to find that his ship, the *Sylvania*, had survived the night. It still rode to its anchor despite the mountainous seas. Jones noticed the fatigue of his crew. "Most of the men having been up all night long waiting either for the crash or the probable sinking of the vessel," he said. "The anchor was so secure that we were enabled to turn the boat around and again attempt to go on our way. By 10 o'clock Monday morning we had hardly covered any distance at all."

Not far away the steamer *Edenborn* was also battling Lake Superior waves after leaving the protection of Whitefish Point just after midnight Monday morning. From the start the ship was in trouble. "It was almost impossible to make any headway," said Captain T. J. Cullen. Like masters of other vessels wrestling with the storm, Cullen tried anchoring. "We allowed our anchor to drag along and in this way avoid an accident. Time and again we would pull up the anchor only to throw it in again a few minutes later. It was the worst trip I have experienced in the twenty-two years of my service," he told the *Duluth Herald*.

At the northern end of Lake Huron in Cheboygan, Michigan, Miss Violet Wood read the message from Weather Bureau headquarters in Washington, D.C. As the local deputy weather observer, she tended the signal flags when the male station chief was not available. Bracing herself against the gale-force wind, she began lowering the old flags. A sudden gust carried the bunting upward with the young woman clinging tightly to the halyards. Her feet rose off the platform and she flew skyward, lifted by the 8-foot-square signal flags, which acted like kites. Her shrieks brought help, and she was quickly pulled back to earth by her heels.

Lake Superior — Apostle Islands
WILLIAM NOTTINGHAM

Yet another ship came to grief on the Lake Superior shore while Captain Mosher was waiting for a break in the storm. The 376-foot steel freighter *William Nottingham* was tossed unceremoniously onto a rocky reef between remote Sand and Parisian Islands in the Apostle Island chain located just off Wisconsin's scenic Bayfield Peninsula.

Lacking radio gear, the *Nottingham's* crew decided to send a lifeboat to summon assistance even though their ship seemed firmly wedged on the rocks. Three volunteers climbed into the frail craft as it was lowered into the waves. The falls were not even disconnected when a breaking wave crashed the lifeboat and its occupants against the steel side of the ship. The boat teetered, then rolled over as the wave surged back from the stranded freighter. The three men were thrown into the near-freezing water, where they instantly disappeared. Shaken by the sudden deaths of their shipmates, the remaining *Nottingham* castaways retreated to the relative safety of the stranded vessel. All were rescued the following Wednesday.

Lake Superior — Gull Rock and Bete Grise Bay
L.C. WALDO *and* GEORGE STEPHENSON

The swirling snow and high winds on Lake Superior continued to frustrate Captain Mosher, the would-be rescuer of the *Waldo's* stranded crew. He waited impatiently aboard his anchored ship, the *Stephenson*, for a chance to rescue the survivors of the broken ship. Every hour that passed made it increasingly unlikely that anyone would still be alive in the wreck. Even the heartiest of sailors might have frozen to death by now. Meanwhile, pieces of the smashed pilothouse from the *Waldo* washed ashore near Marquette, Michigan, and were discovered by commercial fisherman Jim Burns, who reported his find to authorities. People on shore immediately assumed the *Waldo* had foundered. The wreckage seemed to seal the fate of both the ship and its crew. A Chicago news service dutifully announced that the *Waldo* was lost with all hands.

In fact, the crew had survived the demolition of the pilothouse, the grounding, and the breakup of their ship. Captain Mosher of the *Stephen-*

son had seen survivors raise a distress signal. When Mosher had answered that signal more than 24 hours earlier, he considered it a promise not to abandon the men and women who remained huddled in the freighter's windlass room. Mosher knew it must be freezing aboard the battered hulk of the *Waldo*. Perhaps the survivors were already dead. The captain refused to let such thoughts enter his mind. He had promised to rescue those sailors, and he would not go back on his word.

A momentary lull in the snow flurries at dinnertime Monday encouraged Captain Mosher to get the *Stephenson* underway again. He headed straight for Gull Rock and the wreck. Mosher had to know—was the battered and broken ship still lodged on the rocks, and were any of the crew still alive after all those hours in the cold?

The *Stephenson's* engine throbbed as the ship headed onto the sullen lake. Although Captain Mosher's intentions were good, he was being lulled into a trap by what is called around the lakes a "sucker hole" in the weather. The brief lull in the blizzard was soon torn apart by renewed gusts from the northeast, and blinding snow once again filled the air. Mosher was plagued by dark thoughts as he navigated through the high seas running past the rocky Keweenaw Peninsula. It was entirely possible that the wreck had washed into deep water. If that happened, there would be no one left alive to rescue.

What Captain Mosher saw through the darkness and flying snow was disheartening. "I hove up at 9:20 P.M., came through Gull Rock and saw the *Waldo* still with her decks above water. She was lying lifeless and silent in the night." Taking the *Stephenson* close enough to look for survivors at night was a daring bit of seamanship, especially with high seas running. The area around Gull Rock and Manitou Island is marked by shoal water and unseen rocks. Ordinarily, Captain Mosher would never have taken his freighter into such a dangerous place, but not a man in the *Stephenson's* crew objected to the dangerous maneuver. The decks of the broken hulk were devoid of life. Aside from the distress flag still flying from the foremast, there was no sign of a living soul.

This personal visit to the wreck did not end Captain Mosher's frustration. He could not go aboard the wreck to see for himself what had become of the *Waldo's* survivors. His freighter was too big to get close enough to board the wrecked steamer. Any rescue effort would have to wait for the arrival of a smaller surfboat from the Lifesaving Service. Faced with the primary responsibility for the safety of his own ship in the rebuilding gale, Captain Mosher reluctantly headed offshore. The *Waldo* disappeared astern, but the captain's fears for the stranded sailors remained.

Collin Westrope and the other members of the Portage Canal Lifesaving Station were now well on their way to Gull Rock in their motorized lifeboat. They had been beaten back earlier in the day and did not want it to happen again. No one suspected that the trip would take 14 grueling hours with the boat constantly icing over. Unknown to the Portage Canal crew, the Eagle Harbor lifeboat had finally been repaired and was also heading toward the wreck through the night darkness.

Lake Superior — Whitefish Point
J.T. HUTCHINSON

Captain Yacques of the *J.T. Hutchinson* was more fatigued now than he had been back at Caribou Island. Shortly after 11:30 P.M. Monday he brought his ship to within sight of the Whitefish Point lighthouse. It had been the hardest trip down Lake Superior of his life, and he had never been as tired. Now, the protection of Whitefish Bay was at hand, and the pressure seemed to lift from his shoulders.

"See Whitefish Point light and make entrance all o.k. and everybody is happy," he wrote in a letter reproduced in the *Detroit News*. "Little we thought that in less than five hours we would be on the rocks and have the ship going to pieces under us."

Lake Michigan — Chicago, Illinois
J.G. BOYCE

At first light on Monday, Captain N. G. Norlem and his six-man crew were still struggling to stay alive aboard their lumber schooner. On the previous evening they had anchored the *J.G. Boyce* just off the city's harbor entrance. Norlem had refused to abandon the ship even after a motorized lifeboat from the Chicago Lifesaving Station responded to his distress signals. The reluctant captain and his men chose to spend a cold night on Lake Michigan riding out the storm.

"The schooner dragged," Captain Norlem admitted later. "About day-break we were getting close to shore where we could plainly see the breakers." In a desperate effort to survive, the crew of the *Boyce* climbed into the schooner's rigging. Freezing spray quickly encased both the men and the rigging in a cocoon of ice. The nearly frozen survivors quickly accepted rescue the second time the Chicago's motorized lifeboat arrived. The abandoned lumber schooner remained afloat without its crew. After the storm it was towed into port in good condition.

Lake Erie — Erie, Pennsylvania
SANTA MARÍA

Christopher Columbus experienced tropical hurricanes during his four trips to the New World, but the Admiral of the Ocean Sea never saw anything like the ice and snow of the White Hurricane. A replica of his flagship, the *Santa María*, was wintering in Erie, Pennsylvania, accompanied by reproductions of the *Niña* and the *Pinta*. The trio of ships had been en route to San Francisco by way of the Panama Canal when they were caught by winter on the Great Lakes. The wooden replica of Columbus' caravel was torn from its moorings and thrown onto a sandbar outside the city harbor. This 1913 accident was eerily reminiscent of the grounding that wrecked the original *Santa María* on Columbus' first voyage to the New World. The 1913 replica was more fortunate than its famous predecessor, however. Tugs worked all day to free the *Santa María*, which was refloated without serious damage.

CLEVELAND, OHIO

ON TUESDAY MORNING, CLEVELAND, OHIO, was no longer a functioning city. It was buried beneath a veritable glacier of snow and ice that squashed utility poles and plunged much of the city into darkness. Telephone service, which shared the utility poles, became spotty or nonexistent. Snowdrifts closed the city's major avenues and obliterated residential streets. Cleveland's famous streetcar system was frozen to its tracks. Huge railroad locomotives found themselves powerless against the snowdrifts.

Not even the city's drinking water was safe from the storm. Monster waves on Lake Erie churned up muck from the bottom more than 30 feet down. Cleveland's water supply turned a muddy color, and officials openly feared a typhoid epidemic from polluted drinking water. "Boil the water," went out the order from the Cleveland Health Department on Monday. Later in the day, health concerns eased somewhat when the city bacteriologist, R. G. Perkins, issued his statement regarding the condition of the drinking water. Quoted in the *Cleveland Plain Dealer* on November 11, Perkins said: "I do not believe that sewage from the river has been carried out. If there is a thaw, however, this is likely to occur and the water will then be unsafe for drinking." Despite Perkins' assurances, many housewives continued boiling the off-color water that came out of their kitchen faucets.

Tuesday morning's newspaper was almost poetic in its description of the city's plight:

> Cleveland lay in white and mighty solitude, mute and deaf to the outside world, a city of lonesome snowiness, storm-swept from end to end, when the violence of the two-day blizzard lessened late yesterday afternoon.

Cleveland Plain Dealer, NOVEMBER 11, 1913

It is doubtful the John D. Rockefeller family found the storm quite as disruptive as most other people. According to news accounts, the household retired at 5 P.M. Sunday when the lights in their Forest Hill estate residence went out. The staff was said to have made "several ineffectual sortees" to stores in the neighborhood seeking candles. None could be purchased, so the Rockefellers went to bed in the dark.

The storm pulled a practical joke on Tuesday by forcing the cancellation of a lecture scheduled that evening at the First Baptist Church. The topic was to have been "weather," and the scheduled speaker was Cleveland's official observer, William H. Alexander. As it turned out, at the scheduled hour of his speech the meteorologist was occupied keeping track of the 21.2 inches of snow that had fallen on the weather station from Sunday evening until Tuesday morning. According to the November 11 *Cleveland Press*, Alexander estimated the average depth of snow on the ground in the Cleveland area at 18.4 inches.

Alexander didn't have to check his books to know this had been a record snowfall. The old record had been set the previous March by a spring storm that caused catastrophic floods throughout Ohio. Cleveland's chief weather observer had compiled the statistics on the March storm himself. Before that, the previous snowfall record of 13 inches had stood for seventeen years. Forecaster Alexander told a Cleveland newspaper that the White Hurricane was the worst blizzard in the city's history:

> Take it all in all—the depth of the snowfall, the tremendous wind, the amount of damage done and the total unpreparedness of the people—I think it is safe to say that the present storm is the worst experienced in Cleveland during the whole forty-three years the Weather Bureau has been established in the city.
>
> *Cleveland Plain Dealer*, NOVEMBER 11, 1913

Another of Alexander's duties was checking the maximum wind velocity. According to his instruments, at 4:40 P.M. on Sunday—during the height of the storm—the wind reached 79 miles per hour. "This is easily a record for the Cleveland station for continuous high velocity," Alexander told the *Cleveland Press*. The average velocity from 4:40 to 4:45 P.M. that day had been 62 miles per hour. And from Sunday evening through Monday morning the wind had blown at an average speed of 51 miles per hour through the city streets.

Alexander also noted that the station barometer showed an uncorrected low of 28.35 inches of mercury Sunday evening as the low-pressure center passed over Lake Erie. That was just slightly above Cleveland's record low in the storm of February 21, 1912, when the uncorrected station pressure dropped to 28.28 inches.

Bright blue electrical flashes had illuminated the night sky prior to dawn on Monday. They did not come from the carbon arc streetlights invented by local resident Charles F. Brush. These flashes came from Cleveland's electricity distribution system, which was collapsing into the streets, brought down by the gale. For most people electricity was more of a convenience in 1913 than a necessity. It provided illumination and operated the occasional small appliance, but electric power was not relied on for heating or cooking. Before the blizzard ended, more than three thousand utility poles had collapsed under the combined weight of ice-covered wires and the force of the high winds.

The Illuminating Company, Cleveland's largest supplier of electricity, was forced to shut down many still-working power lines to protect public safety. "Light is less important than the safety of citizens," the company said in newspaper advertisements. "Caution children not to touch hanging wires."

Although they did not spark as they fell, the wires of Cleveland's telephone system also crashed to the ground. At least 20 percent of the city's phones were cut off as wires tangled in the streets on Sunday evening and all day Monday. "Neither the Bell nor Cuyahoga telephone companies would hazard a guess as to when they would be operating normally again," explained the *Cleveland News*. Telegraph service was equally disrupted. "Not a telegraph wire to any point was available up to noon," the paper said. "The Postal Telegraph Company in Cleveland was entirely out of commission Tuesday."

Wireless telegraph—radio—was Cleveland's only reliable means of long-distance communication from Sunday night until late Monday afternoon. For a while the storm even threatened to cut that tenuous link. High winds and ice forced A. E. Jackson, the chief engineer of the local Marconi Wireless Telegraph office, to walk out on the roof of the Schofield Building to examine his antenna. Clearly, repairs were needed. Despite the wind and snow, he started climbing. Hand over hand, he pulled himself up what was called the "wireless pole" 250 feet above the street. "With sleet driving into his eyes and cutting his face, and a 60-mile gale swaying his body and threatening to dash him to the pavement," the *Cleveland Plain Dealer* reported, Jackson "climbed to the top . . . and clung there for a quarter of an hour making repairs."

Considering the severity of the storm, the death toll in Cleveland from the blizzard was slight. Seventeen-year-old Carl Bourgeois, the son of a lake captain, was shoveling snow from the walk in front of his family's home on Monday. He bent over to move a downed wire and was electrocuted. High winds blew a railroad worker to his death from the top of a boxcar. A train conductor walking ahead of his engine to check the safety of the track was struck and killed by an oncoming train on a parallel line. One man escaped death when he was trapped under a tangle of live electrical wires. He received burns to one eye but was otherwise unhurt.

Confederate veteran William Lambert lived in what was called a "little hut" on an alley behind Eagle Avenue, downtown. The alley was referred to as Cleveland's "Skid Row," and the men who lived there were usually called "bums" by the people who shopped in the department stores on Public Square. For eight years the seventy-eight-year-old Lambert's only companion had been his shepherd dog. The two were last seen together just before the storm swallowed the city on Sunday afternoon.

Two days later, on Tuesday, a police officer was snapped at by the growling shepherd outside Lambert's ramshackle dwelling. The dog was faithfully guarding the now-frozen body of its master. Lambert had apparently succumbed to the storm on Sunday at some distance from his hut. His unconscious form was dragged to the door of his dwelling by his faithful companion. "The dog could do no more, so remained faithfully on guard throughout the blizzard," reported the *Cleveland Plain Dealer* on November 12, 1913.

Another man found in a snowdrift during the blizzard was luckier. Paul Burke apparently fell and knocked himself unconscious on Sunday afternoon. A drift built over him, hiding his body for several hours until he was discovered by James Mack. With no other help available, Mack hoisted the nearly frozen man onto his back. Carrying the victim piggyback, Mack staggered to a nearby fire station. The path was often blocked by blue sparks from downed electrical wires. Once, Mack slipped into a snowdrift with the inert body of the victim on top of him. After digging both of them out, the rescuer kept going. Thanks to Mack's efforts, Burke was revived once they arrived at a nearby hospital.

Surgeons at the Eddy Road Hospital normally worked under modern electric lights in their operating room. As utility poles fell around the hospital, those lights went dark right in the middle of a surgery. Candles were quickly brought into the operating room in order to continue the procedure. Doctors and nurses worked under the flickering light, successfully completing their task. Down in the Eddy Road Hospital's boiler room, another situation developed Sunday night that threatened disastrous consequences for sick and injured patients. The medical complex was nearly out of coal to feed boilers that heated steam for sterilizing instruments, made patients' rooms comfortable, and kept medical supplies from freezing.

Hundreds of men and women were caught away from their homes. Many of them sought hotel rooms only to discover there were none to be had at any price. Hotel staffs made their overflow guests as comfortable as possible by turning lobby furniture into makeshift beds. Taverns, movie theaters and even drugstores also became overnight shelters for people made temporarily homeless by the blowing and drifting snow.

> Unable to return to their homes, many persons who visited the Gordon Square theater . . . Sunday night did not leave it until yesterday morning. They found it a haven of shelter from the blinding, drifting storm which tied up traffic and, to many, made walking home impossible.
>
> A drug store in the neighborhood harbored snowbound pedestrians until early yesterday morning. In the crowd were children whose parents were ignorant of their whereabouts.
>
> *Cleveland Plain Dealer*, NOVEMBER 11, 1913

Tavern owners put their businesses at risk by allowing patrons to remain in their establishments past the legal closing hour. The national temperance movement was burgeoning in 1913, and Ohio was in the process of licensing taverns. Many of Cleveland's existing saloons had been forced to close during the past summer after they failed to obtain licenses. Those lucky enough to obtain liquor licenses faced instant bankruptcy if they lost that status due to an infraction of the new laws. One stipulation was that patrons could not remain inside bars after hours. Despite the risk, many saloon owners disregarded the law and allowed customers all the sleeping comforts of a warm barroom floor.

One famous traveler trapped in Cleveland by the storm was lecturer Helen Keller, who had just completed a public speaking engagement. Although blind and deaf, Keller said she was aware of the maelstrom outside her hotel. "I knew it was storming before I was told," Keller told a reporter for the *Cleveland Press*. "The rooms, the corridors, everywhere within this building vibrates with the power of the storm outside. The storm waves, like sound waves or the waves of the wireless, will not be denied by stone walls and plate glass windows."

Also forced to spend an extra day in Cleveland was English comedienne Marie Lloyd. She attempted to depart the city by train on Sunday after completing an engagement at the Hippodrome Theater. Her goal was Cincinnati. Instead, she spent Sunday night on a train that never got beyond the outskirts of Cleveland. In the morning, the comedienne returned to the Statler Hotel, where she waited while the tracks were cleared.

Even weather observer Alexander was not immune from disruption of his personal life as a result of the storm. He spent at least one night away from his own bed. Recorded in his official notes for the day is a simple statement that he engaged lodging at a nearby hotel instead of going to his home 5 miles away. "It being evident he would have trouble getting in [in] time next morning for his observations," he entered in the station's official daily record.

Two Cleveland police officers were trudging through the newly fallen snow Sunday night when they noticed flames coming from the windows of a rag company on Cleveland's west side. They found a street corner fire alarm callbox, then ran shouting through the floors of a flophouse hotel next to the burning building to wake sleeping guests. More than twenty yawning tenants left the warm danger of their beds for the cold safety of the blizzard. They shivered in the snow for more than five hours while firefighters worked to contain the blaze. News reports said firefighters were unable to make headway against the fire in the 70-mile-per-hour wind until the building was consumed. No one was injured.

There was an amusing aspect to this fire. The fractured state of communications caused newspapers in Detroit to receive reports of the fire but no details of its size or scope. So, the Detroit papers speculated that the whole of downtown Cleveland was on fire. These exaggerated reports hinted of a Chicago-style conflagration. In truth, an orange reflection of flames off low-lying clouds over the city was seen by people in outlying communities. This orange glow was probably misinterpreted by those observers and magnified in the retelling. The *Cleveland Plain Dealer* took some delight in exposing the errors made by the rival Michigan newspapers.

Firefighters battling the rag-company fire discovered that locating fire hydrants buried beneath mounds of snow was an almost impossible task. Cleveland's fire chief responded by calling out the Boy Scouts. On Wednesday, young men showed up with shovels to dig the familiar hydrants out of the drifts. After that, Boy Scout shovels helped clear intersections and busy sidewalks.

Emergency services were paralyzed as much as transportation. At the height of the storm an explosion rocked an east side Standard Oil plant. One man was seriously burned. This accident itself was not caused by the storm, but snow and high winds nearly resulted in the injured worker's death. One by one, six gasoline-powered ambulances tried to reach the victim, and one by one each became mired in snowdrifts. Finally, a draft horse was hitched to one of the ambulances, and the victim started slowly on his way to the hospital. It didn't take long before pulling the makeshift ambulance became too much for one horse. Another draft animal was commandeered and a makeshift wagon pole invented on the spot. When they finally drew the mechanized ambulance to St. Alexis Hospital, both exhausted horses were covered by steaming white sweat in which snowflakes melted as they landed.

The tremendous loss of sailors' lives and ships topped headlines in Cleveland on Tuesday morning. The biggest news for most city inhabitants, however, was the sudden lack of fresh food at neighborhood grocery stores. City households in 1913 did not stock large amounts of meat, milk, or other perishables. These items were routinely purchased daily from neighborhood markets, because stores had refrigeration to keep perishables, while homes relied on the less-satisfactory icebox. On Monday morning thousands of families discovered themselves facing shortages of staple food items as a result of the overnight avalanche of snow.

Provisions were running low in many snowbound households Tuesday. Members of thousands of families ventured out for the first time since Sunday. Their quest out into the deep drifts was in search of food.

Most folk still sought in vain under four and five feet of snow on their back porches for the sign of their old familiar milk bottle which up to Sunday had never failed them.

Cleveland Press, November 11, 1913

Hardest hit were children when the city's supply of milk simply disappeared. Cleveland mothers were forced to ration the last bottles in their home iceboxes. No more milk was to be had. Not only were the neighborhood stores closed, but roads were blocked. Lack of transportation prevented raw milk from being brought into the city's dairies. The snow-clogged streets also stopped the horse-drawn wagons from delivering bottled milk to Cleveland's homes.

Unless the big dairy companies are successful in their efforts to obtain an additional supply of milk, hundreds of babies will face privation. The reserve supply is almost exhausted.

President J. H. Coolidge of the Belle Vernon-Mapes Dairy Company . . . Tuesday abandoned all attempts to make deliveries, concentrating all efforts and the company's entire force of men, trucks and teams on trying to break through snow drifts between Cleveland and Willoughby for a fresh supply of milk.

"Our supply will last until late Tuesday. Those who want it must come for it. Babies are to be considered first and those who do not want the milk for babies are asked not to come for milk."

Cleveland News, November 11, 1913

Restoring the supply of dairy products took a herculean effort by hundreds of dairy employees. Men on horseback rode out of the city, past abandoned trucks and cars, past snowbound steam locomotives, and into the country. Only four-footed mounts were capable of moving though the mounds of drifting snow. The plan was for the riders to man-haul sleds carrying emergency supplies of milk back into the city.

Late yesterday men on horseback were sent out by the Belle Vernon company to the Belle Vernon farm at Willoughby, O., to the nursery milk farm of John Sherwin and to the Walker-Gordon certified milk farm at Novelty—all east of the city—with instructions to men in charge of the farms to bring all milk on sleds early this morning as far as Euclid Creek, Euclid Avenue, where the Belle Vernon will have trucks to haul the rest of the way. Men on the farms were instructed to take shovels with them and all the men necessary to make way through the snowdrifts.

The horseback messengers and sleds, it is thought, will aid greatly the situation today and tomorrow as to milk for babies.

. . . There was no longer much hope that trolleys would move any milk. Powerful auto trucks sent into the country early Monday by the Belle Vernon company were reported stuck in snowdrifts in the afternoon.

Cleveland Plain Dealer, NOVEMBER 11, 1913

Grace Hospital on the city's west side ran out of milk on Tuesday. An emergency request for replenishment went to C. E. Richards of Cloverdale Farms Dairy. He and an assistant chose the dairy's biggest, heaviest truck and loaded it with the precious white fluid. They started without hesitation, knowing the roads between the dairy and the hospitals were virtually impassable. The pair was not surprised when snowdrifts blocked their truck only a short distance from the dairy.

Not wanting to give up their mission, the two dairymen looked for an alternate route. There was only one open path: the Nickel Plate railroad tracks. Without hesitation the two determined men drove their big truck onto the tracks and began bumping their way down the wooden sleepers. They had not rattled any great distance when the familiar sound of a steam whistle announced that a locomotive was gaining on them. The emergency milk delivery took on the appearance of a Mack Sennett silent movie, with truck outracing train through a blizzard. Fortunately, the Lorain Avenue grade crossing appeared ahead of the frightened men, and they were able to swerve out of harm's way seconds before the locomotive snorted past. It was a close call, but there was no time to think about that. The milk still had to make its way to the hospital, which it did without further incident. In all, what was normally a short 20-minute trip from dairy to hospital required more than 2 hours of hard driving.

The Telling Brothers dairy processing plant on Cleveland's east side suspended normal operations Tuesday morning. Instead, at least two hundred employees and the company's herd of a hundred draft horses were pressed into service delivering milk to stores and homes. It took three-and four-horse teams to pull a milk wagon normally drawn by a single animal.

Wholesale deliveries of meat, fish, potatoes, onions, and other food-stuffs were also curtailed by the blizzard. "There may be a temporary shortage in some lines," said A. C. Blair, owner of a produce distribution company, "but there need be no fear of a famine." He was responding to newspaper headlines screaming that Cleveland faced a famine because of the snow. In fact, food did go into short supply for a day or two, but the city did not starve. The only commodity to disappear as a result of the blizzard was, despite the heroic efforts of the dairies, milk.

M. D. Renkenberger operated a grocery store on the city's west side. Although he was unable to get fresh stocks of meat and vegetables through his regular suppliers, he did receive an unwelcome delivery of pork and poultry. A Nickel Plate train consisting of forty cars, many loaded with chickens and hogs, struck a frozen switch on Sunday. The steam locomotive jumped its tracks and slammed into the side of Renkenberger's store. One man received a minor leg injury in the crash, and the resulting fire was quickly extinguished. The leaning locomotive was left where it landed by railroad workers, who headed for their homes in the swirling snow.

By Tuesday morning, animals trapped inside the cars of the derailed train were starving as well as freezing. A humane officer attempted to obtain chicken and hog feed to ease their suffering. He found many animals already dead from exposure and lack of food. Grain dealers refused to give the officer any animal feed on credit. The dealers demanded cash, which the man did not possess. He had been unable to telegraph for money because of the downed Western Union wires. News reports said chicken and ducks died "by the dozen" while the humane officer hag-gled with the feed companies.

Surprisingly, the price of food for people rose only slightly during the shortage caused by the blizzard. Fresh eggs disappeared, but storage eggs were a penny or two more expensive, at 37 to 40 cents a dozen. Tomatoes went up 5 cents a pound, and cabbage advanced a penny. Potatoes remained plentiful at $1.20 a bushel. The Nickel Plate derailment at Renkenberger's store was typical of problems the railroads faced battling ice and snow on their tracks. Grocery prices continued upward until the trains were able to resume regular service late on Wednesday.

Homer McDaniel, manager of Cleveland's Sheriff Street Market, said that the lack of fresh meat would not be noticed until the existing three-day supply was exhausted. He also said there was an adequate supply of butter, eggs, and cheese because these items had been stored in large amounts. According to the *Cleveland Plain Dealer*, he predicted a "famine in green things," however, until normal deliveries resumed.

Other than milk, the chief shortages were of bread and other baked goods. Not only did bakers have difficulty receiving new supplies, but their electric mixing equipment was useless during the massive power outages. Bakers were forced to knead and mix their dough by hand, a tedious process that severely limited production. There was plenty of natural gas to heat bakery ovens, but bread fresh from the oven faced the same delivery problems as milk. The Speck Bakery resorted to pulling its wagons through the snow with four horses instead of one. Grocers in the suburb of Newburg refused to sell more than one loaf of bread per customer.

Although marooned in their Forest Hill estate on the city's east side, John D. Rockefeller's family was not forced to change their diet. The farm behind the mansion provided an uninterrupted supply of food. "Chickens and fresh cream were just as plentiful on the oil magnate's table Wednesday as before the storm," reported the *Cleveland News*. "The miles of roadways through the estate were well shoveled. . . . Telephone and telegraph communication at the Rockefeller home was unbroken."

Cleveland had a highly efficient street railway system in 1913. Streetcars were the primary means of transportation for workers, shoppers, and even young couples heading to the nickelodeon. Trolleys were scheduled to run day and night, seven days a week. As a result, many traction cars were making normal rounds on Sunday evening when the blizzard began to clog city streets. Streetcars lacked the power to push through the snowdrifts, but bigger problems resulted when the overhead catenary power wires began falling in a shower of sparks. Blocked by snow and fallen utility poles and deprived of electric power, Cleveland's famed streetcars rumbled to a halt.

> Crews of a cluster of Detroit-av [sic] cars stalled at Detroit-av and W. 38th-st. have built rude bunks out of boards in one of the cars and are living there waiting for the street gang to dig them out of the snow.
>
> Crews of all cars stalled along their lines are sticking by their cars, getting what sleep they can on the seats at night.
>
> *Cleveland Press*, NOVEMBER 11, 1913

Another news story reported that a half-dozen "elderly" women were trapped in one of the stalled cars on the city's west side. J. B. Merriman realized they might not survive long in the cold and wind, so he took action. One at a time he gently lifted the women to the back of his horse and carried them to the warmth of his home. In addition, he brought lunches back to those younger passengers who remained in the cold streetcar.

Of the 1,200 employees at the Winton Motorcar Company, fewer than 500 were able to struggle through the plant gate on Monday. That was not enough workers to operate the assembly line, so Winton shut down for the day. Only the American Steel & Wire Company's central works operated at full capacity on Monday. All other Cleveland steel mills were virtually out of production due to shortages of both workers and fuel. "The supply of factory coal is always low until just before navigation closes. The coal now on hand must be used to heat plants and keep our pumps in service," said one wire company official.

But thousands of hourly workers walked to their jobs through the snow because staying home was unthinkable. They needed eight hours of pay every day to meet their family bills. In 1913, workers were paid only for the hours they actually worked. Time lost to the storm came at a worker's expense. Anyone not showing up at work was docked a day's pay. Union officials estimated that hourly workers in Cleveland lost at least $200,000 in wages as a result of the storm. All outside construction jobs were halted Monday, and P. J. Smith, head of the Structural Ironworkers Union, estimated the one-day loss in wages to his members at $20,000 (about $250,000 in 2002).

Cleveland's normally bustling downtown was deserted Monday and

Tuesday as the storm howled around Public Square. The bronze statues on the Soldier's and Sailor's Monument seemed to shiver in the swirling snow. The city's major department stores tried to open Monday morning but were forced to close at noon by the combined lack of employees and absence of customers. One enterprising advertising executive for the Halle Brothers department store placed newspaper ads Tuesday morning that promoted shopping by telephone during the blizzard. Unfortunately, a large number of Halle's customers were without phone service to call in orders.

While most retailers simply never opened during the worst hours of the storm, shoe stores were crowded. People eagerly sought to purchase boots, overshoes, galoshes, or any other protective footwear. One store sold three hundred pairs of rubber overshoes and twenty-five pairs of boots before the lunch hour Monday. The May Company department store saw another opportunity in the blizzard: snow shovels—"all kinds and sizes." Prices ranged from 95 cents for the best shovel with a veneered wooden handle to 59 cents for a galvanized iron "snow plow." The Brothers Opper stores advertised fur and seal caps ranging in price from $2 to $20. Bailey's Department Store trotted out cotton, wool, and fleece blankets.

More than 1,500 Cleveland streetcar employees were pressed into overtime service on Monday clearing the tracks. Many worked into the evening and through the night. By Tuesday morning they had fourteen lines back in service, with only two additional main lines remaining to be cleared. No attempt was made to restore suburban service until later in the week. The immediate goal was to get the streetcars running in the central city. At first, only individual self-propelled motorcars were sent on the various trolley routes. Later, when it was certain the tracks were clear, nonpowered trailer cars were hitched up to create the familiar two-car streetcar trains that were a Cleveland trademark.

The city's streetcars were running again several days before all of the sidewalks could be cleared of snow and ice. People who normally walked a few blocks to work or who walked daily to the neighborhood store found their footpaths blocked. The only solution was to climb aboard a streetcar, even for journeys as short as a block or two. "All the big lines. . .were swamped with people Tuesday morning," reported the *Cleveland News*. "Thousands walked great distances to get to the lines where there was service. As a result, from 50 to 100 people were waiting at every corner for downtown cars. . . . There were many mad scrambles to get aboard."

Just getting the trolley lines back in service did not end the traction company's problems. Blowing wind kept creating new drifts and knocking down the restored catenary wires. Nearly four hundred workers remained busy around the clock through Thursday morning making sure the city's streetcar lines kept rolling. "I've been spending money today like a sailor," Cleveland Railway Company president John J. Stanley joked sarcastically. He estimated the streetcars lost $10,000 in revenue on Monday. Cleanup and restoration of service would add another $30,000 to the cost of the storm. "I guess it will be all right," he told the *Cleveland Plain Dealer*, "even if Pete Witt isn't here."

"Pete" was Peter Witt, Cleveland's street railway commissioner. His name has been immortalized in the "Peter Witt Car," which was the standard design for U.S. trolley cars for half a century. A minor irony of the White Hurricane was that Peter Witt was vacationing on Middle Bass Island in western Lake Erie when the storm struck. High winds and waves kept him marooned on that island during the worst disaster in his streetcar line's history.

The cost of getting Cleveland's streetcars rolling again depleted the traction company's Special Emergency Fund. This fund contained money set aside to pay for events such as cleaning up after a blizzard. Money in the fund came from the price of transfers. When the fund was considered full, the penny charge for each transfer was eliminated. This had been the situation just prior to the storm. The cost of getting the streetcars running again after the blizzard forced the company to dig into its reserves. Once again, Cleveland trolley riders had to dig pennies out of their pockets for their transfers.

Streetcars served the people living within Cleveland's incorporated area. Those who lived in outlying areas relied upon interurban trains for travel. Interurbans were little more than long-distance streetcars on rickety tracks. In 1913, it was boasted that a passenger with enough patience and transfers could go from the Atlantic Ocean to the Mississippi River via these long-distance trolley cars. Interurban lines in all directions from the city were delayed Sunday, but those approaching from the south and east were stopped in their tracks by the storm.

The record for the greatest number of trapped passengers went to an interurban inbound to Cleveland from Chardon, Ohio. More than three hundred people were aboard the four cars of that train when it became snowbound in a wooded area east of Gates Mills, Ohio, on Sunday afternoon. Although the train's exact location was known by officials, high winds and blowing snow prevented all attempts to rescue the marooned passengers. Snowdrifts up to 8 feet tall clogged not only the track but also all highways leading to the train.

"No opportunity to reach them with food or drink has existed," said the *Cleveland News* on Tuesday morning. By that time, the passengers had been trapped for more than 30 hours. "The cars are undoubtedly like refrigerators, as means of heating them would be exhausted in a short time after they stalled," the paper concluded.

Male passengers on one interurban car inbound to Cleveland were forced to stand all Sunday night. Their crowded interurban became snowbound just west of Cleveland near Berea, Ohio. The Cleveland & Southwestern Traction Company hired every available man on Tuesday to shovel snow from the tracks. The flimsy wood and sheet metal sides of the car did almost nothing to prevent the passengers from freezing. Early on Monday the cold and tired riders were taken to downtown Berea, Ohio, where they found warmth and shelter in hotels and residences. Feeding the stranded passengers exhausted the town's meager supply of bread.

About 35 miles west of Cleveland, a Toledo-area football team found it could not make yardage against the storm. The gridders were snowbound for 18 hours in a Lake Shore Electric car stalled within "a few feet" of Lake Erie near Vermilion, Ohio. The car wedged itself into a snowdrift, where it spent Sunday night unable to move. Fortunately, the football team carried blankets normally used to warm themselves on the sidelines of a game. The blankets were gratefully accepted by the women aboard the stalled car.

Riders in the stalled car slept all night to the sound of Lake Erie's pounding surf. In the morning a nearby farmer knocked loudly on the outside of the car. He carried an armload of sandwiches prepared by his wife, who had noticed the interurban car's predicament. The Toledo football team spent nearly 29 hours trying to get home. Their game, of course, had been cancelled due to bad weather.

Outlying routes were served by self-propelled interurban cars fitted with woefully inadequate internal combustion engines. It was expected that these puny machines would have difficulty getting through snow-drifts or that their overhead power lines might collapse. But even old-time railroad men were surprised that the blizzard proved no less vexing to powerful steam locomotives. At one point, railroad service on all lines into the city was either curtailed or completely disrupted. Not only did the lack of trains cause havoc with the city's food supply, but it also reduced incoming mail to a trickle.

"Not over 20 percent of the usual volume of mail is arriving in Cleveland," explained the city's postmaster, Ray G. Floyd, to the *Cleveland News* at the height of the storm on Monday. "Fifteen mail trains, long overdue, have been delayed on the road. There is practically nothing from the southeast. There is nothing from southern Ohio and Indiana. The office is skinned. Everything on hand has been delivered."

Coal was still king in 1913. Not only did it power factories, but coal also kept the majority of homes warm. One of Cleveland's major industries was the Iron Fireman Company, which produced automated stoking equipment for commercial and residential heating systems. When the blizzard began on Sunday there were fewer than two hundred railroad cars of coal available for domestic and factory use within the city. Once the storm blocked rail connections to the Appalachian coalfields, there was little hope of getting more.

However, there were about a thousand carloads of coal on the docks awaiting shipment by straight-deck freighters to ports on the upper lakes. Technically, this fuel was already "owned" by the people who were to receive it. City officials planned to get around this technicality by simply expropriating the industrial coal right from the docks and sending it to homes around the city for heating if the predicted "coal famine" actually materialized.

All railroads entering Cleveland were still paralyzed by the storm Tuesday. The only roads on which efforts to keep trains moving have met with any success are the Lake Shore and Nickel Plate. Other railroads answered all inquires with a vague reply that they had trains coming somewhere, but didn't know when they would arrive.

Cleveland News, November 12, 1913

Drifting snow on the rails was not the only reason that locomotives rolled to a halt during the storm. Dispatching orders necessary to prevent train collisions and other accidents depended upon a complex web of telegraph wires strung along every mile of track. This railroad network of wire was just as vulnerable to storm damage as were public telephone and telegraph wires. Wooden poles 18 inches in diameter supporting the railroad wires cracked under the combination of ice and high winds. As those wires tumbled down, railroad dispatchers lost control over their trains.

> Cleveland was almost completely isolated from the rest of the country. A few trains passed in and out of the city, but they ran many hours behind schedule and had to proceed without dispatching orders.
>
> Enginemen had to use the utmost caution to prevent not only smashes with other trains, but with poles across the tracks.
>
> . . . "Not a single train going out or coming in," was the report from the Erie passenger station last night.
>
> Tracks are snowed under and wires in bad shape.
>
> *Cleveland Plain Dealer,* NOVEMBER 11, 1913

On Sunday evening the famous *Twentieth Century Limited* passenger train managed to chug through Cleveland, heading east. This most famous of American passenger trains ran from Chicago to New York via Toledo, Cleveland, Erie, and Buffalo—all cities engulfed by the White Hurricane. Nothing more was heard from the *Limited* until Monday afternoon. The train seemed to have disappeared into thin air. In reality, it had been forced to stop somewhere east of Cleveland by blizzard conditions and snowdrifts. Downed telegraph wires prevented news of the famous train from getting back to the city.

The first passenger train into the city on Monday came from Wheeling, West Virginia, on the Wheeling & Lake Erie line. It arrived almost 90 minutes late at Canton, Ohio, which was normally about a two-hour run from Cleveland. As the train rolled northward, conditions worsened. According to newspaper reports, the train passed through drifts as tall as the engine. The single passenger locomotive was not enough, so a larger freight engine was coupled ahead of it. Another locomotive came up behind to push. Even with the motive power from three engines, progress was no faster than a man could walk.

The final obstacle was an iron bascule lift bridge over the Cuyahoga River that had been raised during the storm to permit passage of a ship. Nobody suspected that hurricane-force winds would twist its steel girders to such an extent that, once it was lowered, the tracks on land would not align with those on the bridge. Passengers could see their destination while they waited for the bridge to be inspected. If they had wanted, they could have shouted to friends awaiting their arrival at the depot on the other side of the river.

The bridge was found to be unsafe, so the locomotives began backing away and the passengers watched their destination go out of sight. Detouring a train is not a matter of backing up to the next intersection. The train needs miles of track to loop around to another bridge. It took another hour or so to find a new path to Cleveland's depot. When the passengers finally arrived on the platform, they were more than nine hours late.

A company of actors almost went hungry during its visit to Cleveland because of the White Hurricane. The cast and crew of *The Garden of Allah* had just finished playing a week in Toledo and were supposed to open in Cleveland on Monday evening. The trip from Toledo should have taken a bit more than two hours. Instead, it stretched into six as their train bulled its way through the snowdrifts along the lakeshore route. Once the train arrived in Cleveland, teams of horses were needed to drag wagonloads of scenery through the snow-filled streets. The last load did not reach the Cleveland Opera House until 5:30 P.M. on Monday, too late for the first scheduled performance.

The troupe's real problem, however, was not scenery. It needed to find special cuts of fresh meat for the non-Christian actors. According to press reports, "Mohammedan religious beliefs forbid the Arabs from eating any food other than mutton and rice." Contracts with local theaters required that these items be supplied daily. So, at the request of the Cleveland impresario, teamster Charles Read went to the stockyards on West 65th Street Sunday afternoon to load six fat sheep. He hauled the squirming animals in a stake wagon to Union Depot, where he patiently waited for the theatrical company. Read did not know the Arab actors had been delayed in the blizzard. According to news accounts, at about 8 P.M. Read became concerned for his draft horse, which was suffering in the cold and snow.

Read started back for the barn with the six wooly animals. Half way up the slippery slope of W 3d-st, Read looked back into the wagon.

Three of the sheep were missing.

The driver threw the reins over the horse's back, and jumped from the wagon just in time to see three short wooly tails disappear around one of the bends in the street.

A strong blast of wind sent Read's hat rolling. The horse began to rear and started up the hill.

Sheep, horse, and hat all were going at the same time in different directions. Read paused a moment, then ran to his wagon and drove on.

Three sheep in the wagon were better than three sheep and a hat driven at the will of the storm, Read thought, as he bent his uncovered head to the wind.

Cleveland Plain Dealer, NOVEMBER 10, 1913

The Mohammedan actors were only slightly more discomforted by the storm than the rest of the city's inhabitants. Nearly everyone in Cleveland was forced to do without something during the storm. Children had to forgo their milk. Adults found green vegetables had disappeared from their tables. Bread was scarce for everyone. Despite these shortages, the predicted famine never materialized. By Thursday the streetcars had returned to almost their normal schedules, and milk deliveries were getting caught up.

The blizzard was still at its peak when weather observer Alexander began to think more about the storm's aftermath than the current speed of the wind. Once the telegraph wires were repaired, he received weather predictions from Washington that called for a rapid rise in temperature. A quick thaw triggered unpleasant memories of the 1913 spring floods, when raging floodwaters destroyed Ohio's canal system and put communities from Lake Erie to the Ohio River under water. Fears of a reprise of that flooding were quelled on Thursday when the city's forecaster confidently predicted there would be no runoff. "There is practically no danger of flood in the melting of the heavy snow," Alexander told *Cleveland Plain Dealer* reporters. "The ground, warm and soft before the snow arrived, has not frozen and will absorb the water almost as quickly as the snow melts." Fortunately, his prediction was correct. There was no flooding after the storm.

All of Cleveland's streetcar lines were running by Thursday morning, when Cleveland's schools opened for the first time since the previous Friday. Interurban service was also back to normal on all lines except those heading east from Cleveland along the lakeshore. Railroads once again were able to run all freight and passenger trains on schedule. Electric and telephone service was slowly being restored, although replacing poles and stringing new wires took longer than shoveling snow off tracks. By Thursday workers were back at their jobs in factories and homemakers were restocking their iceboxes with milk and other perishables. The rush for boots and galoshes was over.

The White Hurricane altered Cleveland's appearance forever. Utility poles stacked with crossarms full of electric, telephone, and telegraph wire had been symbols of technological progress during the first decade of the twentieth century. The fragility of those poles had proven to be a major problem when they snapped by the thousands in the sleet, snow, and wind. Pieces of broken poles disrupted more than just utility service. Broken poles lying across railroad and interurban lines were the cause of more transportation problems than snowdrifts were.

Snow was still swirling on Monday when city councilman John Andrews offered a resolution to put Cleveland's electric and telephone wires underground. He proposed that the city install "tubes" beneath major streets. These tubes would be rented to the electric, telephone, and telegraph companies for their wires and cables. Cleveland's constructing engineer, F. W. Ballard, improved the idea by suggesting that the tubes be installed in tunnels large enough for city crews to work standing upright.

Cleveland's campaign to put utility wires underground could not be completed in a single year. It took half a decade. But the prestorm forest of utility poles and wires never reappeared in the downtown area. Modernization of Cleveland's telephone and electric cables dates from the period immediately following the 1913 White Hurricane.

TUESDAY, NOVEMBER 11

BY MIDMORNING TUESDAY the storm was moving rapidly away through eastern Canada, losing power as it traveled overland, unable to tap the still-warm waters of the lakes to replenish the energy it had expended. The once-deadly storm was just another November gale as it moved toward Canada's capital city, Ottawa, but it was still dangerous. Ottawa received a heavy fall of snow, though nothing like what Cleveland experienced—in part because the storm was moving more quickly and in part due to the absence of lake-effect snow. All day Monday and well into Tuesday snow and high winds stopped all shipping on the St. Lawrence River around Montréal, Québec. One vessel sank on the St. Lawrence in the aftermath of the storm, although its loss may not have been weather related.

Lake Superior had been the first lake affected by the weather events already being collectively termed the White Hurricane, and it was the first lake on which conditions began returning to normal. That process started on Monday while the southern lakes were still in the grip of snow and hurricane-force winds. At 8:40 A.M. Monday, weather observer P. J. Johnson measured the wind in Marquette, Michigan, at 48 miles per hour out of the northwest, suggesting that out on the water it might still have been gusting over 60 miles per hour. But gusts began decreasing during the noon hour, and by evening the wind at Marquette was below 20 miles per hour. Only the bitter cold remained. Johnson calculated the mean temperature for Marquette that day at 23 degrees, some 11 degrees lower than normal.

Improving weather on the Great Lakes revealed the magnitude of the disaster. Scores of frozen bodies washed onto the beaches of southeastern Lake Huron. They were found both huddled together and alone. Some appeared to have struggled, while others were composed and serene. From Cape Ipperwash to Grand Bend, Bayfield, and beyond, the beach held one gruesome discovery after another. Sometimes, a stretch of beach would be cleared of bodies only to have new ones appear as the waves brought them to shore.

Wreckage was everywhere. Pieces of broken cabins and superstructure were found strewn on the beach. Occasionally a lifeboat, liferaft, or life ring would float ashore, and with it would come confirmation of the loss of another freighter. Ketchup bottles from a crew's mess were mixed in with broken crates from package freighter cargo. Broken oars landed in heaps with unrecognizable scraps of ships. News reporters who viewed the scene groped for adjectives to describe the magnitude of the disaster. Words did not seem adequate. The first news bulletins claimed twenty ships were missing. When the truth was known, the toll would be far worse than anyone could imagine.

Lake Superior — Keweenaw Peninsula
L.C. WALDO *and* LIFESAVING SERVICE RESCUE BOATS

Darkness still covered Lake Superior during the very early hours of Tuesday as two ice-covered, motorized lifeboats finally approached the broken wreck of the *L.C. Waldo*. Although each boat had come from a different lifesaving station, the two arrived on scene almost simultaneously, just after 3 A.M. They saw a silent hulk encased in ice. There were no signs of life. Shouts of the rescuers came back as hollow echoes from the cold steel wreck. They saw only the ice-covered boilerhouse and the crumpled remains of the pilothouse.

As the rescue boats circled the hulk they noticed that the crack in the deck had been accentuated by an awkward, unnatural bend amidships. They could read the name now, *L.C. Waldo*. At least the fate of that ship was no longer a mystery. Men in the boats thought back to the horrible stories surrounding the loss of the *Mataafa* off Duluth eight years earlier. That ship had been half awash through a gale, just like this one. The men of the *Mataafa* were found frozen in place where they died, some encased in ice so thick it had to be chipped from the deck. Would rescuers find the same here? It appeared the three-day rescue effort involving boats from two lifesaving service stations had arrived too late.

Suddenly, a voice from within the ice-covered bow shouted, "Ahoy!"

Through an opening in the forecastle rescuers got a peek at grizzled faces staring out from the smoky interior. The voice shouted down to the rescuers that the *Waldo* survivors were locked into their steel prison by a coating of ice on the broken hulk. It took several minutes for a group of sailors to first break themselves out of the windlass room and then smash the ice off the doors to free the rest of the crew. In the meantime, the two rescue boats waited patiently while spray built layers of ice on the wet clothes of the lifesavers.

As the ice fell away and the door to the windlass room swung open, the men in the lifeboats began hearing voices, lots of voices—even women's voices. "So haggard and worn from starvation and lack of sleep that they were more dead than alive," the official report noted, "and their faces were ghostly white from frostbite." At that instant, there was no happier place anywhere on earth than the ice-covered deck of the *L.C. Waldo*. Everyone was alive.

Joy quickly turned to concern. Finding the survivors was one thing. It was quite another to get them into the motorized lifeboats and then transport them to safety on the tugboat waiting offshore. Ferrying the *Waldo's* crew took two more hours. The motorboats had to bash through sloppy waves left over from the gale. Thomas McCormick was in charge of the Portage Station boat. "Part of the *Waldo's* crew was taken on board by means of a rope ladder. Others leaped from the deck. Ten men were taken into our boat without serious accident," he wrote in his official report. "The rest, including the two women, were taken into the boat from Eagle Harbor."

Once in the lifeboats, the survivors gratefully wrapped themselves in blankets for the short trip through the Lake Superior surf. "They were all nearly frozen. Some had towels wrapped around their heads and some were wearing mittens. Most had neither. We put our mackinaws and caps on them until we managed to get them to the tug," said surfman A. F. Glaza, who was part of the Eagle Harbor crew. "The women cried for joy when we wrapped them in blankets."

The tug *Hebard*, under the command of Bert Nelson, had towed the Portage Station lifeboat the last few miles to the scene. Now, the tug became a safe haven for the *Waldo's* hungry, tired, and half-frozen crew. The cook went to work turning a crate of eggs and 100 pounds of ham into breakfast for the survivors. (Special provisions had been carried for this purpose.) A few of the *Waldo*'s crew were too weak to eat, but most of them "crammed food into their mouths like cannibals," recounted one crewmember.

Despite being castaways in a blizzard for almost 90 hours, no one suffered lasting injuries. Seventy-year-old Captain Duddleson summed up their common ordeal by saying, "It's the closest call I ever had in all my life." Duddleson and others were packed onto a passenger train for Cleveland, Ohio, where they were, in nautical parlance, "paid off." Their wages were paid by the lost ship's namesake and owner, L. C. Waldo himself. A news conference of sorts was held in the law offices of Harvey W. Brown & Company.

> The two women . . . had words of praise for the conduct of the crew during the time of the wreck. The crew spoke of the bravery of the two women. All had only the highest praise for the lifesavers who rescued them, for those aboard the tug *Hebard* of Houghton, Michigan.
>
> Her deck buckled, the battered and broken *L.C. Waldo* still lies on the ridge at Gull rock, a bit of evidence mutely testifying to a small part of what happened in the worst storm in the history of—navigation on the Great Lakes.
>
> *Cleveland Plain Dealer*, NOVEMBER 14, 1913

Lake Superior — Copper Harbor, Michigan
TURRET CHIEF

While the crew of the *Waldo* was gobbling down ham and eggs, the lifesaver crews were bashing their way back to their respective stations through a still-angry Lake Superior. Now that it was daylight, the Eagle Harbor crew could see the hulk of the *Turret Chief* with its nose smashed into the Keweenaw. They had passed the ship in the darkness without realizing it was there. Although cold and tired, the lifesavers recognized their duty. They went back to work, searching the wreck for survivors. They found none, because the crew by now had abandoned its rude hut and was struggling inland, searching for warmth and food. The lifesavers beached their boat to examine the wreck before resuming the long, wet, cold journey back to their station.

Lake Superior ── Point Iroquois, Michigan
J.T. HUTCHINSON *and* F.G. HARTWELL

Also in the small, dark hours of Tuesday morning Captain Yacques found himself past the point of feeling tired as he guided the *J.T. Hutchinson* down Lake Superior. He was working through numbing fatigue that dulled his senses and slowed his thinking. The anchorage at Whitefish Bay was just ahead. He had promised his crew a good night's sleep after the ship was safely anchored, but that promise was not to be fulfilled. Perhaps it was fatigue, or it could have been a navigation error caused by the rough seas. Whatever the cause, a sickening lurch told Captain Yacques and all the other weary sailors that their ship had gone aground on the rocks off Point Iroquois.

"We have all done our best," Yacques wrote to his wife. "We have not any thought of losing out, within half a mile of good dry land. We can't launch any of our lifeboats—too much sea running."

Normally, a captain would have ruined his career if he allowed his ship to ground on well-known shoals. But the fierceness of this storm coupled with its duration created an alternate reality for tired sailors and for ship owners. More than one captain lost his way after 24 to 36 hours of fighting the White Hurricane. Landmarks were obliterated by blizzard snow. Men in the pilothouses did the best they could, but success or failure was more a matter of chance than skill.

The steamer *F.G. Hartwell* also crashed onto the rocks off Point Iroquois. The two stranded ships were discovered by Captain Wheeler of the revenue cutter *Mackinac*. "We found the *Hutchinson* and the *Hartwell* hard aground. The bottoms of both steamers were badly torn by the big boulders which lay along the shores. The *Hutchinson* lay above the point while the *Hartwell* lay below. The first thing the masters asked was, 'Have you anything to eat? We're all out.' The *Hartwell*'s crew was worn and tired. The big steamer lay on her side with a heavy list to port."

Lake Superior ── Marquette, Michigan
HENRY B. SMITH

On Tuesday the *Henry B. Smith* was officially listed as "overdue." Nothing had been seen of it since Sunday afternoon, when the ship had departed

Marquette harbor with its hatches only partially secured. Captain Jimmy Owen and his beloved ship had simply sailed away. Some said the *H.B. Smith* went as far as Standard Rock before foundering. Other local observers thought the vessel came to grief in deep water just off Marquette harbor. Nobody knew for certain what had happened to the *H.B. Smith* and its crew of twenty-five men.

The *H.B. Smith* was owned by two brothers, W. A. and A. H. Hawgood, of Cleveland. Worried over the fate of their vessel, the brothers began sending a stream of telegrams seeking news of their missing ship. Hope was dashed on Tuesday when what appeared to be a lifeless member of the *H.B. Smith*'s crew and pieces of wooden wreckage were spotted floating on Lake Superior.

Any doubt over the fate of the ship ended when lumberman Dan Johnston came across parts of a cabin, a broken lifeboat, and other debris from the *H.B. Smith* on Shot Point, about 13 miles east of Marquette. He walked a mile in either direction from the wreckage but could find no bodies. It was speculated—but never proven—that Jimmy Owen and his ship disappeared sometime Sunday night at the height of the storm. All that is known for certain is that no one else ever took command of Jimmy Owen's ship.

A⊤ 6:30 P.M. ON TUESDAY EVENING, weather observer P. E. Johnson in Marquette, Michigan, noticed a halo around the moon. Although he was paid to do scientific observations, he could not help recalling the folklore concerning such halos. Was more foul weather on the way?

Lake Superior — Angus Island
LEAFIELD

Ship captains on Lake Superior were asked to be on the lookout for wreckage or bodies from the steamer *Leafield*. That ship was known to have been aground on Angus Island near Thunder Cape during the height of the storm. Now, as the waves abated, there was no sign of the unlucky vessel. Most people believed that the storm had pulled the *Leafield* back off the rocks. If that happened, it was surmised that the cargo of steel railroad rails would have caused the vessel to founder almost instantly. All hope was abandoned for the fifteen-man crew.

The grounding of the *Leafield* was not a first-time event for the Canadian ship. In August 1912, the hapless vessel had run onto heavily wooded Beausoliel Island, inside Lake Huron's Georgian Bay. The ship's bottom had been heavily damaged, and the *Leafield* had come to rest on the bottom. It was refloated and repairs were made during the previous winter, and the ship had been placed back into service.

Lake Superior — Apostle Islands
WILLIAM NOTTINGHAM

Off Sand Island, near Bayfield, Wisconsin, the location of the steamer *Nottingham* was never in any doubt: it remained hard aground. News reports claimed the ship's bottom was "gone," but enough of the vessel remained intact to shelter those members of the crew who had remained on board. In the end, everyone who stayed aboard the *Nottingham* survived. The only deaths were the three men lost on Monday during an abortive attempt to launch a lifeboat. During their ordeal, the remaining members of the crew kept warm by firing the ship's boilers with wheat taken from the cargo hold. Although the *Nottingham* was visibly buckled amidships, it was successfully removed from the reef and towed to Toledo, where it took a winter's worth of work by shipfitters to make it seaworthy again.

Lake Superior — Whitefish Bay
HURONIC *and* MARSHALL F. BUTTERS

Another steamer, the *Huronic*, arrived safely in Sault Ste. Marie after being aground for two days in Whitefish Bay. This Canadian-built passenger ship had the good fortune to strike on a sandy bar rather than a rocky reef. The ship's bottom had been largely undamaged by the accident, and none of the passengers or crew were injured during their frightening adventure.

The largest lumber carrier on the Great Lakes, the steam barge *Marshall F. Butters*, was more than two days overdue on Lake Superior. The best guess, reported in the November 12, 1913, *Port Huron Times-Herald*, was that the wooden vessel had foundered with its crew of twenty men. The *Butters*, however, would be one of the few derelict stories with a happy ending. The ship survived the storm and sailed for three more seasons before coming to grief off Kelleys Island in Lake Erie.

Sault Ste. Marie — Soo Locks
GEORGE C. CRAWFORD

Captain Walter C. Iler knew his ship, the *George C. Crawford*, had taken a terrible beating on Lake Huron during the worst hours of the White Hurricane. Perhaps it was fortunate that darkness and the ship's covering of ice prevented anyone in the crew from learning the truth. The *Crawford* had almost crumpled in the storm like the *Argus*, the ship they had seen collapse and sink in front of their eyes, but this startling fact was not revealed until after the *Crawford* left Lake Huron and began steaming up the protected St. Marys River.

Calm conditions on the river allowed men to use steam hoses to melt tons of ice off the ship's decks. As the ice disappeared, the crew began discovering missing rivets in the *Crawford's* deck plates. Hundreds had apparently sheared and were now missing. Even more disconcerting were the cracks that traced their way across several of the ship's inch-thick steel deck plates. The crew marveled at their amazing good luck. The *Crawford* had survived the storm, but barely. Perhaps one more sea sweeping over the deck would have caused it to collapse and disappear like the *Argus*. Nobody wanted to think much about that possibility.

From passage records published in newspapers, it appears the *Crawford* did not complete its last voyage of 1913. Instead, it seems to have turned around and headed back down Lake Huron for the shipyard at Toledo, Ohio. It took most of the following winter for shipbuilders to replace the cracked plates and missing rivets. As a result, the ship came out in the spring of 1914 somewhat stronger than it had been when it steamed through the worst storm in Great Lakes history.

Lake Michigan — Menominee, Michigan
JAMES H. MARTIN *and* PLYMOUTH (BARGE)

There was surprise in Menominee, Michigan, on the shore of Green Bay, when the tug *James H. Martin* appeared in the harbor battered and almost sinking. All nine men aboard were safe. They were treated like men raised from the dead because both their tug and its barge, the *Plymouth*, had been thought lost at the height of the gale. Captain Louis Stetunsky related a tale of horror that had begun the previous Thursday as an ordinary trip from Menominee. The tug and its tow were bound for Search Bay, on Lake Huron, when the storm caught them.

By Saturday morning, it became obvious that the tug and barge could not make headway against the building storm. Tug captain Stetunsky first tried to anchor both vessels in the lee of St. Martins Island, at the mouth of Green Bay. When that proved unsatisfactory, he took the barge to a better anchorage off Gull Island. Once the barge seemed to be riding comfortably, the tug sought better refuge in Summer Island passage. Captain Stetunsky said that when he went back to pick up the *Plymouth*, there was no sign of the barge or its seven-man crew.

The captain was not casting the barge to its fate. His tug simply did not have the power to fight the storm while towing the barge. Both would certainly have foundered had they remained connected. Even without the barge, the battered *James H. Martin* barely survived.

No trace of the barge was found, but bits and pieces of wreckage were discovered floating on Lake Huron. Eleven days after the barge disappeared, a message was discovered in a bottle. The following words were written on the letterhead from a Menominee company and signed by Chris Keenan, a federal marshal who had been in charge of the *Plymouth*:

> Dear wife and Children. We were left up here in Lake Michigan by McKinnon, captain *James H. Martin* tug, at anchor. He went away and never said goodbye or anything to us. Lost one man yesterday. We have been out in storm forty hours. Goodbye dear ones, I might see you in Heaven. Pray for me.
>
> Chris K.
>
> P.S. I felt so bad I had another man write for me. Goodbye Forever.
>
> *Cleveland Plain Dealer*, NOVEMBER 13, 1913

Although it was in another man's hand and certain details were fuzzy, the validity of this message has never been questioned. The wording makes it plain that the crew of the *Plymouth* felt abandoned to their fate by the tugboat. The loss of one crewmember prior to the barge's foundering indicates it took quite a pounding before succumbing to the waves. The body of Chris Keenan was found on the shore of Lake Michigan later that month.

Lake Huron — Point Aux Barques, Michigan
MATOA

Tuesday morning the men of the Point Aux Barques Lifesaving Station managed to repair the storm damage to their equipment enough to launch their motorized lifeboat and head for the battered hulk of the *Matoa*. That ship was still hard aground almost two miles offshore from their station. While the lake was no longer experiencing storm conditions, the seas were far from calm as the fragile wooden lapstrake rescue boat pulled alongside the steel bow of the broken freighter. The crew of the *Matoa* looked down at the surfboat and to a man decided they were better off where they were than in that cockleshell. "No thanks" was the unanimous response to offers of rescue from the lifesavers. Instead of going ashore himself, Captain McLeod sent a request for the salvage tug *Favorite*. The men in the lifeboat agreed to the request and headed back to their station.

Lake Huron — Port Austin, Michigan
HOWARD M. HANNA JR.

At dawn Tuesday on Lake Huron, rescuers from Port Austin launched their hastily patched surfboat in yet another effort to reach the sailors trapped aboard the wrecked *Howard M. Hanna Jr.* Almost at the same time, one of the *Hanna's* mates and several other members of the crew cleared their ship's port lifeboat from the wreckage on top of the boilerhouse. Nine men began rowing ashore to seek help for the rest of the crew, who remained aboard. The *Hanna's* lifeboat passed the outbound Lifesaving Service surfboat at midmorning.

Sadie Black, the wife of the *Hanna's* steward, struggled in the ship's nearly demolished galley throughout the ordeal, fixing potluck meals for her fellow survivors. She did not stop even when for a time waves filled her work area almost waist deep with freezing water. For better traction on the wet deck she toiled barefoot, wearing a woolen skirt and pea jacket. "Mrs. Black was the only cool one on the vessel after it went on the reef," said boatswain Arthur Jacobs. Throughout, Sadie encouraged and nursed the men. After their rescue, the male members of the crew claimed they were sure she never slept until their rescue.

"When it came time for us to leave the ship and get into the lifesavers' boat, Mrs. Black refused the courtesies extended to a woman in the time of danger at sea," said Jacobs (*Cleveland Plain Dealer*). "She took her turn in the order of her position and went over the side clad in the fireman's heavy shoes, and with all the earmarks of a real sailor."

The hasty repair job on the Port Austin surfboat was not adequate to face the sloppy waves on Lake Huron. Water began welling up inside the frail wooden craft even before the first *Hanna* survivor managed to climb down the side of the ship. Continuous bailing gave the surfboat crew enough time to run their boat onto the sandy beach before it sank. There was no time to make any new repairs, so the battered and patched boat was bailed and the rescuers set out for the wrecked steamer once again. This time, their leaking surfboat nearly sank before it reached the *Hanna*. Only by hoisting sail were they able to return to shore fast enough not to sink with the last of the stricken ship's crew.

As a result of her efforts to feed the castaways, Sadie suffered from hypothermia, a lowering of the body's core temperature. The *Hanna's* crew had become concerned that Sadie might not survive long enough to be rescued, which is one reason they wanted her among the first taken to safety. Immediately after everyone came ashore the crew took up a small collection for her benefit.

Lake Huron — Harbor Beach, Michigan
ARTHUR (BARGE)

Barges and small steamers were strewn about the shore at Harbor Beach, Michigan. Normally, the port offered a protected harbor for its fleet, but not during the White Hurricane. Storm waves had roared over the protective breakwater. The resulting surge inside the harbor tore vessels loose from their moorings. For the crew of the barge *Arthur*, however, their vessel being driven ashore was not the worst news. A member of the *Arthur's* crew, Thomas Porter, had been helping double the ship's docklines at 1 P.M. on Sunday afternoon. High winds simply lifted him off the pier and dropped him in the angry water. He had not been seen since and was presumed drowned.

Storm waves nearly destroyed the seawall. Four small steamers, the *M. Sicken*, *Rhoda Emily*, *Wyoming*, and *Edward Buckley*, were all deposited on shore alongside the *Arthur*. It was estimated that $25,000 worth of damage (in 1913 dollars) had been done to buildings and docks in the small port town. Several commercial fishermen lost their boats, nets, fish sheds, and homes as well.

Lake Huron——Port Franks, Ontario
NORTHERN QUEEN

The crew of the *Northern Queen* finally came ashore through the pounding surf on Tuesday, having survived in the bow of their wrecked vessel since its stranding Monday evening. By morning their ship was nearly pounded to pieces, and the survivors had to leave the wreck before it was totally destroyed. They gingerly hoisted a lifeboat and lowered it into the pounding surf, using great care to prevent the boat from being dashed to pieces against the ship's steel hull. Ten frightened men pulled on the oars as the boat inched its way toward the Canadian beach on southeastern Lake Huron. They timed their approach to ride the back of a swell as far ashore as it would take them. Men who had been watching from shore rushed into the near-freezing surf to pull the tiny boat safely beyond reach of the waves.

Two of the lifeboat's crew refused to stay on shore. They asked the crowd to help push their tiny craft back into the surf to get the rest of the crew from the *Northern Queen*. Things did not go as planned.

> They started out but when some distance from the shore a heavy sea capsized the lifeboat and they were seen struggling in the heavy surf. Women turned their heads and men snapped their jaws. Finally one of the sailors was seen a little ahead of the other. The second man was in distress. The man in the lead turned back and locking hands with his sinking companion they made their second fight for life. Slowly they neared the shore and men ran into the surf and brought them safely to land.
>
> *Port Huron Times-Herald*, NOVEMBER 11, 1913

When the first lifeboat capsized in the surf, the dozen men remaining on the *Northern Queen* thought it had been destroyed. They decided their only salvation lay in launching the ship's second boat and rescuing themselves. Nine sailors climbed into the frail craft and began the long pull to shore. Captain Crawford and two of his mates remained on the crumbling ship until after 8 P.M., when they were taken off by a return trip of the second lifeboat. Despite the capsize of the first boat, all members of the crew were landed safely.

Lake Huron — Port Franks, Ontario

SAILORS ON THE BEACH

Dozens of other sailors also returned to shore on Tuesday, but under less happy circumstances. Frozen bodies began rolling onto the cold sand of the beach near Port Franks. The first lifeless sailors were discovered at noon on Tuesday. As was the custom in those days, a local physician, Dr. C. Clerk, was called to examine them. The men were obviously sailors from some lost ship. The doctor realized these unfortunate victims would not have been alone in the storm. There must be other sailors farther up or down the beach. Dr. Clerk enlisted the help of J. B. Woodhall, the local coroner, and undertaker William Jennings to organize a systematic search of the Canadian shoreline. Before the day was over they had collected ten bodies within a five-mile radius of Port Franks. Mixed among the human debris were bales of hay, broken crates of Canadian canned goods and other packaged freight.

> The bodies were scattered and some of them were high on the beach while others were still lying in the water. Life belts encircled the dead men and from their drawn faces and cramped bodies it was evident that they had made a gallant fight before giving up.
>
> Port Huron Times-Herald, NOVEMBER 12, 1913

Any mystery over the origin of the dead sailors seemed to end when one of the searchers found a lifeboat lying partly on its side. Clearly visible on its bow was the name "Regina." The lifeboat's rudder was found a bit farther down the beach along with several oars. This equipment was also stamped "Regina." As beach patrols ended at dark on Tuesday, it seemed to searchers that only the remains of a single wreck had come ashore. Several days would pass before they learned the full magnitude of the destruction that had occurred just a few miles offshore.

Coroner Woodhall began the grim business of identifying the dead men. Their frozen bodies were placed on the floor of a makeshift morgue created in the back of a Thedford, Ontario, furniture store. Woodhall searched through the contents of their pockets looking for clues, but he found little beyond a few coins. Only one body found on the beach had positive proof of its identity.

Wheelsman Walter McInnes carried a letter from his mother in Owen Sound, Ontario. According to press accounts, the sailor's mother had appealed to him to be a "good boy." Also found on the wheelsman's body was a personal diary that contained a complete accounting of money he spent on such mundane items as underwear and tobacco. Alex T. Stewart, a reporter for the *Port Huron Times-Herald*, quickly toted up the numbers. McInnes had sent his mother more than $400 during the 1913 sailing season.

Reporter Stewart then telephoned the owners of the *Regina*. He described the appearance of McInnes and several other victims over the telephone. "My God, that's them!" came the startled reply over the scratchy earpiece. "You have got them. No need of going any farther. We must get to Port Franks at once. The boat's gone."

The body of Dave Lawson was tentatively identified from a postcard in his pocket addressed to a Mr. Harry Lawson in New Brunswick, Canada. Harry was Dave's brother, so it was surmised that the dead man had written the card prior to the storm and intended to mail it at his ship's next port of call. Coroner Woodhall gently dried the soggy card before dropping it in a nearby postbox as a final favor to the drowned sailor.

While the *Regina* drama was unfolding, more bodies were discovered on the southeastern shoreline of Lake Huron. Seven dead sailors from the steamer *Charles S. Price* came ashore just south of Grand Bend, Ontario, and only a few miles north of Port Franks. Searchers who came upon them also discovered a liferaft marked with the name *Argus*. At first, no one along the Canadian shoreline recognized that ship's name. The mystery was solved when Lynn Marine Reporting Agency confirmed the *Argus* had left Port Huron just ahead of another steamer, the *John A. McGean*. Both ships were missing. Finding the liferaft confirmed the *Argus* as lost, but what of the *McGean*?

Not everyone combing the beaches on the Canadian side of Lake Huron was there on honest business. Along with the official searchers, there were looters looking for booty on the bodies of victims. News reports claimed that one dead sailor had been looted of a belt containing $800 in cash. To calm public anger over the thefts, authorities said they knew the names of the looters.

Pocket watches found on the frozen bodies of sailors killed by the storm had stopped ticking between 8 P.M. and midnight, bearing mute testimony to the deadliest period of time ever recorded on the Great Lakes—four hours during which eight modern steel ships foundered on Lake Huron. Each took with it a full crew of sailors, almost two hundred souls in all. Only a handful of those unfortunate victims made it to shore, none alive. Most of the dead sailors remained with their ships on the bottom of the lake.

Lake Huron — Goderich, Ontario
JAMES CARRUTHERS, JOHN A. McGEAN, WEXFORD, *and* ARGUS

Searchers were stunned Tuesday afternoon when they discovered furniture, lifeboats, and other wreckage from the brawny 529-foot Canadian straight decker *James Carruthers* on a beach near Goderich, Ontario, 30 miles north of Grand Bend. Many Canadian sailors refused to believe that this particular ship—the strongest and newest in their fleet—had foundered, until actual pieces of identifiable wreckage came ashore. The *Carruthers* had been launched just the previous May at Collingwood, Ontario. Until the wreckage was discovered, no one doubted that Captain W. H. Wright and his crew of twenty-three men had survived the storm.

Other discoveries hinted of untold hardship. The bodies of three sailors lashed to a liferaft were found near Goderich. What were those men thinking as cold water sapped their strength? Did they expect to be found alive tied to the liferaft, or did they just want to make sure their lifeless bodies would be given proper burial ashore? The raft carrying the dead sailors bore the name *John A. McGean*, proof that this ship had also foundered. One man was identified as Thomas Stone; his brother, James, confirmed that Thomas had been among the *McGean*'s crew.

Identifying Stone was but one accomplishment in a busy day for the

Goderich coroner. Several more bodies from the *McGean* were found a short distance from the liferaft. Then came reports of a new group of bodies wearing life preservers from the steamer *Wexford*. That ship, which had been listed as "overdue," was now put into the official record as "lost" during the storm. The location of the sunken *Wexford* remained a secret for eighty-seven years, until it was discovered by sport angler Don Chalmers. He was searching for fish when his depth-sounder showed an anomaly on the bottom not far from Grand Bend, Ontario. Unlike so many other wrecks from the White Hurricane, this ship was sitting bolt upright on the bottom.

Two sister ships seemed determined to be close to each other at the end. A lifeboat from the steamer *Hydrus* washed ashore amid wreckage from its sister, the *Argus*. The two vessels had been bound for opposite ends of Lake Huron. Somehow, their paths must have nearly crossed during the most deadly hours of the storm. The two sisters must almost have been in sight of each other as each succumbed to the waves. Strapped to the seats inside a lifeboat from the *Hydrus* were five bodies—four men and one woman. One of the victims was the ship's captain, Paul Glitch. All wore life belts except the captain. The lone woman, the ship's second cook, Mrs. William Walker, was found wearing a life belt with the word *Captain* stenciled on the back.

Lake Huron — *Goderich, Ontario*
SEARCHLIGHT

Across the lake at Harbor Beach, Michigan, the storm solved a seven-year-old Lake Huron mystery. The tug *Searchlight* had disappeared without a trace in 1906 with its crew of five. This disappearance was unusual because it happened on a clear fall day and in sight of people on shore.

> The boat was heading towards the breakwater when sighted by the lookout in the tower of the life saving station. He turned away for a minute, and when he looked again the boat had disappeared. That was the last ever seen of the *Searchlight*. No trace of her was ever found.
>
> *Port Huron Times-Herald*, NOVEMBER 12, 1913

Following the storm, fishermen found a grisly discovery in their nets. It was the partially decomposed body of one of the *Searchlight's* crew. Almost simultaneously, people on shore discovered the tug's smokestack and pieces of its cabin on the beach. The whereabouts of the small vessel was now known, but one question would remain unanswered—why did it founder so suddenly in good weather?

WEDNESDAY, NOVEMBER 12

THE "UNSETTLED CONDITIONS" predicted by the Weather Bureau for Lake Superior on Wednesday consisted of westerly winds gusting into the mid-20-mile-per-hour range, then dropping in the afternoon to almost calm. Then a new wind from the south moved in, gusting into the mid-20s. Leftover storm waves were still rolling out of the northwest when the wind shift took place, and the southerly winds created new waves at an angle to the existing waves. Known as a "cross sea" by sailors, waves of this type make navigation difficult and conditions uncomfortable.

Lake Superior —— Near Whitefish Point
A.M. BYERS *rescues* MAJOR

Captain A. Craigee was summoned to the pilothouse of the *A.M. Byers* after his crew spotted another ship wallowing in Lake Superior off White-fish Point. The hulk was the 283-foot *Major*, the largest-capacity wooden vessel on the lakes. Obviously without power, it was listing heavily and appeared to be helpless in the choppy cross sea.

"They had a close call," Alex Mouck, the *Byers'* first mate, said later (*Toledo Blade*). "According to the officers and men, the seas got into the *Major's* engine room, put out the fires, and with insufficient steam the men were unable to control the vessel, which was being pounded by the seas."

The cargo of loose coal in the *Major's* hold had already shifted to one side by the time the *Byers* happened along, which explained the derelict's list. Even the machinery in the engine room was starting to come loose as the hulk rolled violently. Sailors moving about on the decks of the waterlogged ship were in danger and could not remain aboard. Captain Craigee knew that lower Lake Superior was still too rough to launch a lifeboat. He decided instead to use his freighter in an imaginative rescue attempt. He would put the nose of his 525-foot steel ship gently against the wooden bow of the waterlogged ship in order to take the *Major's* crew aboard.

It was an impossible thing to do. Thousands of tons of steel had to be controlled to within inches despite the wind and waves on Superior. Impossible, perhaps, but the *Byers* nudged gently against the wooden ship and men began to jump for their lives. Only one sailor from the *Major* was injured during the rescue, a cook who slipped on the rescue ship's steel deck.

One frightened member of the *Major's* crew remained in the after deck-house, watching his shipmates escape. He lacked courage to jump to the rescue ship until it was obvious that every one else had made the leap; then, throwing caution to the winds, he made a sudden dash for the bow. Lake Superior combers washed across the midsection of the *Major*, horrifying the rescuers on the *Byers* who watched green water pour over the wooden hulk. But the runner reappeared and with a flying leap landed on the steel deck, where he shook water out of his fur. Jack, the *Major's* hound mascot, had rescued himself. He was frightened, wet, and obviously suffering from canine seasickness.

Just as the wooden *Louisiana* was the storm's first victim, the wooden *Major* was its last. On the following Thursday the hulk was towed to Sault Ste. Marie, where the coal was removed from its hold. Its last battle with the sea had been too much for the ship's oak frames and pine planking. The ship was declared a total loss and sent to the breakers.

Lake Erie—*Buffalo, New York*
LIGHTSHIP 82

Reports that *Lightship 82* was missing from its station off the Buffalo harbor were passed to Inspector Roscoe House, who personally boarded the lighthouse tender *Crocus* to begin a fruitless search of Lake Erie for the lost floating beacon. His effort had barely begun when word was received that pieces of the lightship were coming ashore at the foot of Michigan Street in downtown Buffalo. The flotsam included a door and other wreckage identified as part of the lightship. One of the missing vessel's lifeboats also was recovered. A broken oar was still attached to one of the boat's oarlocks.

It was now all but certain that *Lightship 82* and its six-man crew had been claimed by the White Hurricane. Later that Wednesday Lake Erie gave up either a poignant piece of wreckage or the cruelest hoax to arise from the storm. On the beach was a broken section of cabin door with a message scrawled in crayon:

GOODBYE NELLIE, SHIP IS BREAKING UP FAST. WILLIAMS

This message appeared to be a final farewell from *Lightship 82*'s captain, Hugh M. Williams, to his wife in Manistee, Michigan. Ever since its discovery there has been controversy over the message's authenticity. Would a man about to die be inclined to sign the final message to his wife with only his last name? Married couples are generally on a first-name basis. Most curious is the use of "Nellie" for Williams' wife, whose name was Mary. A friend of the couple later claimed that he had heard Williams address his wife as "Nellie" on several occasions. Mary Williams steadfastly denied that such a thing ever occurred. She claimed her husband always used her correct first name, "Mary." Authentic or not, the scrawled message to Nellie became part of Great Lakes lore.

Lightship 82 was almost new at the time of the storm. Built of steel, it had only one flaw: a wooden superstructure. The job of lightship required that it remain anchored in an exact location to guide other mariners. As the storm built, waves undoubtedly began crashing over the top of the 150-foot lightship. The anchor chain that kept it on station would have prevented the ship's hull from rising up and over waves. Apparently, the battering of the storm was too much for the wooden superstructure, which finally collapsed. Water entered and the ship foundered. The crew of six were drowned.

Lake Huron — Port Huron, Michigan
"MYSTERY SHIP"

The thing rose out of Lake Huron like the back of a steel whale. Sailors who saw it never quite believed that such a sight was possible. Yet, it was real. Swaying in the diminishing waves Wednesday was the overturned bow of a large freighter. How did it happen? What ship was it? What about the crew? The silent black steel plates lolling in the waves gave no answers to any of these questions. Lake Huron's "mystery ship" instantly became the focus of nationwide speculation.

"How big is this mystery ship?" That question became a popular topic of conversation in beaneries around the lakes. The best clue was the depth of the water beneath the overturned bow, which was estimated to be about 60 feet. Based on that depth, most people guessed the hull had to be at least 250 feet long, with 100 feet of its upturned belly exposed. Self-proclaimed experts were quick to point out that the sunken stern of the vessel must be smashed into the mud bottom of the lake. Newspapers jumped on every new theory or speculation in a rush to satisfy the curiosity of their readers. Speculation quickly focused on events that might have caused the ship to "turn turtle."

> It is thought by some that her cargo shifted as she was caught in the trough of the sea. The bow of the boat is turned toward the north and east which also indicates that control was lost of her and that she swung around at the mercy of the mountain high waves.
>
> *Port Huron Times-Herald*, NOVEMBER 11, 1913

Captain Thomas Reid, owner of the salvage tug that had discovered the mystery ship, was eagerly sought by reporters. As an experienced salvor, he was considered an expert on shipwrecks, and it was his nature to speculate freely about marine matters such as what caused the ship to roll over. "There will be another ship on the bottom nearby," he confidently told reporters on Tuesday morning. He theorized that the ship had rolled over when its cargo shifted. The only reason he could imagine for such a rapid shift would have been a collision with another vessel during the height of the storm.

> The captain believes that the two vessels met in a collision during the fiercest storm ever experienced in the great lakes region yesterday, and that one, a 600-footer is resting on top of a smaller boat with part of her bow protruding from the water. The names of the vessels are unknown.
>
> *Cleveland Press*, NOVEMBER 11, 1913

So many ships were known to be lost and so many more were still missing that any one of them could have been the mystery ship. The list of candidates was too long for any particular ship to stand out as most likely. Yet, no other question was asked more often than, "What's her name?"

Lake Huron's mystery ship was the topic of conversation even among the beach patrols searching for bodies of frozen sailors. Officially, the Life-saving Service refused to join the speculation, saying that it did not want to create "unnecessary anxiety" on the part of sailors' relatives. In truth, government officials knew nothing more about the ship's identity than the average waterfront barkeep.

"I have no doubt that every soul on board has been lost," Captain Reid pronounced somberly to reporters. He was no longer speculating, and everyone knew it.

THURSDAY, NOVEMBER 13

SENDING A DIVER DOWN was recognized as the only way to solve the identity of the mystery ship. The ship's name must have been painted on the bow as required by law. A few minutes' work by any good diver would reveal its identity. Unfortunately, high winds and plunging breakers on Lake Huron prevented diving on the wreck. It would have been too dangerous in the cumbersome "hard hat" diving suits of 1913. The operation had to wait for better weather. But would the mystery ship remain afloat that long?

> The overturned wreck opposite the light ship still holds its secret closely and this morning banks of fog settled down around it as if to further shield its identity. As the morning wore on and the clouds of fog dispersed, an effort was being made to get another tug to go to the scene of the wreck with a diver.
>
> *Port Huron Times-Herald*, NOVEMBER 13, 1913

Some inkling of the identity of the overturned ship came on Tuesday from the Canadian shoreline near Port Franks, Ontario, where bodies and wreckage continued to be driven onto the sand by Lake Huron waves. Among the bales of hay and Canadian canned goods was a lifeboat from the package freighter *Regina*. Life preservers from that ship also were found in the debris, and tentative identification of the bodies showed they were from *Regina*'s crew. There was no longer any question as to the package freighter's fate: it had foundered.

Officials of the Merchants Transportation Company, owners of *Regina*, boarded an express train from Toronto to the Lake Huron beach. The somber owners confirmed the identities of several dead crewmembers now resting in a makeshift morgue. Was the overturned hulk their freighter? The *Regina's* owners did not even bother to venture out on the lake to examine the mystery ship, because they knew for certain that it was not theirs. *Regina* had green bottom paint, while the paint on the upside-down wreck was coal black.

Two of the *Regina's* dead crew had been found in their ship's lifeboat. One was draped over the gunwale, and the other was staring up from the bottom. More bodies of *Regina* sailors were found lying on the beach nearby. It was assumed that these men had been in the lifeboat before it rolled over in the pounding surf.

Finding the *Regina's* lifeboat had fueled early speculation that the package freighter was the overturned mystery ship. But within hours the Canadian beach yielded new evidence. A little north from Port Franks the bodies of crewmembers from other ships were also washing ashore. Seven of them were from the *Charles S. Price*, a ship that had not been reported since it departed the St. Clair River on Sunday morning. An empty and battered lifeboat from the *Price* was also discovered in the debris. Speculation about the mystery ship quickly changed. If it was not the *Regina*, then could it be the *Price*?

> Not far away on the same Canadian shore near Kettle Point five sailors were found in life preservers that saved them not. Those were the life preservers that gave the clew [sic] to the identity of the mysterious ship that lies upside down north of Port Huron, Mich.
>
> *Cleveland Plain Dealer,* November 12, 1913

Milton Smith had thought he was through with the *Price* when he climbed off the ship in Ashtabula, Ohio, the previous Wednesday. He thought he was going home to rest and look for a new job that would not take him away from his family for weeks at a time. Smith had been the *Price's* first assistant engineer for all but the final trip of the 1913 season. Now, less than a week after quitting his job, he found himself the vessel's sole survivor.

"I am indeed a fortunate man," Smith told his hometown newspaper, the *Port Huron Times-Herald.* "I left the *Price* . . . just before she started out on her last and fatal trip. There is no doubt the *Price* is gone. It is awful to think of it."

Out of respect for his former shipmates, Smith took upon himself the grisly task of identifying the frozen bodies that washed ashore. He boarded a train in Sarnia, just across the St. Clair River from Port Huron, and headed for the makeshift morgue at Thedford, Ontario, a scant 30 miles from his home. The number of bodies on the furniture store floor had reached eleven by the time he arrived at his destination. Nine of the bodies had been wearing life belts from either the *Regina* or the *Price*. Two victims were found in life belts that carried no ship's name. Wreckage had washed ashore from yet another ship, the *Wexford*, and it was thought the victims in the unmarked life belts might have come from that vessel. Smith began the grim task of identifying dead shipmates.

THE MYSTERY AROUND THE HULK deepened when three more lifeless sailors were found lashed to a liferaft from the *John A. McGean*. Its frozen crew was found not far from Goderich, where wreckage from the steamer *James Carruthers* also was discovered. Debris from these two ships was slightly north of *Regina's* lifeboat, but close enough that either the *Carruthers* or the *McGean* could have been the mystery ship. Both were large vessels, and the overturned hull was obviously that of a good-sized straight decker.

Lake Huron was still giving up the bodies of dead Great Lakes sailors when a major conference on safety at sea opened across the Atlantic Ocean in London. Lord Mersey was in charge of the event. He was still well known by the public on both sides of the ocean as the man in charge of the British Board of Trade hearings into the sinking of the *Titanic*, which had taken place some sixteen months prior to the White Hurricane. Mersey's report on the tragic *Titanic* sinking created a worldwide demand for passenger ships to carry enough lifeboat capacity for everyone on board.

Concurrent with Lord Mersey's conference, the U.S. Senate began considering a measure called the La Follette Bill, which would require full lifeboat capacity on all U.S. ships. Passenger-vessel operators on the Great Lakes immediately opposed the measure, claiming it would put them out of business. There was no "grandfather clause" in the proposed legislation to exempt existing ships from the new requirements. Ship owners said there was no practical way to put so many lifeboats on the passenger ships already sailing the lakes.

Cleveland city councilman James McGinty decided to become involved in the controversy and offered a resolution in council opposing the so-called La Follette Act on the grounds that it would virtually end passenger service on the Great Lakes. McGinty pointed out that Cleveland was home to more passenger vessels than any other Great Lakes port city. Any downturn in passenger ships on the lakes would have an immediate impact on his city's economy. In those pre-automobile years, a greater number of passengers traveled on Great Lakes passenger ships each season than crossed the Atlantic Ocean. Travel by ship was considered less hectic and cleaner than travel by railroad. Also, an overnight cabin afloat was sumptuous compared with the cramped confines of a Pullman berth.

"The bill does not justly cover conditions on the Great Lakes," argued James F. Mulholland, general manager of the Eastland Navigation Company. He was particularly concerned about the effect of the legislation on one particular passenger vessel owned by his company. "If the bill is passed it would require the *Eastland* to have 100 lifeboats and a crew of 200 men for lifeboat service only. The bill says nothing of wireless appliances and it says nothing of fire protection apparatus and life preservers. These things are as important as lifeboats. There should be a separate section of the bill dealing with the Great Lakes."

Although they did not know it at the time, McGinty and Mulholland were on the losing side of a debate that would become a contributing factor in the deadliest single-ship disaster in Great Lakes history. The passenger steamer *Eastland* had always been considered a "tender" vessel by its crew. When the weight of lifeboats and davits were eventually added to the top deck, they simply made this problem worse. Some historians have credited the weight of those boats as a factor in the capsize of the *Eastland* in the Chicago River on July 24, 1915. An estimated 840 people, mostly women and children, were killed when the ship rolled over while still tied to its downtown Chicago wharf.

IN NOVEMBER 1913, however, heated debate over lifeboat requirements could not shift the headlines from Lake Huron's mystery ship. The color of its bottom paint had ruled out the *Regina*, but six others ships were still likely candidates. A total of seven freighters were known to have foundered within a 90-mile radius of the entrance to the St. Clair River. In addition to the *Regina*, they were the *Charles S. Price*, *John A. McGean*, *Argus*, *Hydrus*, *James Carruthers*, and *Wexford*. With each discovery of new wreckage or another lifeless victim, the mystery deepened.

"What is the name of the overturned boat?"

This is the question that is being asked a hundred times a day not only in Port Huron, but in every port along the lakes.

No man knows the name of that overturned steel boat and what is more, no man will know until a diver goes down in sixty feet of water and wrests the secret from the waves.

Port Huron Times-Herald, November 13, 1913

Newspapers went to extremes to create fresh developments for each edition. The *Port Huron Times-Herald* sent a reporter by tugboat to the overturned hull on Wednesday. He was accompanied by a diver, but the pair could only get within 15 feet of the mystery ship. Sea conditions continued to make it impossible for the diver to go over the side.

To send down a diver is one of the hardest propositions that confront the marine men and *The Times-Herald*. On Wednesday this paper had a reporter and a diver within fifteen feet of the wreck but there was not a chance on earth to send down the diver. To have let him take the chance would have been practically sending him to his doom as well as imperiling the lives of those on the tug.

Port Huron Times-Herald, November 13, 1913

The *Times-Herald* slightly inaccurately explained that the diver would have to go "underneath" the ship to find its name. In truth, the name of the ship was expected to be in plain sight on either side of the bow. Although 60 feet is not deep, the 1913 writer questioned whether a man could work at that depth. Nitrogen narcosis, known as "the bends" to divers, was not well understood in 1913. Hard-hat divers feared the painful illness that we know now is caused by nitrogen gas bubbles in the bloodstream.

Another problem was the clumsy diving suit of the day. Divers wore weighted boots to keep them upright while walking on the bottom. Their heads were encased in a metal helmet with only tiny viewing ports. Because the suits were so clumsy, it was necessary to wait for a relatively calm day so that the diver would not be upset by a surge of the vessel that was tending the diver's air hose and tether from the surface. The *Times-Herald* also explained to its readers that the boat from which the diver would hang suspended must anchor no farther than 15 feet from the wreck. The clumsy equipment made a dive on the wreck a dicey proposition.

Despite the fact that the hull's bottom paint did not match the color of the paint on the *Regina*, some people argued that the shape of the mystery ship's bottom did in fact match that of the Canadian vessel. *Regina's* owners remained adamant that the overturned hulk was not their ship. According to the November 13, 1913, *Toledo Blade*, they pointed out that their steamer had a "marked bow" as the result of a collision. The exterior plating of the overturned hulk was smooth and undamaged.

Even that physical evidence did not quell the controversy. Captain George Plough of the Lakeview, Michigan, lifesaving station, Captain Thompson of the wrecking tug *Sport*, and Captain Carmine of the revenue cutter *Morrill* were all quoted on Wednesday night as saying they believed the mystery ship to be the *Regina*. Captain Plough claimed he had measured the beam of the overturned wreck at just over 42 feet. The beam of the Canadian package freighter was reported to be 43 feet, similar enough to lend believability to Plough's claim.

The almost hourly discovery of additional bodies continued to confuse the situation. Coroners working in the temporary furniture store morgue were starting to admit they were having difficulty deciding from which ship each victim had come.

> Little credence is given to the report from Goderich, Ont., that the seven bodies found on the Canadian shore of Lake Huron below Grand Bend were sailors on the steamer *Charles S. Price*, reported lost. The *Price* may have sunk, marine men admit, but it is believed the bodies were of members of the crew of the *Regina*.
>
> *Cleveland Plain Dealer*, NOVEMBER 13, 1913

Automobile driver licenses with photographs were sixty-five years in the future, so identifying the bodies of storm victims was often little more than a guessing game. Few people carried positive identification. Coroners attempted to match the frozen bodies to photos or descriptions of men known to be missing, or they tried to find papers on the bodies that might shed light on the victim's identity. Postcards written but not mailed were sometimes the key to a victim's identity. An inscribed ring or pocket watch occasionally linked a body to a name.

Although not at first obvious, another mystery was developing. It slowly became apparent that sailors from two particular ships had been intermingled in death. Bodies of men from the *Charles S. Price* were continually being mixed up with dead sailors from the *Regina*. The main reason was that victims from both ships had come ashore along the same stretch of beach, sometimes almost in one another's arms. And there were other confusing factors. One of the dead *Regina* sailors had apparently served on the *Price* earlier in the season before switching to the Canadian package freighter.

Milton Smith finished the sad task of identifying his former shipmates on Thursday. Like everyone else visiting the morgue, he noticed the way in which victims from the *Regina* were intermingled with the bodies of his former shipmates on the *Price*. It did not seem like an accident of wind and wave. Rather, it appeared to Smith and the morgue workers as if the dead sailors had come ashore in a single group, perhaps in the same lifeboat. Smith outlined his theory for reporters as he prepared to return to his home in Port Huron.

"The two ships collided in the storm," Smith explained, causing both of them to sink. In Smith's view, only a collision between the two vessels could explain why bodies from the ships were found together on the beach. "They didn't have any warning," Smith said. He used the body of steward Herbert Jones as proof. Jones was found still wearing his white apron, as if preparing a meal.

"Jones, the steward, was clothed in his working uniform," Smith pointed out. "This would indicate to me that Jones had to leave the boat very suddenly as it was always the rule of this man to take off his working clothes the moment he was through with tasks. Evidently Jones did not have any time for himself, but at the moment that something happened to the boat he went directly to his wife's assistance. This proves to me that something of a sudden nature occurred to the *Price*."

Sports fans in Cleveland, Ohio, were saddened by the identification of Steward Jones' body. He had been a well-known amateur hockey player during the winter months, when his ship was laid up. From 1907 to 1910 he played center on three different teams in the Cleveland city hockey league.

Reporters questioning former engineer Smith were naturally curious about one thing: why had he resigned his job with only one more trip to go? Smith shrugged. He had a wife and six children, the oldest just eleven years old. "I just had a premonition," he said about his ship. "I might have been in her. I was getting tired of sailing anyway and I realized this was my best chance. I knew every boy on the *Price*. I'm especially sorry for poor Arze McIntosh of St. Clair, our wheelsman."

Smith was not the only one advancing the *Price-Regina* collision theory. Captains who survived the gale pointed out that visibility had been almost nil that Sunday. The two ships could not have seen each other until it was too late. When the ships collided, they averred, one probably sank immediately while the other rolled over. It was considered certain that the diver would find another wreck beneath the mystery ship.

FRIDAY, NOVEMBER 14

DISTURBING REPORTS emanated from Canada on Friday. U.S. newspapers claimed the Thedford morgue had been careless in marking bodies. According to the *Port Huron Times-Herald*, identification papers and other valuables taken from the bodies were not kept separate. Instead, they were "massed together." That mistake, it was asserted, now made it nearly impossible to relate these critical items with their original owners. And, the newspapers pointed out, this added to the confusion regarding the mingling of victims from the *Regina* and the *Price*.

One example was the body of John Groundwater, the *Price*'s chief engineer. Some people claimed that his body was found wearing a life preserver from the *Regina*. They backed these claims by saying that the ship's name on the life vest explained why Groundwater's body was mistakenly placed with those of the Canadian ship's crew. Milton Smith had correctly identified his former shipmate, and the body was now moved into the group of victims from the *Price*.

"I have studied the matter carefully," Smith said. "And I have taken into consideration the facts that were given to me by those who found the bodies from the *Regina* and the *Price*. While I cannot state positively, the position of the bodies and the manner in which they were mixed, indicates to me that there could have been a collision between the two boats."

Another American drawn to the Thedford morgue was Mrs. Howard Mackley of St. Clair, Michigan. Her husband was second mate on the *Price*. The grieving widow was accompanied by her sister and a neighbor lady. The trio of women did not find Howard Mackley's body on the furniture store floor and were about to return home when news came of more victims being found farther north. To spare the woman further emotional trauma, Mrs. Mackley's sister proceeded to Goderich, while the widow and her other friend returned to St. Clair, on the U.S. side of the border.

On Friday, newspapers around the country carried the first photo-graph of the overturned mystery ship. It had been made by an enterpris-ing photographer who hired a tugboat to go to the wreck. The *Cleveland Press* used the occasion of this first photograph to speculate on the mech-anism by which a modern steel freighter might capsize. The *Press* pub-lished a set of drawings down the left column on its front page that illustrated how ballast water could have begun sloshing from side to side. According to the newspaper, sloshing ballast could have rolled the ship on beam ends, causing the boilers to break loose. To back up the drawings, the paper quoted an unnamed shipbuilder.

> "If the boat had been loaded the upsetting of that steamer would have been simple enough," said a Cleveland vesselman Friday. "She was not loaded, however, because if she had been, her forward end would not have floated at all. Had she been loaded she would have gone down instantly when she went over and the spar forward nor anything else would have held her up.
>
> "She could not have been loaded, however, and about the only theory to advance in this case was that the high seas which must have been running 20 or 21 feet, got under her and sent her over. Going out into a gale like that, the master of the vessel undoubtedly let water into her to be used as ballast.
>
> "Rolling in the heavy seas the water ballast would rush from one side of the vessel to the other and the more it rushed back and forth, the farther over the vessel would list."
>
> *Cleveland Press,* November 14, 1913

This same story was carried word for word in Friday's edition of the *Detroit News,* except that the person quoted was not "a Cleveland vessel-man." He was correctly identified as Earnest Ketchum, secretary-treasurer of the Detroit Shipbuilding Company. (The *Cleveland Press* had apparently altered a wire service story to give it a more local slant.) Sloshing ballast seemed to rule out the *Price,* which had been fully laden with soft coal when it left Ashtabula on Saturday.

The mystery of the overturned ship took another twist when the steamer *W.H. Gratwick* arrived in Duluth, Minnesota, on Thursday. The *Gratwick's* captain reported passing a second overturned vessel on northern Lake Huron. The identity of this second capsized ship has never been established. It apparently sank without being spotted by any other ships and before it could be explored. Early speculation held that the second capsized hulk was the *James Carruthers*, which had apparently foundered nearby. Later, as more wreckage of other ships floated ashore, it seemed more likely in 1913 that the second capsized hull belonged to the *Wexford*. Both of these lost ships were last reported near the area where the *Gratwick* made its grim discovery. It was thought that either one could have been the second mystery ship.

Lake sailors had always known that if damaged their straight deckers would sink quickly. The long holds of these ships were divided, semi-watertight bulkheads intended mostly to help control the cargo. Each compartment was large enough that the flooding of one would sink the ship. There was no profitable way to build a bulk freighter without this defect. The *Titanic* proved it was impossible to build an unsinkable ship, but no one wanted to believe that a modern steel bulk freighter could be rolled belly-up by a storm on the lakes. Suddenly, they had proof that Lake Huron had capsized not one but two big ships. It was not a comforting thought.

The hulk of the mystery ship on Lake Huron remained an unmarked hazard to navigation. Honest fears were raised that a freighter might strike the overturned wreck during the night.

SATURDAY, NOVEMBER 15

LAKE HURON FINALLY CALMED on Saturday morning, almost a full week after the storm began. Captain Bob Thompson skillfully nosed his salvage tug *Sport* against the steel sides of the overturned black leviathan. On deck was William H. Baker, a diver from Detroit who was considered to be among the best on the Great Lakes. He was familiar with working in the treacherous currents of the fast-flowing Detroit River. This experience was put to the test by diving on the mystery ship in open Lake Huron.

Baker carefully checked his equipment one last time. He slipped his legs into the rubberized fabric of his diving suit until his feet fitted into the attached lead-weighted boots. Additional lead weights went around his waist on a special belt held up by wide canvas suspenders. A bronze collar bolted to the suit circled his neck. Once dressed, Baker was almost unable to move, so he sat on a convenient crate while the tugboat maneuvered into position over the wreck. He cradled his globe-shaped bronze diving helmet in his lap.

Thompson, Baker, and the crew of the *Sport* had spent all night on the lake in order to be ready at first light. "I got in touch with diver Baker on Friday afternoon," said Captain Thompson, owner of the tug. "The weather has been so bad that you had to have somebody that you could depend on. I had to have a diver that could do the work and I got the best one on the lakes, Mr. Baker."

By 6 A.M. the tug was finally in position and anchored. A helper lifted the hard hat over Baker's head and locked it in position. Tap, tap, the helper rapped on the bronze dome. Baker waved in acknowledgment. Everything was working. Two men, one on either side, steadied the diver as he lumbered across the deck, his heavy boots making an odd shuffling sound on the metal. With obvious effort Baker was able to swing his weighted feet across the tugboat's bulwark and climb down a ladder installed over the tug's stern. He disappeared into the murky water, leaving behind only a trail of bubbles.

Normally, the surface of Lake Huron is a deep cobalt blue because of its almost crystal clear water, but not that morning. The mud and sediment churned up from the bottom by 35-foot storm waves was still suspended—something few Great Lakes sailors ever see in a lifetime afloat. Baker discovered he could hardly see his fingers at arm's length. He would have to do most of his work like a blind man, using his hands in place of his eyes.

"I felt her sides all the way down for 20 feet. Then I lost it again, but I kept on going down, expecting to run into it," he recalled. "When I discovered that I was too far down I started to come up again and found the wreck again coming up. I ran into the pipe rail around her texas work. I hung on there until I found out where I was at. Then I went down that pipe rail until I ran into the bulwarks of the wreck. The bulwarks were painted white."

Only Baker's air hose and emergency rope were visible to the anxious men on the tug. They judged the diver's progress by the location where bubbles from his exhaust air broke the surface. The tense atmosphere on the tugboat's deck was punctuated by the mechanical sounds of the air pump. Peter Bachus dutifully turned the pump wheel, sending air down to the diver with each "wheeze-thunk" of the triple-cylinder device. A meter on the front of the wooden pump box allowed him to check the air pressure in Baker's diving suit. What was happening down there? Had he found anything? Only Baker knew the answers to those questions, but he could not communicate to the surface.

Wheeze-thunk. Wheeze-thunk. Wheeze-thunk.

"There was a round railing around her bulwarks and I went around that railing until I ran across her name," Baker said. "There I stopped and took my time." Limited visibility forced him to read one letter at a time. Just to be sure, he repeated the laborious process. "I read her name twice," he would tell men on the tug after emerging from the water.

Wheeze-thunk. Wheeze-thunk.

Now that he knew the mystery ship's true identity, Baker wanted to find an explanation for how it came to be floating upside down. "I went on further forward to the stem to see if there were any damaged plates to indicate if there had been a collision or if the boat had been damaged in any way. While going around there I found two rows of deadlights forward on the starboard bow. The deadlights were all closed and the glass is in them. They are not broken. One curtain was hanging out of one of the deadlights, but it was closed. The curtain evidently having become jammed when the deadlight was closed."

Wheeze-thunk.

With no damage found forward, Baker turned around. "Then I started and went back aft. I was pulling myself along this rail all the time. I went to the after side of the forward house. I found nothing there that showed any signs of a collision."

Wheeze-thunk. Wheeze-thunk.

Lake Huron's early morning calm was beginning to break. By 7 A.M. a choppy sea had arisen with the wind. Baker was forced to leave the overturned hulk and return to the surface. "I was under water in all about an hour and the length of the wreck that I investigated was about 48 feet of the starboard bow. I did not have a chance to go any further on the wreck and I did not get inside of her as the sea began to toss me about and I had to give it up." Although his exploration of the wreck had been cut short, the diver's primary mission was a success. The identity of the mystery ship was known.

Baker emerged from his suit without saying anything. Quietly, he gave the name of the overturned ship to Captain Thompson and then whispered it to a reporter for the *Port Huron Times-Herald*. The tug hoisted anchor and headed back to the St. Clair River, where diver Baker made an appearance at Lynn's Shipping Agency. He refused to divulge the name of the mystery ship until he was paid. The price was $100. Baker counted his money carefully before speaking: *"Charles S. Price."*

BOAT IS PRICE
Diver Is Baker
SECRET KNOWN

Learning the name of the capsized ship did not solve the ultimate mystery of how the *Price* had come to be floating upside down. No one had thought a fully loaded straight decker could roll completely over and still remain afloat. Somehow, the storm had rolled a fully loaded 504-foot steel ship that was less than three years old and had done it quickly enough to trap the air that kept the bow afloat. How could this have happened?

"The boat's hatches have been washed off in the heavy storm," Captain Thompson theorized. "Water poured into the hatches. The cargo has been shifted over so that the steamer was turned over on its side at such an angle. This, together with the fact that her watertight compartments which are in the bottom of the steamer were filled with air, instead of water, turned her over." It is as good a theory as any.

"The boat is gradually settling as the air which is buoying up her bow is leaking out. The boat has settled two feet since Wednesday," Thompson explained. Then, he put in a thinly veiled pitch for the services of his salvage tug. "In a few days the *Price* will be beneath the water unless some means is taken to save her at once. I am of the opinion that some of the bodies of the crew are still in the boat."

Salvaging the overturned hulk was never attempted. Perhaps it was not even possible. The ship filled slowly and now rests on the bottom of Lake Huron, still upside down. It is often visited by modern scuba divers. In its way the capsized hulk of the *Charles S. Price* is a perfect monument to a storm that left so many mysteries in its wake. Not far away are the rusting remains of the salvage tug *Sport*, which sank in yet another Great Lakes gale several years later.

The mystery of the intermingled crews of the *Price* and the *Regina* has never been resolved to everyone's satisfaction. Over the years, historians have tended to debunk as myth the claim that the *Price's* chief engineer, John Groundwater, was found wearing a *Regina* life preserver. Current belief is that his body was just found near equipment from the Canadian ship. It is possible that a life vest from the *Regina* simply washed on top of his body as wreckage came ashore. Because of the looting and the confusion in the Thedford morgue, there is no way to determine with certainty what Groundwater was wearing when his body was found.

November 1913

"The month was dry and much warmer than usual with about the normal amount of sunshine," recorded Duluth weather observer Ralph W. Smith in his station's end-of-month report. "From the 16th to the close of the month and extending into December the excess of the daily mean above the normal has been continuous and ranged from 8 degrees to 24 degrees above the normal. At the close of the month reports were common of trees and shrubbery budding and flowers appearing in the yards. Superior reported a lilac bush in one of the yards of that city as being in bloom." Smith also noted one thunderstorm, only the second in November during the forty-two years there had been a weather station at Duluth.

The unusually warm and humid weather of November 1913 caused fog problems for the city of Detroit and its crowded river. On the evening of the 19th, the city's favorite passenger steamer, the *Tashmoo*, collided with the steamer *Essex*. The accident took place at the dock between Chene Street and Joseph Campeau Avenue at about 5 P.M. Unbending the stem of the sidewheel passenger vessel cost about $3,000. Damage to the *Essex* was reported as "light." Another heavy fog on the 20th brought vessel traffic on the Detroit River almost to a halt. Only two ships were reported to have passed through the city that day. Ship traffic the following day was an astonishing 121 vessels.

"The month was considerably warmer than the average, the highest temperature 71 degrees on the 21st was a record breaker for any November since the establishment of the station," wrote Buffalo weather observer F. A. Math in his station's record book. At Chicago, weather observer A. R. Thompson noted that November 26 was an unusually dark day, "a mixture of light fog, city smoke, low hanging clouds and light mist, together with a very humid atmosphere, caused a long period of darkness today, from 9:25 A.M. until after sunset.... Electric signs and lighted windows in the business heart of the city were as conspicuous as at night."

Commercial traffic on the Great Lakes did not pause its rush to complete final voyages during the aftermath of the storm. Ships kept to their appointed routes despite the fact that bodies were still washing ashore. And Great Lakes weather continued its age-old November pattern of major changes every four days. The calm after the White Hurricane was broken by another stint of foul weather as the 1913 shipping season came to a close.

Two weeks after the "big blow," a lesser storm on Lake Michigan stole a measure of Christmas from families in Chicago. It had been a Windy City tradition to purchase Christmas trees from Captain J. Schuneman, owner of the schooner *Rouse Simmons*. For a decade or more, he had obtained a load of cut evergreens in Wisconsin on his last downbound trip of the season. After docking in downtown Chicago, he would sell these Christmas trees right off the deck of his schooner.

Schuneman sailed from Thompson Harbor near Manistique, Michigan, on November 25. Loaded on deck was his usual collection of cut trees. A storm was already brewing, so the experienced captain headed well offshore before turning downbound to Chicago. A member of the Lifesaving Service later reported seeing the *Rouse Simmons* off Sturgeon Bay during a momentary lull in what was by then a full-blown storm. The ship displayed distress signals, but there was no way for the men on shore to reach the tree-laden schooner. Instead, they phoned the station at Kewaunee, Wisconsin, for help and a lifeboat put out from there. Despite the storm the crew of that boat managed to catch a glimpse of the struggling schooner. Then, the "Christmas Tree Ship" was gone from human sight. Commercial fishermen out of Two Rivers, Wisconsin, reported their nets were fouled with cut evergreen trees all during the summer of 1914.

AFTERMATH

THE FINAL TOLL WAS SOBERING. From Saturday, November 8, through Monday, November 10, the cascade of weather known as the White Hurricane had attacked ships on Lakes Superior, Michigan, Huron, and Erie. At least seventy freighters and manned barges were caught out by this "blow," of which an even dozen were sunk and thirty-one more were tossed onto rocky shoals or stranded on beaches. Of the seventeen ships known to have been on Lake Huron between the hours of 8 P.M. and midnight on November 9, only two arrived at their destinations, and both of those lucky ships sustained serious damage. Officially, 248 sailors were killed by the storm, but the actual toll was much greater.

Putting exact numbers to the carnage is difficult because no single agency in 1913 kept track of vessels lost or sailors killed. The Lake Carriers Association numbers appear to be the most accurate, but they focus almost entirely on the damage to large steel vessels. The association's year-end report for 1913 virtually ignores sailing vessels, tugs, and powered barges. No official tally of the dead includes the commercial fishermen, hunters, or anglers who also lost their lives.

> There have been many storms in the past supposedly violent, but this one was unprecedented. It raged with uncommon force, especially on Lake Huron, and proved to be the most destructive in the history of the lakes. As nearly as can be traced, 235 sailors lost their lives in this storm, 44 of them on Lake Superior, 7 on Lake Michigan, 6 on Lake Erie, and 178 of them on Lake Huron.
>
> The storm threw a great pall over lake shipping and practically demoralized lake trade for the balance of the season.
>
> ANNUAL REPORT, LAKE CARRIERS ASSOCIATION

The following tables listing the large commercial freighters and their crews lost or stranded during the storm are based on the Lake Carriers Association report, newspaper accounts, and other sources.

SHIPS FOUNDERED

Lake & Ship	Gross Tonnage	Lives Lost	Approximate Location
LAKE SUPERIOR			
LEAFIELD	2,900	18	Angus Island
Henry B. Smith	10,000	23	Marquette, Mich.
LAKE MICHIGAN			
Plymouth (Barge)	600	7	Gull Island
LAKE HURON			
Argus	7,000	28	Point Aux Barques
James Carruthers	9,500	22	Goderich, Ont.
Hydrus	7,000	25	Goderich, Ont.
John A. McGean	7,500	28	Sturgeon Pt., Mich.
Charles S. Price	9,000	28	Port Huron, Mich.
Regina	3,000	20	Harbor Beach, Mich.
Isaac M. Scott	9,000	28	Sturgeon Pt., Mich.
Wexford	2,800	20	Port Franks, Ont.
LAKE ERIE			
Lightship 82	n/a	6	Buffalo, N.Y.
TOTALS	68,300[1]	253[2]	

1. The Lake Carriers Association claimed 69,100 tons of shipping lost, but the association's figure includes the barge *Donaldson*, which stranded on Lake Erie without loss of life, and the *C.W. Elphicke*, which had gone aground prior to the storm.
2. Total does not include three men lost from steamer *Nottingham*.

SHIPS STRANDED

Lake & Ship	Damage Value ($US)	Approximate Location	Notes
LAKE SUPERIOR			
F.G. Hartwell	30,000	Point Iroquois	rebuilt
Huronic	30,000	Whitefish Point	
J.T. Hutchinson	40,000	Point Iroquois	
Major	unknown	Crisp Pt., Mich.	rebuilt
William Nottingham	75,000	Apostle Islands	three men lost
Scottish Hero	500		
Turret Chief	unknown	Copper Harbor, Mich.	rebuilt 1914 as *Salvor*
L.C. Waldo	unknown	Gull Island, Mich.	rebuilt 1916 as *Riverton*
ST. MARYS RIVER			
Meaford	500		
LAKE MICHIGAN			
Halstead (Barge)		Green Bay	
Louisiana		Death's Door	
Pontiac	7,500	Simmon's Reef	
LAKE HURON			
Acadian	30,000	Thunder Bay	
Matthew Andrews	2,500	Corsica Shoal	refloated
H.M. Hanna Jr.		Port Austin, Mich.	rebuilt 1916
H.A. Hawgood	7,000	Weis Beach	refloated
J.M. Jenks	25,000	Georgian Bay	
Matoa	117,000	Point Aux Barques	total loss
D.O. Mills	45,000	Harbor Beach	refloated
Northern Queen	25,000	Kettle Point	
A.E. Stewart	30,000	Thunder Bay	refloated
ST. CLAIR AND DETROIT RIVERS			
W.G. Pollock	5,000	St. Clair Flats	
Saxona	1,500	Lake St. Clair	
Victory	12,000	Livingston Channel	
LAKE ERIE			
Donaldson (Barge)	800	Cleveland, Ohio	

SHIPS STRANDED

Lake & Ship	Damage Value ($US)	Approximate Location	Notes
C.W. Elphicke[1]		Long Point, Ont.	
Fulton	2,500	Bar Point	
G.J. Grammer	1,500	Lorain, Ohio	refloated
Pittsburgh Steamship Co. Barges	100,000	Cleveland, Ohio	unmanned

1. The steamer *C.W. Elphicke* had gone aground prior to the storm, but salvage was prevented by the White Hurricane. The ship was destroyed by the gale.

BOILERS IN THE SUNKEN SHIPS were hardly cool before the U.S. Weather Bureau was accused of bureaucratic bungling. The Great Lakes maritime community refused to shoulder any blame for the death toll. To them, it seemed senseless and cruel to hold the drowned masters and frozen crews responsible for the disaster. Government forecasters were legally required to post storm warnings, so Weather Bureau meteorologists became the logical targets of recrimination.

Ship owners argued that the storm warnings issued on November 7, 8, and 9 had not come close to suggesting the true ferocity of a storm marked by sustained 70-mile-per-hour winds in several locations and gusts reported by ships to be as high as 90 miles per hour. Never once did the Weather Bureau suggest that a gale of hurricane magnitude was possible.

The Weather Bureau's own publications promised sailors that a hurricane warning—two red flags with black centers, displayed one above the other—would be hoisted on the Great Lakes to warn of just the kind of destructive weather that claimed so many lives and ships in 1913. In the bureau's words, these flags would "indicate the expected approach of a tropical hurricane, or one of those extremely severe and dangerous storms which occasionally move across the Lakes and Northern Atlantic coast."

Eight days after the storm, the *Duluth News-Tribune* interviewed that city's local weather forecaster, H. W. Richardson. He told the paper that the storm was one of the worst, if not the worst, to strike the lakes. Then, without direct attribution, the *News-Tribune* published what every Great Lakes sailor accepted as the truth: the lakes had actually experienced nothing less than a storm of hurricane intensity—a White Hurricane.

The storm from the southeast must have been a hurricane, according
to the figures given, which show an extreme low pressure of 28.76
inches, and a wind velocity of 76 miles, recorded at Buffalo on the
10th.

Duluth News-Tribune, NOVEMBER 16, 1913

The Duluth newspaper tried to give the impression that forecaster Harrison had called the storm a "hurricane." In truth, however, the statement came from the anonymous reporter who wrote the article. The livelihood of almost every resident in both Duluth and neighboring Superior was related in some measure to lake freighters. To the majority of the paper's readers it seemed logical that the Weather Bureau should have put up hurricane warnings.

Ohio Congressman William Gordon was quick to seize a political opportunity. On November 16, he grabbed headlines by announcing plans to investigate the Weather Bureau. Gordon's stated intention was to determine if the proper warnings had been posted. "The government is expending great sums of money to conduct the Weather Bureau," Gordon told reporters. "We have a right to expect accurate and adequate service from it. If these charges are true, the Bureau is a menace rather than a help to navigation."

The next day, the U.S. Department of Agriculture (within which the Weather Bureau operated) responded to Representative Gordon's charges by announcing an investigation of its own. The department's news release said this internal probe would determine if the forecaster at Cleveland had issued sufficient warning of the storm. Cleveland forecaster William H. Alexander was ordered to prepare a report on his actions. As the head of the Cleveland bureau office, the primary responsibility for warning the majority of Great Lakes ship owners about the coming storm had been his. Washington wanted to know if he had done his job.

Alexander had not waited for instructions from Washington to begin defending both himself and the Weather Bureau in statements to Cleveland reporters. Speaking out was a potentially career-ending move in the heavily bureaucratic weather service. "Daring disregard of government storm signals are the main causes of the latest disasters on the Great Lakes," he told the *Cleveland Plain Dealer* on November 15. "Had the same storm prevailed in foreign waters with government storm signals placed in every port three days ahead of the storm, sounding the warning, a catastrophe never would have happened."

> It seems singular to me that lake captains should take their ships out in the face of the warning. They might have avoided the loss of lives and property and it seems as though the disaster was almost without excuse.
>
> WILLIAM H. ALEXANDER, FORECASTER, CLEVELAND, OHIO, NOVEMBER 15, 1913

Criticism of the Weather Bureau grew despite Alexander's protestations. Ship owners and captains continued to dodge their responsibility for loss of life by claiming that official warnings were inadequate for the size of the storm. The shipping companies argued that they would have responded properly—keeping ships in port—if hurricane warnings had been hoisted instead of the simple storm warnings actually displayed.

In part, this argument was correct. The actual conditions on November 9 and 10 were far worse than ordinary storm warnings implied. Wind velocities and barometric pressures recorded on Sunday show that Lakes Superior and Huron were battered by a winter storm of an intensity equal to a Caribbean hurricane, and the Weather Bureau's publications promised that hurricane warnings would be displayed for such storms regardless of their origin. But weather prognostication was at a critical point in the early twentieth century—an evolving but still fledgling science—and forecasters zealously guarded the principles and definitions of their trade. Knowing what they knew, they could no longer apply the term *hurricane* loosely. It appears that while the scientists had agreed to reserve the word *hurricane* to mean only storms of tropical origin, this decision had not been passed down the line. Weather Bureau publications still promised that hurricane warnings would be posted when conditions became dangerous enough, and Great Lakes sailors still held the traditional view that a hurricane was any storm of killer intensity. Outside the small community of weather forecasters, no one seemed to know or care about the distinction.

"Hurricane signals have not been hoisted in years," said one unnamed Weather Bureau official in Washington, D.C. This true but meaningless argument obviously did not impress the editors of the *Duluth News-Tribune*. The newspaper was unabashedly on the side of the captains and sailors caught in the storm.

Captains of vessels arriving in the Duluth-Superior harbor since the
memorable storm say that a display of hurricane warnings instead of
the usual storm warnings undoubtedly would have prevented any
such large loss of life.

What boat owners are eager to see is such change in the operation
of the weather bureau as to make it possible for local forecasters to
warn vessels of the tendency to lightning shifts of the wind, and also
be so equipped that they may put out warnings of "unusual" storms.

Duluth News-Tribune, November 19, 1913

Sailors were still being rescued and bodies recovered when Congressman Gordon sent a telegram to President Woodrow Wilson announcing
his investigation of the Weather Bureau. The White House responded by
threatening a counterinvestigation aimed at probing the actions of Great
Lakes ship owners. In a news release, the White House said the president would direct special attention to the custom of permitting ships to
make trips long past the date when navigation had been declared "dangerous." Specific mention was made of vessel owners who allegedly
offered bonuses to captains for making extra trips after the end of the
regular shipping season.

On November 18, the Weather Bureau finally responded to its critics
by issuing a statement from Washington, D.C., headquarters that took full
responsibility for the storm warnings and forecasts issued from November
8 onward. The Agriculture Department absolved the individual forecasters in Cleveland and other lake ports of all blame:

> The records show that every weather bureau took precautions. Sig-
> nals were displayed at 112 points along the lake shore, including nine-
> teen weather bureau stations from any one of which special
> information could be had upon request. The severity of the storm
> was fully recognized by officials in Washington and no information
> concerning it was concealed or withheld.

According to the Department of Agriculture, forecasters had issued the
proper warnings under the existing regulations governing their operation.
(The initial announcement of an investigation into the adequacy of

William Alexander's actions to warn Great Lakes shipping may only have been an attempt to deflect criticism away from the bureau's Washington office.) Storm warning flags hoisted by day and lanterns displayed by night were the only signals available to the Weather Bureau in 1913. If the storm grew an order of magnitude greater than the size implied by the official warnings, the Weather Bureau was not responsible. Forecasters had followed regulations.

The press was struck by the implicit irony.

> From the foregoing facts, it seems that it would have been impossible for the weather bureau to have given more adequate or timely warning of the approach and dangerous character of these storms.
>
> *Duluth Herald*, NOVEMBER 18, 1913

A similar debate over the adequacy of the storm warnings was joined in Toronto between shipping interests and the Canadian weather bureau. R. F. Stupart, director of that bureau, stated in a letter published in the *Duluth News-Tribune* on November 19, 1913, that "the captains of vessels lost in Lake Huron and Lake Superior during the recent terrible gales disregarded the 'heavy gale' warnings given by the meteorological office in Toronto, and ignored the heavy gale signals which were flying everywhere on the lakes is shown everywhere by the weather forecasts of the days preceding the storm."

The conflicting arguments on both sides had validity. To weather observers on land, neither of the two weather systems that created the White Hurricane warranted more than ordinary storm warnings until Sunday, and even then, the hurricane-strength gale was not an official hurricane because it did not start as a tropical storm.

Captains also were correct in claiming they should have received the equivalent of a hurricane warning no later than Saturday noon. This storm that sank a dozen ships, stranded thirty more, and killed at least 253 sailors did, in fact, produce wind velocity, precipitation, and waves equal to those of a hurricane. Quibbling over the minor technicality that the deadly gale was only an "extratropical cyclone" ignored reality. It had been a White Hurricane by any standard of measure except the official "tropical storm" definition.

But this argument over the definition of "hurricane" missed the deeper truth, which was that the Weather Bureau had been a critical step behind the storm from the beginnings of the Superior gale on Thursday through the devastating weather over the lower lakes on Sunday and Monday. Ship owners preferred to focus on the narrow question of what signals were hoisted because doing so might absolve them of responsibility for losses.

For its part, the Weather Bureau did not want to acknowledge that it had no foreknowledge of events and could not have predicted how severe the storm would become. The bureau, perpetually scrambling for funding, sought always to emphasize its abilities and usefulness, not its limitations. As in the aftermath of the New York blizzard of 1888 and the Galveston hurricane of 1900, the bureau's instinct was to shift attention away from its fallibility. In November 1898, when a low moving over the Great Lakes had combined with a low moving up the East Coast to wreak havoc on Massachusetts and sink the steamship *Portland* with great loss of life, the Weather Bureau mounted a post-storm offensive to prove that forecasters had seen the storm coming and predicted it correctly. It wasn't true. During that storm the bureau had been tracking the Great Lakes low but not the East Coast depression, which had moved north offshore and escaped their notice. Lacking satellite photos, modern communications, and upper-atmosphere weather data, they could not have predicted the ferocity of the combined low. In 1913 the same was true, and the Weather Bureau's insistence on a narrow definition of "hurricane" was in part a semantic fig leaf to hide behind.

Ship captains may have been right in saying they did not get sufficient warnings, but they were wrong in blaming government forecasters. The problem was simply a general lack of knowledge and data. The U.S. and Canadian weather bureaus had done their best considering their limited resources. The opposite cannot always be said of the captains. Some sailed despite obvious signs that they were facing more than just an ordinary November gale. A few editorial writers recognized this, which is why not all newspapers were as favorable to the mariners as those in Duluth. On November 14, the *Cleveland Press* ran an editorial criticizing ship owners for their greed.

GREED

Just one more trip—just a little fatter dividend—just a hundred or so seamen floating dead in the lakes.

Children are fatherless and newmade widows are thrust out into the world to wring from it a hard living because rich vesselmen are willing to imperil the lives of their employees in the name of greed.

All of the world knows that death lurks upon the Great Lakes in November. None know it better than the boat owners, but their boats are insured.

So nine great Cleveland vessels are lost or missing and 168 members of their crews have died.

The November dividend has been paid, in coin of human life and suffering.

Cleveland Press, November 14, 1913

Accusations that ship owners and captains ignored storm warnings cannot be dismissed. There was no significant change in vessel departures as the result of the warnings posted at 10 A.M. Friday. Most embarrassing to the shipping companies was the revelation that bonuses were paid to captains who squeezed extra trips into the end of the navigation season. Newspapers of November 17 carried the story of Captain Jimmy Owen being pressured to sail despite the weather. Owen commanded the steamer *Henry B. Smith*, which departed from Marquette, Michigan, on Sunday and disappeared. The implication was that other captains were under similar pressure to sail.

By November 19 the political process in Washington, D.C., had shifted blame away from the Weather Bureau and its employees. Instead, the Agriculture Department's investigation focused on proving that regulations governing storm warnings were at fault. "There is no question but there should be signals showing more than the usual storm is expected," said one unidentified high-level Weather Bureau official.

"The warning indicated by the small craft signal is for the smaller boats to seek shelter or take necessary precautions, and the other signal—the one which is used to warn the larger craft, is for the purpose of informing the lake maritime world that a severe storm is due, there being no suggestion as to the severity of the storm aside from the fact that there is danger," the unnamed official admitted, as reported in the November 17, 1913, *Toledo Blade*. "I think everyone concerned is of the opinion that regulations should require special warnings for the particularly dangerous storms where wind and snow combine."

■ ■

WHILE DEBATE OVER WARNINGS RAGED, one of the lakes' leading vessel owners proposed a theory as to why this particular storm had become so severe. "The cause of the gale reaching cyclonic proportions on Lake Huron, as it must have done to create the havoc it did with the big ships, was that two gales collided," G. Ashley Tomlinson theorized in the *Duluth Herald*. Although not a trained weather observer, Tomlinson was remarkably close to the truth. A cold November gale had preceded the warm, moisture-laden southern storm. In 1913 it certainly appeared the two storms had collided.

The meteorologists in Washington did not do as well as Tomlinson in analyzing the storm. Weeks later, the bureau routinely plotted the paths of all the storm systems that had moved across North America during November 1913. This sort of summary map had been made every month since the late 1870s as part of an ongoing effort to learn more about the patterns of storms. In the track of the gale over Lake Superior as shown on the 1913 map, none of the plotted positions from Wednesday evening, November 5, through Saturday morning, November 8, agree with the actual weather encountered. The summary map shows a low of Canadian origin over southern Minnesota, well below Lake Superior, on Thursday morning. Its track was then plotted almost due east across Green Bay, Wisconsin, and Traverse City, Michigan, before arriving over Lake Huron on Saturday.

Almost fifty years after the event, as part of a weather briefing paper for saltwater ships that would be using the newly opened St. Lawrence Seaway, a panel of U.S. meteorologists took a second look at the 1913 records and concluded that their predecessors had placed the storm track too far south. Replotting the storm in a 1959 technical paper, the Marine Area Sector, Office of Climatology, within the U.S. Weather Bureau, moved the November gale track hundreds of miles north of that shown on the 1913 summary. This northerly path more closely predicts the conditions encountered by mariners on Superior in 1913. The 1959 review also identified the low moving north from Georgia, but even forty-six years after the storm meteorologists still could not offer a credible description of the interaction between the two systems that turned Lake Huron into a killing zone Sunday night, November 9, 1913.

From contemporary ship reports and weather observer records, it now appears probable that the northwesterly gales blasting upper Lake Superior Friday morning, November 7, were an invasion of arctic air from a powerful high in western Canada, and that invasion was announced by the passage of a cold front trailing from a low that might have been centered over Hudson Bay or northern Québec. The weather science of 1913 included no clear understanding of frontal mechanisms. Jacob Bjerknes was still a fifteen-year-old boy at the time, and his paper introducing the concept of warm, cold, and occluded fronts and their relation to extratropical cyclones was still six years in the future.

There may have been a secondary low embedded in the cold front when it reached Superior, but if not, one developed and strengthened over the warm lake water. Ahead of the cold front, the lakes region had been dominated for several days by an area of high pressure over the East Coast that was wafting southwesterly winds and above-normal temperatures onto the lakes. As the low deepened over Superior and moved east Friday, the regional pressure gradient steepened and the southwesterly winds ahead of the front increased to gale force, while the northwesterly winds behind the front did the same.

The Superior low moved east-northeast across Ontario and toward Québec Saturday afternoon and night while the cold front swept southeast over the lakes, gradually weakening as it went. And that might have been the end of it—one more November gale on Superior—had it not been for the atmospheric chain of cause and effect that had been set in motion.

To have had any chance of predicting that chain, the Weather Bureau would have needed upper-atmosphere data and a fully developed knowledge of atmospheric waves, fronts, and interactions, none of which it had. Even today, with satellite photos, reams of upper-atmosphere data, hurricane-hunter planes, and multiple predictive models running on supercomputers, forecasters are sometimes fooled by hurricanes. In 1913, despite its protestations to the contrary, the bureau could only play a constant game of catch-up from Friday, November 7, through Sunday, November 9.

The key to the storm of 1913 was in the upper atmosphere, and lacking any upper-atmosphere data we cannot know for certain what transpired. Very likely, however, there was a sharp and deep equatorward dip in the jet stream on Friday from the Hudson Bay region south-southwest into the central United States. This trough probably supported the surface low over northern Québec with which the Lake Superior cold front was associated. The wind to the west of the trough would have been north-west—possibly for some distance through the Yukon region and into the Arctic—transporting cold air southeastward behind the front. The trough shifted east-southeastward through Friday and Saturday, and on Friday it supported the development of the secondary low over Superior.

Meanwhile, farther south, another upper-atmosphere wave—much smaller than the jet stream trough—may have moved through Texas on Friday and into the southeastern United States Friday night, giving rise to a new, weak surface low in Georgia Saturday morning. As it did so, the jet stream trough continued to deepen, extending into the southern states by Saturday morning. The north-flowing circulation on the jet stream's eastern side now "picked up" the surface low and steered it north. In the process this low intensified rapidly. By Sunday morning it was much stronger and centered near Washington, D.C. During Sunday it moved north and a little west and entrained the cold air behind the Great Lakes cold front, which was by then losing its identity. This cold air led to a further rapid strengthening of the low, with surface air being lifted aloft and exhausted by the jet stream.

By the time the low crossed Lake Erie between Cleveland and Buffalo Sunday night, it was highly organized and intense. It also created a steep pressure gradient from the large mass of arctic air and strong ridge of high pressure to the west, so that northwesterly gales assaulted all the lakes. The low also brought with it an unusually wet snow for the region. The amount of water contained in snow varies depending upon its origin. Lake-effect snow typically produces less meltwater per inch than snow that originates with warmer, moisture-laden air. This explains why the sleet and snow on Sunday night and through Monday were so destructive to power and telephone wires in Cleveland.

As late as the 1950s, meteorologists thought the Superior low and the southern low combined into a single storm. In fact, by Sunday, the Superior storm had become a weak vestige well to the north and east of Lake Erie before the southern storm arrived. Although they never met, the two storms were part of an upper-atmosphere sequence of interrelated events the precise details and timing of which haven't been repeated since.

FOR ALL HIS WEATHER SAVVY, ship owner Ashley Tomlinson did not protect his fleet from damage during the White Hurricane. Tomlinson's vessels had sailed into the storm along with those of every other fleet. F. P. Houghton, the secretary of the Tomlinson fleet, told reporters in Duluth that the company had always made every effort to impress upon its company's captains that they alone were responsible for the safety of their ships. "The greatest care should be taken at all times to insure safety to the lives and property entrusted to them," he said.

Houghton did not mention whether or not the Tomlinson company participated in the common practice of paying bonuses to captains for making extra, late-season trips.

To this day, the practice of rewarding captains for exceeding company goals may not have disappeared from the lakes. More than sixty years later, when the *Edmund Fitzgerald* went down in 1975, many sailors expressed private beliefs that performance bonuses were partially to blame. These claims were never proven, but belief in their existence a half-century after the White Hurricane indicates how pervasive the late-season bonus system might have been in 1913. Few sailors doubted that Captain Owen felt at least some pressure from his company to sail despite the storm.

Not every mariner agreed, however. Some told reporters that the dead captain just made an error in judgment. "Naturally I would not want to be quoted on it," one unidentified shipmaster told the *Marquette Daily Mining Journal*. "This is of course a delicate question. Naturally, the owners want dispatch, but they don't want any more dispatch than is consistent with safety. I can't help but believe that the loss of the *Smith* is due primarily to a fatal error in judgment. The storm could not have been under estimated."

Whether or not Captain Owen succumbed to pressure from his ship's owners, the Lake Carriers Association needed to distract public attention from suggestions that late-season bonuses and other rewards may have enticed captains into sailing despite the storm warnings. William Livingstone, president of the association, serendipitously found that distraction in a stunning blunder by the U.S. Revenue Service. The cutter *Morrill* was ordered to leave Lake Huron during the aftermath of the storm on Tuesday, while bodies were still floating ashore and the overturned mystery ship remained a hazard to navigation.

The *Morrill* had been warning vessels to avoid the overturned hulk of the "mystery ship" when some unknown functionary of the Revenue Service inexplicably ordered the cutter to go to the aid of a vessel believed to be stranded on Lake Erie. This aroused the ire of Livingstone:

> With Lake Huron thickly dotted with wrecks I cannot understand the philosophy of the Treasury Department action in instructing the *Morrill* to go from there to the assistance of the steamer *G.J. Grammer,* which was aground off Lorain, but never was in any danger, and which I am advised today is now in port loading a cargo of coal.
>
> Even if the *Grammer* were in need of assistance there are any number of tugs at Lake Erie ports, while tugs cannot be had at Port Huron for love or money. What a colossal joke it is for the *Morrill* to be sent from a place where she could be of service to assist a boat which she will find in the harbor taking aboard a cargo.
>
> The *Morrill* really has done only two things all summer. Part of the time she was securing samples of water for the international joint commission, which is investigating pollution of the lakes and the rest of the time she was tied up with the Perry centennial celebration. Now when she might be of some assistance to the vessel interests, she is dispatched to a distant port on a useless errand.
>
> *Port Huron Times-Herald,* NOVEMBER 14, 1913

Livingstone demanded that control of revenue cutters be removed from the federal government and given to local officials in the individual ports. He suggested that port officials would have a better understanding of local needs than Washington bureaucrats.

> The *Grammer* . . . is ashore but in no danger. The derelict off Port Huron is a menace. With wrecks all over the lakes every tug has been called away and it has been almost impossible to get a boat to go out to the wreck at night and warn other vessels away. Thousands of people are in suspense until the name of the vessel is learned. It may be that on which their kin are sailing. Yet the government sends the means by which they expect to learn the truth away. Bodies of many sailors are drifting in the lake, but the government has removed the means of recovering them. Instead the corpses will drift with the wind until thrown up on the beach, as a score already have been. They may

lie on the sands in some deserted place and rot for all the aid the government gives.

Port Huron Times-Herald, NOVEMBER 14, 1913

Livingstone skillfully moved the public's attention away from allegations of late-season bonuses and other company practices that may have caused ships to depart safe harbors despite deteriorating weather and storm warnings.

LIVINGSTONE ALSO STEERED PUBLIC ATTENTION away from defects in the designs of Great Lakes ships, defects that may have caused many of the founderings and strandings. Time after time, captains reported that their ships lacked the horsepower to make headway against gale-force winds. Anchored ships often found themselves dragging backward onto lee shores even though their engines were thundering at full speed ahead. The White Hurricane proved conclusively that 1913-era straight deckers were woefully underpowered in the face of survival conditions.

Great Lakes freighters of that day had triple-expansion steam engines of between 1,000 and 1,600 horsepower. By comparison, thirty years later, a World War II liberty ship of roughly equal size and speed to a 1913-vintage lake freighter was powered by a 2,500-horsepower engine. This difference in power was not the result of technological improvements. Steam engines in 1943 were not significantly advanced from those of 1913. Rather, the smaller horsepower of engines placed in Great Lakes freighters was a matter of economics. Smaller engines cost less to build and used less fuel over the lifetime of the ship.

Design flaws such as the underpowering of Great Lakes bulk freighters were never officially investigated in the aftermath of the White Hurricane. In its year-end report, the Lake Carriers Association gave only the barest hint that the storm was not the sole cause of the carnage. The document quietly acknowledged that something might have been wrong with the ships, but suggested more "investigation" was needed.

The lessons of the storm, however, will not be lost. It had not been thought possible hitherto that a bulk freighter, with its great flat bottom, could be forced to turn turtle, but some unknown combination of circumstances certainly caused the *Charles S. Price* to do so. How this could possibly be accomplished may be fathomed by those competent to investigate the subject. Certainly the revelation comes to us with something of a shock. As stated, the whole subject will undoubtedly be investigated to determine whether modification of structure or increase in power in our larger vessels is necessary.

ANNUAL REPORT, 1913 LAKE CARRIERS ASSOCIATION

One Cleveland naval architect had the courage to step forward with proposals to improve straight deckers based on knowledge gained during the storm. "For their size, Great Lakes vessels do not have enough power. With their shallow depth and extreme length, they need a great deal of power to make headway against a wind," J. R. Oldham stated flatly. He explained that the average speed of a 1913 bulk freighter was only 9 miles per hour. He suggested that they should be able to make a minimum of 12 miles per hour. The naval architect admitted he was not sure that the additional horsepower to reach that minimal speed would be sufficient during a major storm.

"The reason I say lake steamers should have more power is, that in these enclosed waters they must be able to keep ahead of the wind. A matter of ten miles out of its course and a steamer goes on the rocks. Unless it is powerful enough to drive on, it is sure to be carried by the wind," Oldham emphasized to a *Cleveland Plain Dealer* reporter. Similar comments were made by other ship designers in the United States and Canada.

Even though the inadequate horsepower of Great Lakes ships was made obvious by the storm of 1913, little immediate attention was paid to Oldham's recommendations to increase the size of engines. The 504-foot straight decker *Charles S. Price*, which had a single triple-expansion engine of 1,760 horsepower, was built in 1910 by American Shipbuilding at Lorain, Ohio. Three years after the White Hurricane, the same yard turned out the *Henry G. Dalton*, a 587-foot bulk freighter with a single engine of only 1,800 horsepower, virtually identical to the smaller *Price*.

Except for a handful of sailing vessels, all commercial ships on the lakes in 1913 were steamships. (Diesel and diesel-electric plants were still a generation in the future.) Engine horsepower is only one way of measuring a steamship's power output. Equally important is the combined surface areas of the fire grates in the boiler fireboxes. The area of the fire grates determines how quickly a ship can replenish steam when the engine is running at full throttle. Operating wide open takes heat out of the steam, heat that must be replaced by the fire beneath the boiler. A ship with larger fireboxes below its boilers can sustain high output demands better than a vessel with smaller fireboxes.

Straight deckers like the capsized *Charles S. Price* typically had heating surfaces of 4,500 to 6,000 square feet. The poststorm *Henry G. Dalton* was given only 6,405 square feet to feed its 1,800 horsepower. Significantly, when the *Dalton's* boilers were replaced in 1948, the new installation had 8,712 square feet of heating surface. That represents a 30 percent increase in the ship's ability to generate steam under emergency conditions.

Eventually, lakes freighters did receive larger engines fed by enlarged boilers and fireboxes. In 1942, the 622-foot *Benjamin F. Fairless* was launched at Lorain with a single 4,400-horsepower engine. One reason for the increase in power was to gain speed. This was the first of a group of ships known as the "Supers." Slightly larger than the standard 1942 freighter, the Supers were capable of 14 to 16 miles per hour, compared to the 11 to 12 miles per hour made by the previous generation of Great Lakes bulk freighters. The *Fairless'* boilers had a combined heating surface of 16,992 square feet, almost three times that of a 1913-era ship.

Eight ships were lost with all hands on Lake Huron during the White Hurricane: five were U.S. vessels and three Canadian. Of the U.S. ships, all five were built by the American Shipbuilding Company yard in Lorain, Ohio. Two—the *Charles S. Price* and the *Isaac M. Scott*—were nearly identical 504-foot vessels turned out for the M. A. Hanna Company. Other than the Lorain shipyard, there does not seem to be a common factor influencing the loss of the five American ships. There may be a simple answer as to why so many vessels built by one yard foundered. American Shipbuilding was one of the most prolific yards on the Great Lakes at the beginning of the twentieth century. Most of the straight deckers launched at Lorain served on routes that followed Lakes Huron and Erie. So it was natural that a large number of American Shipbuilding hulls would have been exposed to the storm on Huron.

Naval architect Oldham also criticized the practice of allowing iron ore, coal, or grain to rise in pyramid-shaped piles inside the holds of straight-deck ships. These mounds with steeply sloping sides were the natural result of loading the ships through gravity chutes that extended from dockside hoppers. Oldham worried that the resulting mounds of cargo were unstable when ships began rolling in a seaway.

"Cargoes of these vessels always should be trimmed," he said. (Trimming is the process of leveling the pile in the hold.) "Ore or coal, when loaded into the ships, should be leveled off. There is no doubt in my mind that several of the vessels lost in this storm went on their beam ends in the gale because their cargoes shifted. Shifting of a cargo of ore, coal, or grain will send a steamer over on its side at once."

The capsized hulk of the *Charles S. Price* on Lake Huron has been cited as proof of Oldham's criticisms of cargo handling aboard 1913 straight-deck freighters. To date, no one has suggested a better reason why that ship rolled over in the storm. Additional proof of Oldham's shifting cargo theory may be that most of the wrecks lost during the White Hurricane have been found upside down on the bottom.

One of those overturned wrecks is the 504-foot *Isaac M. Scott*, last seen afloat just before 11 A.M. on Sunday, right before the White Hurricane struck with full force. Although not an exact sister ship, this vessel was nearly identical in size, horsepower, and fire grate area to the "mystery ship," the *Charles S. Price*. Both vessels came out of the American Shipbuilding yard in Lorain, Ohio. Like the *Price*, the *Scott* appears to have capsized on the surface before it sank. The overturned hull was discovered in 1976 half a dozen miles northeast of Thunder Bay Island, not far from where it was last seen. The *Scott* is reportedly half buried in mud.

There is no way of knowing if the overturned hull of the *Scott* floated for any period of time before sinking. It is possible that this ship was the upside-down hulk spotted by the *W.H. Gratwick* on the Thursday following the White Hurricane. If so, it would add another eerie point of coincidence linking the *Scott* with the unfortunate *Price*.

The *Price* and the *Scott* shared one additional similarity. Both were loaded with coal, which is considered a "light" cargo. Most ships could be filled right up underneath the hatches with coal and still not be overloaded. Coal piled that high is effectively trapped on all sides and cannot shift from one side to the other of the vessel. Although trimming cargo is obviously a good idea, Oldham's cargo shift theory may not be the real reason for the capsize of either the *Price* or the *Scott*.

Oldham was hardly the first naval architect to point out that the row of hatches on Great Lakes straight deckers was an inherent weakness of the design. "The greatest fault with the lake steamers lies in the hatches," he said. "The hatch combings [sic] are low—about twelve inches in height. They should be three feet high. The hatches should be stronger and heavier, and more attention should be paid to the hatch coverings."

This leads to the possibility that excessive amounts of water got into the holds of both the *Price* and the *Scott* as combers rolled across their decks. Air is trapped in the spaces between and around lumps of coal in a cargo hold. These spaces could just as easily have been filled with water coming down through leaking hatches. This water would have percolated slowly downward; perhaps it never reached the bottom of the hold where pumps could remove it. Instead, much of the water may have been trapped high in the coal, where its weight added to both ships' instability problems.

Stability has always been a problem in the design of Great Lakes ships because of the shallow waterways they must negotiate. Oldham noted that Great Lakes ships could not be built to the optimal length-to-depth ratio for a cargo vessel. "Lake Steamers are of peculiar construction," the naval architect said. "They are about eighteen times as long as they are deep, whereas the safe ratio of length to depth is twelve or fourteen to one." Oldham pointed out that the shallow stretches of the St. Marys, St. Clair, and Detroit Rivers made it impossible to build ocean-style deep-draft freighters.

"The type won't be changed because it is the only sort of vessel that can navigate on the lakes," Oldham admitted in the November 17, 1913, *Cleveland Plain Dealer*. "The lake steamer must be able to carry a great cargo, but it must be shallow. So, the type and general construction will remain the same. But, the remedies I speak of will be made. They are practical and ship owners could adopt the changes if they would."

Toronto naval architect W. E. Redway pointed out the same list of flaws in the design of Great Lakes vessels. In a letter to newspapers, he noted that Lloyds' rules (specifications required for a ship to qualify for insurance through Lloyds of London) required that the length of ships not exceed 16 times the depth of their hulls. On the lakes, the typical straight decker had a length 17 or more times its depth, which was outside the Lloyds guidelines. Redway published the following table to illustrate his contention.

Redway pointed out in a letter printed in the *Duluth Herald* on December 1, 1913, that Great Lakes ships of 1913 were potentially weaker than their oceangoing counterparts, even though "those two boats are constructed . . . of precisely the same weight of metal." He carefully explained the importance of this difference. "Looking upon them roughly as two girders, we have the ocean boat with about 4,750 tons of metal as a girder 460 feet long, 41 feet deep. The Lake boat with about 4,750 tons of steel as a girder 530 feet long and 31 feet deep. This does not prove that the 530-foot ship is too weak for the work she has to perform, but that is what we want to find out."

Possible evidence of the instability of Great Lakes straight deckers during survival conditions lies at the bottom of Lakes Superior and Huron. The majority of the sunken hulks from the storm have been found upside down on the bottom. No one can say for sure, but this is a good indication that the ships rolled over on the surface and sank inverted. The one glaring exception is the steamer *Wexford*, which was originally built for ocean service. It sits bolt upright on the bottom as if waiting to resume its long-interrupted voyage.

There is always some element of mystery when a ship sinks. That mystery was multiplied a dozen-fold by the White Hurricane. So much mystery surrounding so many founderings did not escape the attention of either

COMPARISON OF OCEAN AND GREAT LAKES FREIGHTERS, PER W. E. REDWAY, TORONTO, 1913

	Ocean Boat	Lake Boat
length, ft.	460	530
beam, ft.	48.5	56
depth, ft.	41	31
draft, ft.	27	19
horsepower	4,000	2,000
depth to length	11.2	17.1
draft to length	20.7	28
watertight bulkheads	6	3

the public or the shipping industry. In its 1913 annual report, the Lake Carriers Association discussed what it quaintly described as the "wastage of
steel vessels" during the first thirteen years of the twentieth century. At
least forty-six iron and steel ships were lost during that period. They
included ships built in U.S., Canadian, and British shipyards. Thirty percent
of those ships—fourteen vessels—foundered during the 1913 storm.

Mystery was common to most of those forty-six losses. No one could
explain the loss of *Bannockburn* in 1902, the *Cyprus* in 1907, the *Clem-
son* in 1908, the car ferry *Marquette & Bessemer No. 2* in 1909, or the *Pere
Marquette 18* in 1910. The thirty-two-man crew of the *Pere Marquette 18*
was rescued, but none of them could say what made their ship founder.
Until 1913 all of the vessel losses had been single-ship events. Suddenly,
eight modern steel ships disappeared almost simultaneously on Lake
Huron and one each on Lake Superior and Lake Erie. Not a single life was
saved from any of them. There were no living witnesses to explain what
had gone wrong.

For its part, the Lake Carriers Association never publicly admitted that
the White Hurricane proved there were defects in the design of Great
Lakes ships. Rather, the organization viewed the storm as a random event.
In a printed report on the storm, the association claimed the storm was
unprecedented.

> No lake master can recall in all his experience a storm of such unprece-
> dented violence with such rapid changes in the direction of the wind
> and its gusts of such fearful speed! Storms ordinarily of that velocity do
> not last over four or five hours, but this storm raged for sixteen hours
> continuously at an average velocity of sixty miles per hour, with fre-
> quent spurts of seventy and over.
>
> Obviously, with a wind of such long duration, the seas that were
> made were such that the lakes are not ordinarily acquainted with.
> The testimony of masters is that the waves were at least 35 feet high
> and followed each other in quick succession, three waves ordinarily
> coming right after the other. . . . They were considerably shorter than
> the waves that are formed by an ordinary gale. Being of such height
> and hurled with such force and rapid succession, the ships must have
> been subjected to incredible punishment.
>
> ANNUAL REPORT, 1913 LAKE CARRIERS ASSOCIATION

While the great storm showed the need for improvements in the design of Great Lakes bulk freighters, it is simplistic to argue that ships of 1913 were categorically underpowered or flimsy. The Lake Carriers Association pointed out that the storm of 1913 was capable of overpowering even the best human machinery. Because that statement was at least partially true, it was easy for ship owners to ignore the need for improvements in the design and construction of Great Lakes vessels.

UNLIKE SHIPS, the system of government weather warnings was improved (if only slightly) under pressure from the investigations, accusations, and rebuttals involving the fledgling U.S. Weather Bureau. In the aftermath of the White Hurricane, the Weather Bureau claimed it had been limited to hoisting only a simple storm warning—even though this claim was belied by the bureau's own published descriptions, which stated flatly that hurricane warnings could be posted for extremely severe and dangerous storms of nontropical origin. Internal bureau policy had apparently outrun bureau publications, and the bureau stood firm on this point. But largely as a result of the 1913 storm, a new level of weather advisory was authorized. Under the new system, predicted winds of 38 to 55 miles per hour were indicated by the posting of a *gale warning*, while *storm warnings* were reserved for winds of 55 or more miles per hour. This was, at least, a clarification of the pre-1913 warning signals. No longer would anything more severe than a small-craft warning be termed a storm; in the future, it was hoped, storm warnings would be taken more seriously.

Even today, however, hurricane warnings are not posted by U.S. meteorologists on the Great Lakes—not even if wind, precipitation, and wave conditions duplicate or exceed those of a tropical storm. By the same definition used in 1913, "hurricane warnings" can only be posted for a tropical storm. Curiously, U.S. meteorologists are permitted to issue exactly the warning that captains of lake freighters clamored for in 1913—"hurricane-force winds"—for extratropical storms on the Atlantic and Pacific high seas. This phrase is also authorized in all Canadian forecasts if conditions warrant, whether or not the storm causing the winds originated in the tropics.

From a practical standpoint, however, discussion over the legitimacy of hurricane warnings on the Great Lakes is no longer significant. The

1913 system of flags and lights is no longer in use. The U.S. National Weather Service (successor to the Weather Bureau) has discontinued displaying those archaic signals. Only a few yacht clubs and other private organizations still cling to the old warning flags and lights, out of habit or tradition. Otherwise, lamps and flags have been relegated to the past along with ringtailed topsails, paddle wheels, Morse code, and manila rope. In place of the antiquated signals, commercial ships receive weather information directly from satellites and ground stations. It is common to hear a coast guard operator reading immediate warnings of threatening weather over the marine radio. Even so, the debate over accurate forecasting continues. As government forecasts improve, the expectations of sailors increase. There is likely no end to this inflationary spiral of increased accuracy followed by higher expectations, simply because weather forecasting can never be a precise science. When predicting weather over a wide area, there are too many variables for even a modern supercomputer to consider.

The financial cost of the 1913 storm was enormous. The Great Lakes Protective Association, a cooperative that carried about 25 percent of the insurance on lake vessels and cargoes, was forced to increase its rates. On December 4, the GLPA announced it would increase the contribution of members by 2 percent to a total of 6 percent of the value of cargoes carried.

> The value of vessels totally lost amounted to $2,332,000, the constructive total losses to $830,900, making the total value of hulls destroyed $3,162,900. The damage to stranded vessels, as nearly as can be estimated, will amount to $620,000, while the losses on cargoes will not be far from $1,000,000, making the aggregate loss of hull and cargo combined $4,782,900.

> ANNUAL REPORT, 1913 LAKE CARRIERS ASSOCIATION

Probably the last storm victim's body to come ashore that year was that of Axel Larsen, captain of the barge *Plymouth*, wrecked in Lake Michigan. He was found half-buried in sand about 15 miles north of Muskegon, Michigan. At about the time Larsen's body was being pulled from the sand, the Lake Carriers Association was adding up the death benefits paid during the 1913 sailing season. The White Hurricane occurred prior to seamen's unions and passage of the Jones Act, which spells out benefits that ship owners must pay to injured American sailors. Although the association paid out $18,245.60, a substantial sum in 1913 dollars, as compensation for the deaths of 253 sailors, that amounted only to an average of $72 per victim—less than a month's wage.

Until the White Hurricane, the year 1913 had been safer than normal on the Great Lakes. Only nine sailors had died on the job prior to the storm. That compared to thirty-three deaths in 1912 and fifty-one in 1911. The size of the financial cost of the death benefits can be gauged by comparing those paid in 1913 against 1914. During the year following the White Hurricane, the association paid only $4,025 in benefits, less than a quarter of the 1913 payments.

The large number of vessels in the 1913 Great Lakes fleet meant that a significant number of ships were operating during that first week of November. This explains why at least seventy vessels were caught on Lakes Superior, Huron, and Erie by the storm. Today the total number of ships in the fleet is smaller, so a storm of equal ferocity would have fewer targets. Yet the threat of another White Hurricane is always present.

Destruction of the modern steel freighter *Edmund Fitzgerald* on November 10, 1975, proved that the five lakes still can overwhelm modern technology. Much like the White Hurricane, that storm began as a run-of-the-mill low-pressure center. The only difference was that the 1975 storm was born over south-central Kansas when warm, moist air from the Gulf of Mexico met cold Canadian air. A jet stream pushed this burgeoning storm into the path of the hapless freighter.

The "*Fitz*" and its twenty-nine-man crew simply disappeared, even though its captain had requested nearby vessels to keep an eye on him. Though immortalized in Canadian troubadour Gordon Lightfoot's ballad "The Wreck of the Edmund Fitzgerald," the doomed ship *Fitzgerald* is only a footnote in Great Lakes history compared with the loss of lives and ships during many other Great Lakes storms. It was only one ship, not a fleet of fourteen vessels. Nothing like the White Hurricane of 1913 has been seen again on the Great Lakes. Every sailor knows, however, that it can happen on any steel-gray November day when major weather systems line up just right.

SUMMER 1986

NOTHING MORE WAS LEARNED ABOUT THE LOSS of the *Regina* on Lake Huron until 1986, when three divers discovered the wreck about 3 miles offshore between Port Sanilac and Lexington, Michigan. Wayne Brusate, Gary Biniecki, and John Severance found the ship using sophisticated side-scan sonar and a bit of luck. Like the *Price*, the *Regina* lies upside-down in about 80 feet of water.

The trio of sport divers had been looking for a sunken tugboat. They were surprised when their equipment showed the silhouette of a large, unknown ship instead of the smaller boat. No one had suspected there was a large wreck in the vicinity. One of the trio suited up and went down to investigate. Within minutes he was back on the surface. Wayne Brusate had become the first person to see the *Regina* in seventy-three years.

During the next two years a careful archaeological investigation was undertaken to explore the wreck and catalog the artifacts found. Recovered items included copper navigation lanterns, electric light fixtures, and the ship's bell. The ship's compass also was recovered in working condition. From the cargo came bottles of whiskey and champagne, still sealed and in perfect condition.

Divers discovered the fatal injury to *Regina*'s bottom as they studied the wreck. A three-foot-long hole was located under the forward end of the center cargo hold. There were also several large dents near the hole, indicating that the ship probably bumped the rocky bottom several times in the shallows between Port Sanilac and Lexington. Divers speculated that the ship's bilge pumps might have become clogged with straw from the cargo, possibly mixed with the roofing tar that was also in the holds.

Stretching forward from the ship's hawsepipe is *Regina*'s anchor chain. It is bar-tight, still under strain from the pull of the hull when the ship was on the surface. This confirms that the crew was successful in anchoring during the height of the storm. The anchor remains lodged where it caught on that fatal Sunday night. Further evidence from the depths confirmed that the crew managed to launch the lifeboat that was later found on the Canadian beach with the bodies of two crewmembers still in it.

Divers discovered nothing to link the sinking of *Regina* to the capsizing of the *Price*. The package freighter's hull is not marked or dented as it would have been if it had collided with a larger ship. However, evidence that a lifeboat was launched from the Canadian freighter caused renewed interest in the possibility that the crews of the two ships did cross paths that fatal night. Based on where wreckage from the ship drifted ashore, the *Regina*'s lifeboat drifted slightly south as it moved east across the lake to the Canadian shoreline. It may well have crossed the path of any steamers heading north from the vicinity of the entrance to the St. Clair River.

The commingled bodies and wreckage on an Ontario beach suggest the fantastic possibility of an impossible rescue attempt at the height of the White Hurricane. *Regina*'s distress whistle was heard on shore at just about 11 P.M. Assuming this marked the time when the crew launched their lifeboat, an hour later the lifeboat would have drifted south and east, pushed by wind and waves, to the place where upbound and downbound steamer tracks converge on the St. Clair River. It is entirely possible that sometime after midnight on Monday the *Regina* survivors saw the bow of a freighter emerging through blinding snow.

That bow would have belonged to the *Charles S. Price*. Based on where the ship was seen earlier in the day by other vessels, the *Price* reversed its course at the foot of Lake Huron and started back northward just before midnight. It is hard to imagine that a small object like a lifeboat could have been spotted at night through the swirling snow and towering waves. Perhaps the men of *Regina* ignited a flare or flashed a lantern. We will never know.

If the crew of the *Price* did spot *Regina*'s tiny lifeboat, they undoubtedly would have felt compelled to rescue its occupants. That is the way of sailors. But how do you take men off a fragile lifeboat in 35-foot seas? To accomplish such a daring rescue would have required maneuvering the freighter to create a protected lee from the wind and waves. In effect, the steel sides of the ship would have been used as a breakwater to give a calm harbor for the transfer of survivors from boat to ship. This maneuver would have been similar to that still used by ships picking up mail on the Detroit River. The *Price* would have made a gentle turn at slow speed to create a tiny patch of water calm enough for a rescue.

The most dangerous part of this maneuver would have been slowing the *Price* to a virtual halt. Without sufficient power from its engine, it would have been extremely difficult to control the heading of the bow during the critical minutes while the crew of the lifeboat were hauled aboard the freighter. A large marine steam engine takes some seconds to go from a dead stop to maximum revolutions, and that would have further extended the period of time during which the ship would not have responded to its helm.

Perhaps the *Price* turned the smallest bit too far. Perhaps the bow was caught by a 70-mile-per-hour gust of wind.

Suddenly, the *Price* was in the deadly trough of the waves with its engine developing no power—the propeller was barely turning. Wheelsman Arze McIntosh reacted instinctively, turning the steering wheel to bring the ship's head back into the wind and sea. The steam-powered steering engine in the fantail instantly responded and the rudder turned in response to the wheelsman, but the hull did not answer its rudder because there was no discharge current from the bronze propeller. Holding the steering wheel hard against the stop, McIntosh may have fervently wished one final time that he had gone ashore with Milton Smith back in Ashtabula.

The men in the pilothouse would have been hanging onto anything handy as the deck tilted out from beneath their feet. The first roll would have been frightening, and the second worse. In the galley, steward Herbert Jones quickly backed away from his stove. He didn't want to be thrown against its hot surface. With each roll the ship turned more into the trough and the tilt of the deck increased. Amid flying dishes and falling tins of food, Steward Jones pulled himself hand over hand across the galley to the outside door. Never in his career had he been on a ship that rolled like this. He wanted to comfort his wife.

The *Charles S. Price* was now caught by a fatal series of sympathetic rolls in the troughs of the passing waves. Momentum from one roll fed into the next, and the next. The angle of the deck at the peak of each roll grew steeper. It was becoming physically dangerous inside the ship as everything not bolted down started flying about: dishes in the galley, books on the navigation table, tools on the engine room workbench.

Then, there was one long roll and everyone knew it was the last. From the *Regina*'s lifeboat the sight of the steel freighter rolling keel over pilot-house would have been more chilling than the arctic wind and glacier waves. For an agonizing moment the men in the lifeboat must have thought the *Price* was about to crush them.

Straight deckers have large doors on either side of their engine room to allow the removal or replacement of broken machinery. These doors also are used for ventilation when waves permit. No other place on the *Price* was close enough to the ship's waterline to pull men aboard from a lifeboat. Chief Engineer John Groundwater would likely have been in that door directing the rescue party when the rolling started. Now, this large square opening was the only escape from certain death in the capsizing ship. Groundwater looked back, but there was no one behind him. He pulled himself through the opening as the stern rapidly settled out from beneath him. Emerging from the heat of the engine room made the freezing water seem all that much colder.

The lifeboat unexpectedly became the rescue vessel. A few survivors of the *Price*, maybe no more than Groundwater, were pulled into the small boat. If the Canadian shoreline had not been so many miles to leeward, there might have been survivors to tell this harrowing tale of rescue-turned-disaster. By the time the lifeboat finally drifted ashore, its occupants were either unconscious or dead—victims of hypothermia. The unguided boat pitched over in the breakers, spilling its frozen human contents onto the beach.

Great Lakes historian and author William Ratigan pointed out in 1960 that while at least one member of the *Price*'s crew was found in a *Regina* life vest, the reverse was never discovered. No bodies from the Canadian ship's crew were ever found in life vests from the *Price*. This seems to indicate that the lifeboat from the package freighter may have rescued some members of the overturned ship's crew, but that *Price* sailors did not succeed in rescuing the men from the *Regina*.

There is no speculation over the fate of *Regina*'s Captain McConkey. He stayed with his ship past the end. His body did not come ashore in November with other members of his crew. It was discovered near Lexington, Michigan, in August of the following year. From the appearance of the crushed forward deckhouse, divers exploring the wreck in 1986 theorize that McConkey was in his cabin when the ship rolled over and sank.

They think that during the winter of 1913–14 the deckhouse collapsed under the weight of the steel hull. By August 1914, lake currents brought the young captain ashore for burial.

Divers combing through the wreckage discovered a shattered piece of wooden cabin with an old-fashioned light switch attached. It appeared to be the one that Captain McConkey would have operated on the night the ship sank, because it came from the area of the captain's cabin in the wreckage. With great reverence, divers retrieved the switch and polished it carefully before presenting the button to Aileen McConkey Reeves, the captain's daughter. The memento would help seventy-seven-year-old Aileen remember her father for the rest of her life.

APPENDIX 1

CAPTAIN LYONS' LETTER

THE FOLLOWING LETTER was written by Captain S. A. Lyons to the secretary of the Cleveland Cliffs Iron Company, the company that owned the steamer *J.H. Sheadle*. In the letter Lyons answers questions about why he turned his ship around three times on lower Lake Huron between the evening of November 9 and the morning of November 10, 1913. The *Sheadle* was one of only two ships known to have survived the lower half of Lake Huron Sunday afternoon and night.

STEAMER J.H. SHEADLE

Ann Arbor, Dec. 24, 1913
Mr. J.H. Sheadle, Secretary
The Cleveland-Cliffs Iron Co.
Cleveland, Ohio

Dear Sir:

Your letter received referring to my statement of the last trip, asking for my reasons for turning around three times during the storm of November 7, 8, and 9.

   The first time, I turned around at the lower end of Lake Huron owing to the circumstances. I did not consider it safe to proceed any further on our course toward the river, or get in the locality of where downbound steamers would likely be at anchor. From the soundings I felt perfectly safe in turning as I did. I had figured for some time previous on doing so, and had given the engineer ample time to be in readiness at such a time to turn around, which we did at the exact time and I have every reason to believe in the locality I had figured on.

You may ask the question why I did not let go my anchors after turning around under such conditions. I did not consider it a safe policy to do so, for had I attempted it there was a long chance of losing them, and at the same time putting the steamer in a position where it would be impossible to handle her. In fact, it has always been my policy not to try to find a harbor or anchorage under such conditions as long as my boat is seaworthy and is acting satisfactorily in every way.

The second time I turned, I figured I was far enough from the river to get back shortly after daylight, and besides I was not going that way with my cargo. I had also given the engineer due notice in regard to time, etc. Of course, we would naturally expect a little more difficulty in turning this time, but by the proper handling of the engines and the helm we turned around and headed back for the river.

The third time we turned there was no sea to speak of and we had no difficulty whatever in turning. The soundings were not satisfactory, and it was still snowing so that we could see no distance, and I did not consider it safe to proceed any further, especially as the soundings I had been getting were not satisfactory. I considered it policy to keep in good water until it cleared up.

About ten minutes after turning the last time it began to clear up so we could make out the shoreline on both sides of the lake.

As to the question of the safety of the steamer other than stranding or collision, I considered her perfectly safe, as we had only run our ballast pump five hours in the twenty-four, and one-half of this time was taken up pumping out the weather side. After covering up the vent pipes on deck leading to the ballast tanks we had very little pumping to do.

At 11:00 A.M. on the ninth I called up the engineer and told him to start the ballast pumps on the weather side, and at 1:30 P.M. he called me and said they had a suck on all tanks on that side, and from that time on we only pumped two and a half hours during the bad weather.

I can truthfully say to you that at no time during this storm did I have any fear whatever for the safety of the steamer, and if any of my crew thought differently their actions did not show it.

Trust this explanation as to why I turned will be satisfactory to you.

Yours very truly,
S.A. Lyons

APPENDIX 2

LAKE LORE

Geography

Massive sheets of ice have flowed down from the polar region to cover much of North America several times during the past 2.5 million years. Geologists estimate that in places these glaciers were up to 2 miles thick. At least four distinct ice ages, or glaciations, have visited the places where Chicago, Detroit, and Cleveland are now built, the most recent of which was the Laurentide ice sheet. This immense glacier scooped and molded the solid rock over which it moved. In geologic terms the Laurentide retreated only the blink of an eye ago, when the earth's climate began its current warming trend. Since that last glacier, the five Great Lakes have seen only a hundred centuries of ice-free summers. This means the lakes are young in geologic terms, not much older than human civilization. The last glacier ice is thought to have melted off the northern shore of Lake Superior ten thousand years ago, about when people in Egypt and the Middle East were forming their first agricultural communities.

Because they are so large, these five sweetwater seas create their own private climate, quite different from that of the surrounding North American continent. Cities around the lakes have a higher percentage of cloud cover than the rainy northwest states of Washington and Oregon. "Snow clouds" pile up over Chicago, Detroit, Cleveland, and Buffalo each autumn. People living around the lakes often find the percentage of cloudy days unnerving.

In a storm, all five inland seas produce waves with steep sides and plunging tops. Unlike the smooth swells of the world's oceans, these steep, choppy seas are characteristic of Great Lakes storms. Nothing is safe from their onslaught. Freshwater storm waves easily alter the rocky shorelines, sometimes causing tens of feet of land to erode and disappear during a single night. A 4-foot-high wave striking a coastline expends more than 35,000 horsepower per mile of beach. During the four centuries of commercial navigation on the lakes, six thousand to ten thousand vessels have succumbed to that kind of pounding from steep, plunging freshwater waves. Remains of these unfortunate wrecks litter the bottoms of all five Great Lakes.

Scientists who study the oceans have developed mathematical tables to predict the size of waves based on wind speed and duration. These tables indicate that a 40-knot wind can produce a wave from 8 to 36 feet in height, depending upon the fetch and duration of the storm. But these predictions are based on salt water and are not accurate for the less dense fresh water of the Great Lakes. There are no tables generally available for predicting freshwater wave heights.

It is known, however, that fresh water responds more quickly to wind than does salt water. The density of water in the lakes also affects the shapes of the waves. Instead of the smooth billows common on the ocean, the Great Lakes develop short, "choppy" waves that slam vessels in rapid succession. Rapid-fire pounding by breaking waves continues to be a significant factor in the loss of ships. These waves have knocked apart pilothouses and other portions of vessel superstructures as thoroughly as if they had been struck by a wrecker's ball.

> To the lesser degree of density of fresh water is due the breaking of the waves with a quicker, pounding motion, quite different in character from the larger and comparatively sluggish billows of the ocean.
>
> JAMES COOKE MILLS, *Our Inland Seas*

Waves on the Great Lakes also are affected by the season of the year, with the most dangerous coming late in the navigation season. Scientists speculate that cold winter winds are denser and thus create more friction on the surface of relatively warm lake waters.

The relatively shallow water in the lakes (compared to the oceans) also contributes to the rapid growth of large, steep waves. Lake billows grow in height and bunch tightly together as they move through shallow water and begin to "feel" the bottom. The visible portion of the wave above the water becomes unstable, and its top begins to outrun its base. At the same time, the sides of the wave become steeper, and wave crests bunch closer together. Water then tumbles off the wave fronts, creating dangerous plunging breakers. These are not the decorative "white caps" depicted by painters of seascapes. The plunging breakers of the Great Lakes are huge, sometimes tens of feet tall.

The geographic shapes of the individual lakes play a large role in both the creation of waves and their size. High winds build the biggest waves when they blow parallel to the long axis of each lake. Since the orientation of the lakes is not uniform, each body of water responds differently to the same storm.

LAKE ERIE

Length: 210 miles
Breadth: 57 miles
Depth: 62 feet average, 210 feet maximum
Water Volume: 116 cubic miles
Elevation: 571 feet

Shallowest of the five, Erie lies in a roughly southwest-to-northeast orientation. Strong winds from either of these directions build large waves.

LAKE HURON

Length: 206 miles
Breadth: 183 miles
Depth: 194 feet average, 748 feet maximum
Volume: 850 cubic miles
Elevation: 581 feet

Lake Huron has a predominant north–south orientation, but the upper end lies almost east to west. Winds from any direction build swells on Huron. The roughest portion of the lake is considered to be off Port Austin where the shallow waters of Saginaw Bay meet the deep lake.

LAKE MICHIGAN

Length: 307 miles
Breadth: 118 miles
Depth: 279 feet average, 925 feet maximum
Volume: 1,180 cubic miles
Elevation: 581 feet

Oriented north to south, winds from either the north or the south quickly create ocean-size waves on Lake Michigan. Neither the rocky Wisconsin nor the sandy Michigan shoreline offers protection for ships from these waves.

LAKE SUPERIOR

Length: 350 miles
Breadth: 160 miles
Depth:4   89 feet average, 1,335 feet maximum
Volume: 2,934 cubic miles
Elevation: 600 feet

This body of water is large enough that high winds from any direction pile up significant seas. However, the western end of Superior has a strong south-west-to-northeast orientation, while the eastern half is tilted northwest to southeast. As a result, sea conditions can be quite different from one end of the big lake to the other.

Lake Superior contains more water than all four other Great Lakes combined.

LAKE ONTARIO

Length: 193 miles
Breadth: 53 miles
Depth: 282 feet average, 804 feet maximum
Volume: 393 cubic miles
Elevation: 245 feet

This lake lies on a southwest-to-northeast orientation, making it susceptible to the prevailing westerly winds. By good fortune, it was largely spared in 1913.

Language of the Lakes

Fresh and salt water are so much alike, yet they cannot be confused. One is sweet to the lips; the other, bitter. A ship sinks deeply in fresh water and rises as it sails into the salty sea. Similarly, the sailors and ships of the sweetwater seas are different from the saltwater companions. Nowhere are the differences more obvious than in the language of the two groups. For those readers who are "salties," the parlance of the lakes may be a bit confusing.

An unusual custom on the lakes involves the naming of ships. While ships are always "she" to sailors, bulk freighters on the lakes are usually given masculine names. The reason is a long-standing tradition to name vessels after executives or investors in the companies that own them. Quite often, the ship and its namesake are active at the same time, which can lead to gender misunderstandings. So, in conversation only the ship's last name is used and it is usually proceeded by "the" to signify that the name refers to a vessel and not a person.

One indicator of the lack of importance that sailors in 1913 attached to scientific weather forecasting was their lack of uniform weather terminology. One man's "gale" was another's "storm." Either word could be used to describe foul weather, as could the more colorful term *blow*. Sailors at the beginning of the twentieth century seem to have paid little attention to their choice of words to describe foul weather. Newspaper accounts also interchanged these words as if they were synonymous. They have no specific definition beyond a chaotic mix of wind, water, and waves commonly known as a "storm."

Great Lakes Glossary

Aft—Toward the stern, or back, of the ship.

Boat—Great Lakes sailors traditionally call their ships "boats." The term is ubiquitous. To differentiate between small craft and true ships, most of the time it is modified by a description of the cargo carried—thus "cement boat" or "ore boat."

Boilerhouse—The deckhouse above the ship's boilers and engine rooms. Usually all the way aft on Great Lakes ships.

BOW CUSHION—The sense that the bow wave of a ship "pushes" against the near bank of a river, forcing the bow to turn away from the bank. This effect "cushions" the bow against striking the near bank.

BREAKWALL—An artificial wall built of stone to protect a harbor from lake waves.

BRIDGE WING—Narrow walkways extending outward from both sides of the pilothouse to the full width of the ship. Officers use bridge wings to when docking of maneuvering in locks and narrow waterways.

CHADBURN—Originally the name of a company that manufactured engine order telegraphs. Now applied generically by Great Lakes sailors to any such device no matter what the company origin.

CROSS SEA—A condition when waves from one weather system continue despite shift in wind. Waves generated by the new wind run at an angle to the old, creating confused water that can be particularly dangerous.

DOWNBOUND—Generally, sailing from Duluth at the head of Lake Superior toward the St. Lawrence River and the sea. On Lake Michigan, "downbound" means heading north from Chicago toward the Straits of Mackinac.

FIDDLEY—An area above the boilers designed for the intake of fresh air. Fiddley grates prevent people or objects from falling into the boiler room.

FLYING BRIDGE—An open area on top of a ship's pilothouse that serves as an operating station for the officers in good weather.

JACKLINE—A temporary wire strung from bow to stern to which a safety harness can be attached to allow a crewmember to move over the deck during a storm.

LIFELINES—A railing on either side of the main deck made of steel cables supported by removable vertical posts. Lifelines are meant to prevent crewmembers from falling overboard.

LIFESAVER—Any member of the U.S. Lifesaving Service.

LIFESAVING SERVICE—In 1913, an agency of the U.S. federal government with the mission of saving the lives of sailors on stranded ships. Now merged into the U.S. Coast Guard.

MATE—A licensed deck officer who stands watch in the pilothouse. Normally three mates are carried, each standing two watches of 4 hours per day.

PILOTHOUSE—A small, glass-enclosed room on top of the texas from which the vessel is controlled. The steering wheel, compass, engine order telegraph, and chart table are here.

SEICHE—A wind-driven change in lake level. It occurs when high winds blow along the major axis of a lake, most particularly east-west on Lake Erie; or north-south on Lake Michigan. Water levels drop at the upwind end of the lake and rise at the downwind. Seiches produce tidelike water level changes, but do not occur on a schedule like tides.

SMOKESTACK—The external pipe taking smoke and firebox gases into the atmosphere. The term funnel is seldom used on the Great Lakes.

STACK ART—Each company painted its stacks in distinctive colors or with special symbols. This was done for quick identification of the owners.

SOO—Sailor's parlance for the area surrounding the cities of Sault Ste. Marie. Most often applied to the locks there. (Sault Ste. Marie is divided into two cities by the St. Marys River, which also serves as the international boundary between the United States and Canada.)

STEERING POLE—A light spar extending from the bow of a straight-deck ship to aid the wheelsman in steering.

STERN SUCTION—The tendency of the stern of a ship to swing toward the near bank when operating in a river or constricted waterway. This is caused by low pressure created between the ship and the bank as the result of Bernoulli's Principal.

STRAIGHT DECKER—Ships built with their pilothouses forward and engines aft to provide a continuous hold between. This design originated to meet the bulk freight demands on Great Lakes routes.

SUCKER HOLE—Colloquial term for a short spate of good weather that "suckers" sailors into leaving port just in time for the storm to resume at full force.

TEXAS—The large deckhouse immediately below the pilothouse of a straight-deck freighter.

TRIP—What would be a "voyage" on the ocean is a "trip" on the Great Lakes. The word most often refers to a two-way voyage, such as from Cleveland to Duluth and back.

UPBOUND—Generally, sailing from the St. Lawrence River and the sea toward Duluth, at the head of Lake Superior. On Lake Michigan, "upbound" means heading south from the Straits of Mackinac toward Chicago.

WATCHMAN—A term often applied to the member of the crew performing lookout duties.

WHEELSMAN—The person at the steering wheel, usually called a "quartermaster" on saltwater ships of the period.

WINDLASS ROOM—A triangular space enclosed within the bow of the ship where the anchor windlasses are located. Often, windlasses for handling docklines are located here as well. This room is where the forecastle of a saltwater ship would be located.

BIBLIOGRAPHY

MOST OF THE QUOTED accounts by witnesses and other principals in *White Hurricane* appeared in newspaper accounts of the day. several, however, are found in Barcus, *Freshwater Fury*, and Boyer, *True Tales of the Great Lakes*.

Primary Sources

Chicago Record-Herald. Chicago, Illinois.

Cleveland News. Cleveland, Ohio.

Cleveland Plain Dealer. Cleveland, Ohio.

Cleveland Press. Cleveland, Ohio.

Daily Local Record. U.S. Department of Agriculture, Weather Bureau. Toledo, Ohio.

Detroit Free Press. Detroit, Michigan.

Detroit News. Detroit, Michigan.

Duluth Herald. Duluth, Minnesota.

Duluth News-Tribune. Duluth, Minnesota.

Geofysiske Publikationer (Oslo) 1, no. 2 (1919).

Lake Carriers Association. Annual report. Cleveland, Ohio: Lake Carriers Association, 1913.

Marquette Daily Mining Journal. Marquette, Michigan.

Monthly Meteorological Notes at Detroit, Marquette, Sault Ste. Marie, Toledo, Chicago, Buffalo, and Cleveland. November 1913. (This is a section of each U.S. Weather Bureau station's monthly report to Washington, D.C., in which the observer was able to make written comments about the weather conditions.)

Original Monthly Record of Observations at Detroit, Marquette, Sault Ste. Marie, Toledo, Chicago, Buffalo, Cleveland, Minneapolis, and Savannah for November 1913. U.S. Department of Agriculture, Weather Bureau.

Port Huron Times-Herald. Port Huron, Michigan.

Russell, Israel C. *Lakes of North America: a reading lesson for students of geography and geology.* Boston: Ginn, 1895.

Superior Tribune. Superior, Wisconsin.

Toledo Blade. Toledo, Ohio.

Secondary Sources

Barcus, Frank. *Freshwater Fury: Yarns and Reminiscences of the Greatest Storm in Inland Navigation.* Detroit, Mich.: Wayne State University Press, 1960.

Bolsenga, Stanley J., and Charles E. Herdendorf. *Lake Erie and Lake St. Clair Handbook.* Detroit, Mich.: Wayne State University Press, 1993.

Bowen, Dana Thomas. *Lore of the Lakes: Told in Story and Picture.* 6th ed. Daytona Beach, Fla.: N.P., 1958.

_____. *Memories of the Lakes: Told in Story and Picture.* 6th ed. Daytona Beach, Fla.: N.P., 1958.

_____. *Shipwrecks of the Lakes: Told in Story and Picture.* 6th ed. Daytona Beach, Fla.: N.P., 1958.

Boyer, Dwight. *True Tales of the Great Lakes.* New York: Dodd, Mead, 1984.

Defense Mapping Agency Hydrographic Center. "Bowditch," *American Practical Navigator,* no. 9 (1977).

Devendorf, John F. *Great Lakes Bulk Carriers 1869–1985.* Niles, Mich.: N.P., 1995. This privately published work is in the holdings of the Toledo Public Library.

Gebhart, Richard. "The Life of the Turret Ship, *Salvor.*" *Inland Seas: Quarterly Journal of the Great Lakes Historical Society* 57, no. 4 (winter 2001): 303.

Great Lakes Commission. *Great Lakes: A Great Place.* Ann Arbor, Mich.: Great Lakes Commission, 1988.

Kotsch, William J. *Weather for the Mariner.* 3rd ed. Annapolis, Md.: Naval Institute Press, 1983.

Marine Area Section, Office of Climatology. *Climatology and Weather Service of the St. Lawrence Seaway and Great Lakes.* Technical Paper No. 35. Washington, D.C.: U.S. Department of Commerce, U.S. Weather Bureau, 1959.

Melville, Herman. *Moby-Dick; or, The Whale.* 1851. Reprint, Cambridge, Mass.: Houghton Mifflin/Riverside, 1956.

Mills, James Cooke. *Our Inland Seas: Their Shipping and Commerce for Three Centuries.* 1910. Reprint, Cleveland, Ohio: Freshwater Press, 1976.

Monmonier, Mark. *Air Apparent: How Meteorologists Learned to Map, Predict and Dramatize Weather.* Chicago: University of Chicago Press, 1999.

National Oceanic and Atmospheric Administration. *United States Coast Pilot 6.* 29th ed. Washington, D.C.: U.S. Department of Commerce, National Ocean Services, 1998.

O'Brien, T. Michael. *Guardians of the Eighth Sea: A History of the U.S. Coast Guard on the Great Lakes.* Cleveland, Ohio: Ninth Coast Guard District, 1976.

Ratigan, William. *Great Lakes Shipwrecks and Survivals.* New York: Galahad, 1960.

Rousmaniere, John. *After the Storm: True Stories of Disaster and Recovery at Sea.* Camden, Maine: International Marine, 2002.

Stonehouse, Frederick. *Wreck Ashore: The United States Life-Saving Service on the Great Lakes.* Duluth, Minn.: Lake Superior Port Cities, 1994.

U.S. Army Corps of Engineers. *Monthly Bulletin.* Detroit, Mich., September 1977.

ACKNOWLEDGMENTS

A SMALL ARMY of people worked to preserve the story of the great storm. To make sure their efforts do not go unappreciated, here are their names in alphabetical order. They have my undying gratitude. To those I have neglected to mention go my sincere and humble apologies.

Denise, Duluth Public Library, Duluth, Minnesota

Ann Blevins, NOAA National Climatic Data Center, Raleigh, North Carolina

Capt. Karl Busam, Schooner *Red Witch*, Port Clinton, Ohio

Capt. Michael W. Carr, meteorologist, Maritime Institute of Technology and Graduate Studies, Linthicum Heights, Maryland

Peg Davis, South Manitou Island, Michigan

Jonathan Eaton, International Marine/McGraw-Hill, Camden, Maine

Christopher Gilchrest, Executive Director, Great Lakes Historical Society, Vermilion, Ohio

Edward Goyette, Museum Ship *Willis B. Boyer*, Toledo, Ohio

Robert W. Graham, archivist, Historical Collection of the Great Lakes, Bowling Green State University, Ohio

Jane John, Peter White Public Library, Marquette, Michigan

Ken McKinley, meteorologist, Locus Weather, Camden, Maine

Mark Monmonier, cartographer, Syracuse, New York

Jeffrey Savadel, meteorologist, Washington, D.C.

Robert Shiels, meteorologist, WTOL-TV, Toledo, Ohio

Capt. Erik Wood, first-class pilot, Great Lakes

INDEX

9 780071 435413